CHARACTERS

WHO CAN MAKE OR BREAK YOUR SMALL BUSINESS

MICHAEL BEST

Characters Who Can Make or Break Your Small Business

First Edition: May 2018

Print ISBN: 978-1-7753077-0-9
Ebook ISBN: 978-1-7753077-1-6

Formatting: Streetlight Graphics

CONTENTS

PREFACE

"Why did you write this book?"

My friend Tom (oil company CEO, geologist, detail-oriented nitpicker, adventurer, and one of my beta readers) is sitting at my kitchen table and has just caught me by surprise with this question.

"Why?" I repeat, stalling for time. For three years I've been concentrating on the content. I've forgotten *why* I'm writing it. With greater poise and presence of mind I would have recalled the reason I offer on my web site where I quote Toni Morrison (Nobel and Pulitzer-Prize-winning author): "If there's a book you want to read, but it hasn't been written yet, then you must be the one to write it."

"Yes, why?" Tom insists. "You need to explain. If people know more about who you are, why you wrote this book, and why they should read it—which I know they should—they'll be more inclined to do so."

So, on Tom's advice, here's what I want you to know.

I'm fascinated by what makes various small businesses tick. I've written magazine articles about it. I blog about it. I could talk with small business owners for days about it. I've spent most of my career, particularly the last twenty-three years of it (during which I owned a small business), soaking up knowledge and experience about business—small business in particular. So what better way to share this than through a book? What better way to reduce the incline of a learning curve for others? I'm tired of all the "my mum's basement to riches" books. Where are the books for the millions of regular small business owners in need of practical advice and encouragement? This book is long overdue.

You might wonder whether I'm qualified to dispense business advice. I'll admit that when at the outset of my career I didn't want to have anything to do with business. I wanted to be a veterinarian. But well before the end of a year of chemistry, physics, botany, and zoology at the University of Cape Town, it was evident that I was going to miss by a considerable margin the admission requirements of the only veterinary college in the country (or any other veterinary college in any other country for that matter).

I resorted to signing articles with an accounting firm (in retrospect it was the beginning of the research for this book though I didn't realize it at the time). I changed faculties at university, eventually graduated and then (to the amazement of many) passed the chartered accountant's board exam at the first try when multiple attempts was the norm. I had become a chartered accountant. And I wondered, where to now?

What followed was a few more years of public accounting in Cape Town for a total of seven years, a two-year assignment of business and share valuations in Toronto, six months with the same international accounting group in London, a year in Tehran managing the internal audit department on a harbour-construction project (until the revolution put an end to it), a few months in Bahrain and Houston wrapping up the Iranian project, a year back in Cape Town working for a small aviation company before emigrating to Canada, six years working for a major oil company in Calgary, and then twenty-three years running a small business head-quartered in Calgary with my wife, Margaret. Chartered accountancy may not have been the original plan but it became the means to a rare and diverse exposure to the world of business in six countries on four continents.

But business is just part of my story. When not absorbed by speaking and writing about it, there's my family and interests like animals (wild, domesticated, and particularly Jack Russell terriers), cricket, rugby, and art.

Now a bit about the book.

For every dramatic small business success story there are hundreds of thousands of small business owners who toil away daily for years without ever appearing in the spotlight. If you're one of them, taking risks and investing long hours because bread must be put on the table and children must be housed, clothed, and educated (while also hoping for some fun along the way and a retirement nest egg at the end), this book is for you.

And even if you dream of building the next Microsoft, Apple, or retail chain—the small business that rockets to stardom—this book is for you too because first there's a learning curve to be engaged. This book is about lowering the incline of that curve.

Take me, for example. By the time I launched my small business, I thought I knew everything there was to know about business. I was, after all, a chartered accountant with twenty years of experience. I'd spent time in public practice auditing and valuing small businesses. I'd held financial management positions in multinational corporations. I'd seen it all. Running a small business was going to be a piece of cake.

How wrong I was.

My steep climb began the moment the idea for my enterprise was conceived, and it never quite ended. A resource such as this book, had one been available, would have lowered the incline of my learning curve considerably.

Regardless of how various jurisdictions define "small business," the precise metrics don't matter. If your business or intended business falls anywhere within the parameters of one of many definitions of "small business" you can dig up, read on.

If you're thinking of starting a business or recently started one, you've probably heard that 50 to 80 percent of start-ups fail in the first five years. Much has been written about why this happens. By telling the story of a twenty-three-year journey in small business ownership, I aim to contribute to the must-read material. I aim to help you avoid the pitfalls so that your small business is one of the 50 to 20 percent still thriving after the first five years, and beyond.

This book won't necessarily apply to all aspects of your particular business. Over the years I've read about a hundred business books, and not one proved to be universally applicable to the circumstances of my business and industry. And I didn't agree with all the sentiments or opinions of any of the authors. But in each book I found something informative.

And so I hope you find this book about characters who can make or break your business informative as well as entertaining. Above all, I hope your small business learning curve won't be as steep as mine was and that this book becomes a companion in your small business ownership quest.

ACKNOWLEDGEMENTS

Red Smith, a renowned sports journalist, once famously said: "There is nothing to writing. All you do is sit down at a typewriter and just open a vein." Writing can indeed be painful work. It can also be depressing, frustrating, uplifting, and exhilarating—sometimes all in the same hour. And you'll often hear people say that writing is a lonely pursuit. This was certainly not my experience, though. Not even close.

While only my name appears on the cover of this book, a number of other names wouldn't be out of place there too. These are the gracious, patient, and talented people without whom I wouldn't have progressed much beyond the starting blocks:

- Margaret, my wife, who encouraged me to write the book, and then served as a memory supplement, cheerleader, and critic.
- Rachel Small, my editor, who patiently endured my deficient grammar and syntax from the first word to the last, and who skilfully reined in my verbosity.
- Angela Merzib, the graphic artist who created depictions of each of my thirty-nine characters.
- Karen Humphrey and Alexander Sakarev, the graphic artists who designed my cover.
- Natalie Conyer, Tom Feuchtwanger, Neil Gardner, David Glassman, Chris Mathias, Sylvia Malinowski, Martin Pollard, and Gordon Robb, who read my manuscript and provided invaluable feedback.

- All those who allowed me to repeat their small business stories and experiences.
- All those who allowed me to quote their writing.
- The specialists and experts who reviewed excerpts of my manuscript for technical accuracy.

In fact, these people not only got me out of the starting blocks—they helped me get all the way to the finishing line. It's with gratitude that I acknowledge their contributions.

INTRODUCTION: WHY CHARACTERS?

Think about it: regardless of the nature of your small business, it's likely that your primary daily activity is interacting with people—partners, employees, suppliers, customers, and a host of others. In fact, as a small business owner, you likely spend most of your day, every day, doing so.

With this in mind, I developed the format of this book. It allows me to recount my experiences, share informative anecdotes, and pass on advice through the characters with whom a small business owner can typically expect to interact—characters who collectively, or even individually, can make or break your small business.

The book is based on the lives and characters of actual small businesses, and often on my small business. Some of the characters might not be relevant to your business, but many will. They are presented in the approximate sequence in which they can be expected to appear in the life of a business, from start to end. That said, each one stands on its own. This book doesn't need to be read linearly. In fact, it may serve you best as a reference book to be pulled from your bookshelf as needed.

Whether you're an old hand or just thinking about business ownership, these characters will give you food for thought, forewarn you, and provide insight, all to help you run a successful small business. I hope they entertain you as much as they entertained me in the process of recalling them for you.

CHARACTER 1: PARTNER

An avoidable mistake

I made an avoidable mistake. I did what so many small business owners do—I entered a business partnership without proper consideration. Consequently, the partnership lasted less than a year. I dare say my ex-partner would agree that he didn't give the matter proper consideration either.

If we had conducted the research and soul searching that I now know is essential, we would have realized that we had different goals for the business, vastly different management styles, and personalities incompatible for a partnership. Had we not erroneously assumed we could turn a personal relationship into a business partnership, we might still be on talking terms today. I have found that it is almost impossible to confine business disputes to the business arena—the acrimony invariably becomes personal and often permanent. We could have avoided all that with quiet contemplation.

Quiet contemplation

Picture yourself in a cottage in the woods. The sound of the lake lapping the sandy shore drifts in through the screen door on the warm, loamy forest air. A chipmunk scurries about on the wooden deck and beyond that, a solitary fisherman sits in a small aluminum rowing boat on the lake hoping for a rainbow trout for supper. Both will soon move on, leaving you to pursue your purpose in absolute peace and without distraction.

This is the type of setting helpful to contemplating the partnership decision: a decision that could have a profound impact on both your personal life and business life; a decision best reached by a completely frank discussion between you and your inner self.

You've bandied about your business model exhaustively, and all that remains is to decide whether you're going to go it alone or enter into a partnership. It makes no difference if yours is a new business about to be launched or an existing business at a crossroad—the decision requires the same degree of contemplation. Should you retain full ownership and hire the expertise and raise the capital you may not have, or should you trade away partial ownership and control to a partner or partners in exchange for expertise and capital?

This decision should not be made lightly. Unfortunately, it often is. In my experience, most people enter small business partnerships not thinking beyond the assumption that they can make more money in a partnership than alone. Much of what needs to be considered though has nothing to do with numbers and money. Commonly overlooked in business decisions of all kinds, including the question about whether or not to enter into a partnership, are the all-important "emotional" considerations. We will explore some of them in a moment.

If you don't have access to a cottage in the woods, a table in a quiet corner of your local library is an alternative—essentially, any place where you can be alone, in peace, and without interruption. But wherever you choose to contemplate the idea, take your time. To partner or not to partner is a big question. The decision should not be hurried.

Deciding

I mentioned in the preface that a high number of start-ups fail within the first five years—estimates range from 50 percent to 80 percent. With this in mind and armed with the research you've conducted on the Internet, in the library, and through conversations with other small business owners, you're ready to consider the partnership question thoroughly.

Examine the numbers and the logic behind them again. If the numbers suggest that a partnership offers a better economic opportunity than a sole ownership, a partnership might be favourable, but this certainly isn't the last word on the matter. The next critical question is whether or not you have the necessary attributes to work within a partnership. Then ask yourself the same question about your intended partner or partners.

Interrogate yourself mercilessly. Are you comfortable trading away control and accepting a degree of relationship stress for the sake of potential economic advantage? How does the proposed partner's personality, work habits, and work ethic fit with yours? Will you be able to stand your ground and protect your interests when you inevitably butt heads with the other party? Can you accept that you'll have to compromise sometimes? Do you have any personality traits that are difficult to work with? Does the potential partner have any such personality traits? Reflect on possible partnership scenarios and be realistic about how you might react to them—and how a partner might react to them if the boot were on the other foot.

You and your prospective partner might also consider an assessment such as the Kolbe A™ Index designed to reveal personality and character traits and determine "what drives you to success." These kinds of assessments can help you determine how compatible you and your potential business partners are. I never participated in such a process and still feel that my partnership miss-match could have been avoided if I'd simply taken the time for some honest soul-searching. However, that doesn't mean that such a process wouldn't be helpful and as many take less than twenty minutes and cost about fifty dollars, you don't have much to lose.

But nothing guarantees partnership bliss. Unanticipated partnership busters can still arise. One partnership buster I've seen more than a few times is seemingly too silly to be real—but it's very real. Two people start a small business partnership. They do everything by the book, including clearly defining their respective roles: one will be the hands-on technical person in the warehouse or factory and the other will be the marketing and sales person out touting for business. Both work long hours. The technical partner is in the warehouse until late at night building product, and the sales partner is in bars and restaurants until late at night with potential clients. There's nothing like slaving away for long hours in a factory or warehouse to generate irritability and frustration. Technical Person's frustration eventually gives rise to resentment: "While I'm getting my hands dirty, my partner is having a good time." Technical Person begins to wonder whether Sales Person is spending time in bars and restaurants drumming up business or drumming up one-night stands. Fatigue exacerbates the resentment, and the resentment leads to confrontation about "unequal" workloads which leads to disharmony which leads to acrimony which undermines and destroys the partnership. Silly? Should be something that adults can resolve? Of course it should. But scenarios such as these are often handled in anything but an adult manner and partnerships collapse.

In the end, a business partnership, particularly in a small business context, boils down to an amalgam of economics and emotion—an amalgam that must be carefully managed so that it yields considerably more than it costs. Otherwise the partnership won't make sense.

Proceeding as a Partnership

If you decide to conduct your business as a partnership, there are several elements that absolutely must be addressed and recorded in a partnership or shareholders' agreement.

A clear understanding of each partner's contribution in terms of expertise, effort, and capital has to be reached. A management and administrative structure should be discussed and agreed upon as well. Then it should all be documented. Document every essential element not because, as many suppose, you should distrust the other party, but because you should distrust the capacity of the other party's memory.

The documentation must include a properly-executed partnership or shareholders' agreement with a termination mechanism (such as a shotgun clause). My properly-executed shareholders' agreement saved me from a lot of potential anguish and expense when I decided to terminate my own ill-conceived but thankfully short-lived business partnership.

The fact is that many business partnerships don't survive for the same catchall reason that so many marriages don't survive: irreconcilable differences. Because the statistical odds are stacked against partnerships, if you enter into one tread carefully and thoughtfully and with a big stick in the form of a comprehensive partnership or shareholders' agreement with an escape clause.

A former customer of mine is a good illustration of how a well-drafted partnership or shareholders' agreement can prevent the instability of partnerships from undermining an otherwise stable and successful business. It is a company that grew steadily under the founder's sole ownership until he retired and sold his shares to three of the management staff. The new owners started out with a comprehensive shareholders' agreement which facilitated the seamless departure of one of the three partners a short time later. The business then continued successfully for a number of years under the two remaining partners' ownership and management.

But as happens more often than not, the relationship between the partners deteriorated, and one made an offer to buy the shares of the other. In terms of the 'shotgun' clause in their shareholder's agreement, the recipient of the offer could either accept it and sell his shares or buy the other shareholder's shares at the same price. The second partner, not wishing to be bought out, countered the offer and thereby acquired sole ownership of the company. Without the shareholders' agreement's clearly defined process for termination—not least of which was the shotgun clause—this successful business could have been jeopardized by an acrimonious and destructive relationship.

On the other side of the coin, I know of small business partnerships that have been very successful and long lasting. The best example I can recall is that of two men who started an offset printing business together while both were in their twenties. Forty years later, when I got to know one of the partners very well, they were still in a harmonious partnership and their business was still thriving. He told me that the secret to their successful partnership was twofold—they had always been clear on their separate and distinct roles in the business, and they had confined their relationship purely to business to the extent that neither had so much as set foot in the other's home. Extreme? Perhaps, but if that's what it takes ...

Family partnerships

It's not unusual for small businesses to start out as family partnerships. However, many don't survive this structure. The problem is that most family relationships carry a lot of baggage not conducive to a peaceful, productive business relationship. In some situations it may be possible to offset this by structuring the business to minimise friction points. But in any case, the decision-making process before entering into a family partnership must include a frank assessment of the nature of the family relationship. Any fractiousness will migrate back and forth from the business relationship to the personal relationship, to the detriment of both.

I failed to give the matter due consideration before entering into a business arrangement with my brother. We had very different ideas about business management that we failed to discuss before entering into our arrangement. In addition, a certain amount of baggage came along in the shape of intra-family tensions. The business relationship was doomed to fail from the outset, and it didn't last long before ending acrimoniously. It just wasn't going to work and we should have known that.

I spoke with many business owners in family partnerships while writing this book, and each one said that if the personal relationships weren't amicable, they wouldn't be able to conduct a business relationship. All also confirmed that a distinct division of duties and responsibilities was a necessary measure to minimize conflict.

I'll address the impact of family relationships on a small business again later in more detail in the Family Member chapter.

All the options and a lot of soul searching

My post-partnership and experience-based preference when it comes to owning a small business is sole ownership that fills the expertise and capital gaps with arms-length arrangements. Only an extraordinarily compelling reason to enter into a partnership arrangement would make me surrender full control of a business. That being said, no options should be pursued until all have been thoroughly explored and some serious soul searching has taken place. There is too much at stake both emotionally and financially to enter into a business partnership without careful consideration.

CHARACTER 2: BANKER

Who needs a banker?

Unless you conduct business entirely in cash and stash it under the mattress, you cannot escape dealing with a banker. For any small business owner, business conducted with the bank breaks down into two main categories: day-to-day banking and longer-term banking.

Day-to-day banking

It's uttered daily in probably thousands of small businesses throughout the land: "I'm running down to the bank." Translated, it means, "It's that time of day again, when I have to take time to battle the traffic, find parking, and stand in line at the bank to make the deposit while I could be catching up on the backlog on my desk instead."

Day-to-day banking—stand in line, hand over deposit book, make small talk with teller, take back deposit book, go back to office—is tedious and usually assigned to the low person on the totem pole. Once in a while there is a cheque to cash for petty cash replenishment, but that's about as exciting as it gets. Nowadays everything else that was once accomplished by visiting the bank, such as wire transfers, is done online.

Many small business owners have found that there are less disruptive and more productive ways of getting that daily deposit into the bank such as a deposit drop box or an ATM located on their route home—much to the chagrin of the low person on the totem pole who could use a midafternoon cigarette break.

Some financial institutions are now, at the time of writing, offering online cheque deposits. By means of an app on your phone, you can take a photo of your cheque and email it to the bank. If you have a very small business or the type of business with few cheque deposits, this might be an attractive option, but for multiple cheque deposits it could be too cumbersome.

In spite of the more productive methods of handling the daily banking, there will still be occasions when you have to line up at the bank. This is when you'll see the rolling of eyes, the sighs, and the if-looks-could-kill expressions from small business owners still doing the daily banking the old-fashioned way. Rita Rudner, the comedienne, has a great line on this topic: "They usually have two tellers in my local bank, except when it's very busy, when they have one."

The Occasional Eventful Bank Visit

Online banking is unarguably more efficient than in-person banking, but it's hardly newsworthy in the way that in-person banking can be. For instance, take my bank and someone we'll call Joe. He owned a business in the general vicinity of mine. Except for the occasional greeting in passing at the bank when I'd see him depositing the contents of a large white canvas bag, I didn't know Joe personally. However, his reputation was that of a likeable but no-nonsense character.

One day as he approached the main entrance of the bank, so did a man with shoulder-length hair, an unkempt beard and a generally scruffy appearance. He held a handgun. It was a short conversation.

Scruffy Man: "Hey, hey!"

Joe: "What?"

Scruffy Man, reaching forward with his free hand: "Gimme the bag!"

Joe, recoiling: "Fuck you!"

I don't recall if the robber was ever caught or if the money was ever retrieved. What I do recall is seeing Joe limping for a year or two after the incident. I guess a bullet in the leg will do that to you.

On another occasion I came close to witnessing an "unauthorized withdrawal" that could have been life threatening. I arrived at the bank only to be denied access by an ashen-faced teller who told me they'd just been robbed at gunpoint. Fortunately there had been no shooting. Even as he was trying to persuade me to come back some other time I heard police sirens approaching. The robbers were caught within an hour or two and the money recovered.

The on-the-job lesson for the robbers: don't attract attention by running out of the bank, jumping into a vehicle and burning rubber—someone is bound to record a description and a licence plate number. The lesson for small business owners: don't try to be a hero—your family and business need you.

Longer-term banking

Small business owners' longer-term banking business primarily involves credit facilities or loans and, if the business is eventually successful, investments.

Robert Frost said, "A bank is a place where they lend you an umbrella in fair weather and ask for it back when it begins to rain." Frost is best known as a poet and playwright, but what is not commonly known is that he farmed for about nine years. One can only assume that he was expressing a frustration born of personal experience—the kind of personal experience common to many small business owners.

If there has ever been a lightning rod for discontent in the small business owner and banker relationship, it has been the potentially thorny topic of small business borrowing. It is here where the banker's proclivity for risk management butts heads with the small business owner's proclivity for optimism. And it's where small business owners can have unreasonable expectations of their banker.

Unreasonable expectations

While many small business owners harbour grudges against bankers, seeing them as indifferent, detached, and short-sighted, they tend to overlook the fact that they and their bankers dwell in different worlds—worlds so different that the inhabitants have trouble relating to each other's circumstances and mindsets. To borrow a popular concept from the arena of the battle of the genders, bankers are from Mars and small business owners are from Venus.

If you've not yet experienced business banking, you might be wondering whether it's an exaggeration to suggest that bankers and small business owners dwell in different worlds. Be assured, it's not. Think about it. Bankers live in a nine-to-five bureaucratic world of policies and procedures, conservative risk management, suits and silk blouses, plush carpeting and furnishings, a guaranteed cheque at the end of the month, and, with some luck, a fat bonus cheque at the end of the year. That's Mars. Small business owners live in a world of long days, risk taking, sleepless nights worrying about making payroll, staff problems, customer retention, late shipments, and overdue receivables. That's Venus.

Under these circumstances, small business owners should not expect bankers to see their world as they see it. Lack of familiarity militates against proper understanding. I audited close to a hundred small businesses, some repeatedly over a period of years, and valued close to twenty during the public accounting and consulting part of my career. As a result, I can assure you that while I spent more time and effort trying to understand these small businesses than any banker ever would, it takes a lot more than an audit or a valuation to come close to understanding a particular small business as well as its owner. Anne Michaels, author of *The Winter Vault*, in commenting on another author's work, wrote that "nothing is known until it is held: in our hands, in our mind, or in our heart."

If it's unreasonable to expect your banker to know your business as well as you do, it's equally unreasonable to expect him or her to understand your challenges and needs as well as you do and, therefore, to be as optimistic as you. That might be why loans officers are not on many small business Christmas card lists.

Ryley visits the loans officer

Whenever I'm in the company of a small business owner and the conversation turns to banking and, more specifically, dissatisfaction with banks' lending practices, I invariably recall Ryley and his visit to the loans officer.

The bank staff had been asking me for some time to bring in my puppy but I was reluctant, as anyone who knows Jack Russell terriers would understand. Turning a Jack Russell puppy loose in the midst of an excitable, fawning crowd can give a whole new definition to "unbridled exuberance."

Eventually I relented under persistent pressure. The predictable excitement started right away. Then when a staff member put a wriggling Ryley down, he naturally took off like a rocket to explore the bank. He dashed in and out of glass-fronted offices until, in full view of everyone, he found the loans officer and cocked his leg against his desk. As I watched a growing wet patch spread out across the carpet it crossed my mind that perhaps Ryley had been a small business owner in a previous life.

An ideal bank

Not all banks are created equal. Nor are all bankers. Some inquiry and thought should take place before selecting a bank. All bank wooing and advertising notwithstanding, some bank branches are not as small business friendly as others. However, sorting the banking wheat from the chaff isn't easy because there are so many variables to consider. For the sake of a relatively worry-free and cordial relationship with your banker, a careful, well-considered choice is worth the time and effort.

As good a way as any to start selecting a bank is to determine your ideal bank and banker. What follows is Jack's description of an ideal small business bank. Jack is actually a composite of a number of small business owners I've known.

"Going to the bank regularly, if not daily, is an intrusion, albeit an unavoidable one, on my otherwise busy day," says Jack. "I want the bank to be close to my business to minimize the time I have to spend in traffic getting there. When I arrive, I need to find free parking close to the door.

When I enter the bank I don't want to encounter a lineup—I want to be able to walk straight up to a teller. I would like the tellers to be friendly and polite without being too familiar. I would like the tellers to recognize me and to be aware of my business and the type of banking business I typically transact. I would prefer that my particular bank not be a training branch with a steady stream of trainee tellers cycling through it. I don't want to be delayed by a trainee teller fumbling around trying to figure out how to process my transactions.

I would like my bank to be a small branch where service is more personalized than it would typically be in a large branch. I would like to be on chatting terms with my banker—either the bank manager or the person to whom my account is assigned. I want him or her to be familiar with my business so that when we meet to discuss my banking needs from time to time we can cut straight to the chase. I would like to know that if and when I need help from my banker, he or she will do whatever is possible to accommodate me.

I would like to feel confident that my banker isn't going to rip the rug out from under my business by unreasonably withholding credit or calling in loans. I would also like to feel confident that should my banker be transferred, the replacement will not arbitrarily change my banking arrangements, particularly funding arrangements, and create a headache for me.

When I call my bank I would like a receptionist in the branch to answer the call and put me through to my banker. Alternatively, if the bank has centralized telephone answering in a location somewhere on the other side of the country, I would like to have the number of my banker's direct line. I don't want to have to explain my reason for calling to a call centre person who has no idea who I am but insists on knowing the reason for my call before putting me through to the branch.

Finally, it's important that my bank offers user-friendly online banking that accommodates most transactions so as to limit my visits to special transactions and the occasional meeting."

A few years ago Ernst and Young published a Canadian banking industry study that echoed Jack's description of a small business owner's ideal bank. The study, which can be found online, includes the following: "Banks need to meet the basic needs of their customers, but beyond that they need to know their customers, reward their loyalty and enable them to interact in a seamless way with the bank—when, where and how the customers want."

All of this might sound very agreeable and encouraging. But even if the banks heeded and acted upon this advice, it would still be unrealistic for a small business owner to expect a banker to be able to relate in any reasonable way to the problems and potential of his or her business—because until the banks recruit small business specialists with many years of hands-on experience running small businesses, bankers will always be from Mars and small business people from Venus.

Play Ball with the Bank

Armed with a realistic understanding of the relationship between banker and small business owner, what can an owner do to help the banker better understand his or her business?

No matter what the banks' PR departments say in their promotional material, the reality is that small business owners need their banks more than their banks need them. The smaller the business, the less the bank needs it as a customer, as the prominent international banking conglomerate with which I bank recently confirmed. It advised some of its small business customers to make arrangements to take their business to another bank. When questioned about it, my bank manager told me that the bank's revised business model did not include servicing "mom-and-pop-sized" small businesses. Then, with a straight face, he assured me that my small business was still very important to the bank. Pure PR and utterly untrue? Absolutely!

Losing one relatively small customer among thousands is not going to be anywhere near the top of a banker's list of concerns. On the other hand, losing his or her only banker and having to find another one will easily top a small business owner's list of concerns. It will always be a disproportionately weighted relationship. And this means that the onus for keeping the relationship with your banker on an even keel falls on you, the small business owner. For example, if you're obligated to periodically produce documents such as a list of receivables that banks commonly require before funding loans or other facilities, then do so exactly as and when required.

Make a point of being on friendly, conversational terms with people in the bank you need to interact with from time to time—it's an easy PR measure. Greeting them occasionally when visiting the bank, even if you're not seeing them specifically, will help maintain an amicable relationship. On the other hand, don't overdo it and definitely don't offer gifts, no matter how insignificant they may be. Even if your particular bank doesn't have a policy against accepting gifts, it would still not be appropriate in what should be an arms-length business relationship.

Another good PR measure to help your banker understand your business better is offering him or her a tour of your premises. It won't make the banker an instant expert on your business, even though he or she might think so, but it will, in most cases, enhance the relationship. This is of course predicated on an assumption that your premises won't undermine the banker's confidence in you or the business. Make sure it's in good condition.

Finally, meet banking obligations such as loan repayments exactly as and when required. While this will consolidate confidence in you and your business, failing to do so will have exactly the opposite effect and raise red flags. Nothing will harm your business relationship with your banker faster than late or missed payments.

BANKING PEACE OF MIND

If you choose your banker well and then work to maintain a congenial relationship, without unrealistic expectations, you will have established an important aspect of successful small business ownership: banking peace of mind.

CHARACTER 3: ACCOUNTANT

ACCOUNTANTS ARE NOT JUST A BIG BUSINESS LUXURY

The mere mention of a chartered accountant (CA), certified public accountant (CPA), or certified general accountant (CGA), depending on country of residence, can send a cold shiver down a small business owner's spine, particularly in the early years after start-up when expenses must be carefully controlled and cash preserved. I know—I've been on both sides of this fence, first as a CA providing small business owners with accounting and auditing services and then as a small business owner.

But, cold shivers notwithstanding, an accountant is one of the more important companions to take along for the journey down the road to small business success. And by "accountant" I refer more to the function than the title. You don't necessarily need a downtown big-firm, big-fee CA, CPA, or CGA. What you need is someone to provide accounting services at a level of expertise appropriate to the nature and complexity of your small business.

Accountants are heroes too

Accountants aren't likely to be particularly exciting or newsworthy in a hero-saves-the-day kind of way. In fact, it seems that when an accountant or accounting firm is mentioned on the evening news today it's in the role of villain rather than hero for having not detected a massive fraud perpetrated at another failed multinational conglomerate.

The fact is, though, thousands of small business owners will tell you that their accountants, while never likely to be publicly hailed as heroes, *are* heroes for a number of reasons. In the small business arena, accountants stand between chaotic and orderly records, late and timely tax returns, well-reasoned and reckless pricing, and in some cases, between survival and failure.

For every stereotypically formal, introverted, humourless accountant in a pinstriped suit with a leather briefcase who spends his or her time nitpicking large corporations' records and then issuing audit letters to management about control weaknesses and errors, there are thousands of other accountants serving small business owners with unheralded dedication. Every small business owner should have such a hero.

Accountants turned entrepreneurs

I need to make a point to do-it-yourself accountants. Take this as advice from one accountant to another—if you're running a small business or planning on it, don't do all your own accounting just because you're qualified to do so, unless your specific role in the business is to be the accountant.

Based on bitter experience, I can assure you that working at being a small business owner is so challenging and time consuming, particularly in the early days of a new business, that you will not have the time or energy to do the accounting as well. Backlogs will build up and eventually create another source of stress you don't need. By all means, stay on top of your financial data, as your background will instinctively drive you to do, but have someone else do the work.

The Type of Accountant You Need

When you need medical services (and all of us do), you choose your practitioner based on the nature of your need. A paramedic might be able to quite easily handle your need, but if it's more complex, you might need a GP. And if it's really complex, you might need a specialist—one of those people in a downtown tower block with an oak-panelled office on the fiftieth floor, a wall full of framed certificates, and a twelve-month waiting list.

Similarly, when you need accounting services (and all business owners do), you must choose your practitioner based on the complexity of your need. You might only need someone with basic bookkeeping skills and the input or review of a fully qualified accountant from time to time. But as your business grows and becomes more complex, you might have to head downtown to the plush offices of one of the big accounting firms.

Regardless of the nature and size of your business though, you'll need accounting services as surely as we all need medical services. No matter how small or unsophisticated your small business might be, you will at least need accounting services to ensure that your tax returns are accurate and submitted on time. Most small business owners will need more than just tax accounting though—not just as the business grows, but indeed, to help the business grow.

Your Accountant as an Advisor

Small business accountants will primarily fulfill the traditional role of maintaining accounting records, preparing financial statements, and completing tax returns, but they can also contribute valuable basic, day-to-day business advice. They can be helpful when you need someone to crunch the hard, cold numbers and shine the light of reality on concepts such as the latest sales-boosting scheme or discounting program.

Failure to consult with someone knowledgeable, most particularly an accountant, on key matters such as costing, pricing, and margin determination can be very costly and, in some cases, disastrous. For instance, for many small business owners, product pricing is like walking a tightrope—you can't lean too far one way or the other. Price too high and you don't make enough sales, price too low and you don't make enough margin. Many small business owners need advice on this but don't seek it and as a result, fall down.

Many will price in a fly-by-the-seat-of-your-pants manner, particularly in the early days. I've known many small business owners to price according to what the competition is doing or what they think the market might bear or some other arbitrary method that doesn't take into account the many factors that should be influencing their particular pricing decisions. Gross – margin expectations, overhead costs, and the business owner's required earnings, among other things, must factor into pricing before comparisons with specific competitors and the general market are considered. A simplistic pricing method that doesn't consider all factors is of course fraught with pitfalls, as Greg discovered.

Greg's "happening place"

Greg was the production manager at a large Canadian textile screen printing company that, for the sake of this story, I'll refer to as Nordic Imprinted Sportswear. Nordic printed large volumes of imprinted sportswear and counted among its customers most of the large brand-name sporting goods wholesalers. Another prized customer was a North American wholesaler of promotional garments for big musical events, primarily rock concerts. They referred to this prized customer as their "rock 'n' roll" customer.

Nordic's customer list was the envy of the company's competitors. Unknown to most though, the enviable volumes were secured by virtue of very low per-unit prices and hence, very tight margins. During negotiations with my company regarding the price of inks and chemicals Nordic bought from us, Nordic's accountant was frank. The figures he disclosed indicated razor-thin margins. That, as you can imagine, placed a lot of pressure on Nordic's management to keep input costs down and production volumes up. They had an extensive infrastructure, including a large number of automatic presses that had to be paid for and therefore kept occupied. This left them with very little leverage in price discussions because their large customers knew that Nordic needed volume to survive and could therefore be ruthlessly squeezed on pricing.

Greg had struck up a friendly relationship with a rock 'n' roll customer executive that led to him leaving Nordic, persuading a few Nordic employees to join him, taking the rock 'n' roll account with him, and starting his own textile screen printing company. It was of course an opportunistic and subversive manoeuvre but, sadly, not an uncommon one in that industry at that time.

Greg leased a six-thousand-square-foot warehouse and a state-of-the-art automatic screen printing press that could churn out a thousand prints on T-shirts every hour. As easily as that he was off and running.

I visited Greg's new business about a month after he started up. He proudly gave me the grand tour, boasting, "It's so totally cool that I've created this happening place." If "happening place" meant a hive of activity in which the press turned without interruption, three press operators worked at a frenetic pace to load and unload shirts, a fourth employee shuffled back and forth keeping the press supplied with ink, a mountain of boxes each containing six dozen T-shirts awaited printing, and stacks of printed T-shirts sat on sorting tables ready to be packed for delivery, then this indeed was a "happening place."

Greg was very pleased with himself for having "stuck it to Nordic." When I asked whether he'd managed to negotiate a good price with the rock 'n' roll customer he said that he'd only had to give them a slightly better price than Nordic was charging.

I asked whether an accountant had checked the viability of his pricing and he assured me there was no need for that because if Nordic was making a lot of money at those prices, then he would too.

I had not been invited to offer business advice and when I sensed that I might be crossing a line I refrained from sharing my immediate thoughts—*You did what? You just assumed that Nordic was making money at that price? You didn't take into account your own overhead structure and cash flow commitments? You didn't consider Nordic's economies of scale? You plunged into this after undercutting Nordic's already low price and without any understanding of how that price was calculated?*

Instead, I just said, "Good luck, Greg," climbed into the rental car, and before even turning the key called the office to tell our accounts receivable person to keep a close eye on Greg's account. Six months later we received a package from a firm of trustees in bankruptcy and wrote off Greg's bad debt of a few thousand dollars. I'll address bad debts later, but for now the point of this tale is that consulting an accountant or someone with similar expertise on something as fundamental as pricing can *make* your business; not doing so can *break* it.

The vexing issue of discounting

Any accountant in public practice can tell you about small business owners who make decisions on everyday business matters influenced more by what everyone else is doing rather than by the impact the decision will have on their businesses in their peculiar circumstances. For instance, a close and equally troublesome relative of pricing is discounting. It's a strategy commonly used to boost sales for any number of reasons.

Discounting can be quite useful in dealing with inventory situations such as overstocking or redundancy. Quite often in these situations, the investment was lost when the product was bought, so any cash one can recover is a bonus. It's certainly not an ideal solution, but recovering some cash is better than having the product occupy space while it ages—unless you're a wine merchant.

Businesses run into trouble with discounting though when using it as a volume-boosting strategy. Typically, small business owners don't properly analyze their discounting schemes and, as a result, these schemes can be more harmful than helpful. If the necessary financial acumen does not exist in-house, then the strategy should be discussed with an accountant or someone with similar insight into the effects of discount tampering. I saw a classic example of the potential consequences of thoughtless discounting in my own business, thanks to Andrew.

Andrew's 10 percent discount proposal

Andrew was running one of our regional operations. With a marketing-focussed MBA from a respected business faculty at a university in the United States, he was more than well equipped for the job. The lesson to be taken from this story is that if the subtlety of numbers can escape an MBA's scrutiny, then small business owners less schooled in the intricacies of interpreting numbers should at least solicit a second opinion from an accountant or similarly qualified source.

I had gathered the staff together for a review and strategy meeting. The topic of sales growth was high on the agenda. Ideas were being bandied about when Andrew suggested offering his customers a discount to attract more sales. I should point out that we were distributing the highest-quality and highest-priced products in a restricted and price-conscious market not particularly concerned with quality—quite a marketing and sales challenge.

Andrew was influenced by the phenomenon we all see quite regularly but never more so than on Boxing Day. However, discounting is not a one-size-fits-all solution. Individual market circumstances can vary greatly and therefore it cannot be assumed that an effective discounting strategy in one circumstance will be effective in another.

Andrew was overlooking the fact that we operated in a restricted market with a finite number of potential customers when he proposed that offering a discount would enable him to attract more sales in his territory.

My immediate question about the size of discount he had in mind and how such a discount would affect our margins, wouldn't have surprised anyone in the room. I was aware of my "Margin Mike" nickname.

"A few points won't get anyone excited, so we'd have to offer something like 10 percent," said Andrew.

Everyone in the room seemed to be comfortable with a 10 percent discount. Considering how accustomed we are to seeing "40 Percent Off" and "50 Percent Off" signs in the malls every weekend, this wouldn't have sounded excessive.

Margin Mike then demonstrated that, given our pre-discount gross margin of 33%, to restore the gross margin given away by the 10 percent discount, we would have to increase our sales volume by 43 percent, i.e., sell 43 percent more product. This would only get us back to where we were in gross margin dollar terms before offering the discount. You can test the arithmetic yourself quite easily.

Andrew immediately poured cold water on any possibility of finding an additional 43 percent of product sales in his territory. We didn't even attempt to determine what it would take to increase the bottom line if we took the additional handling and administrative costs associated with 43 percent more sales into account. It wasn't necessary. The 10 percent discount idea obviously made no sense once it was reduced to numbers.

The moral of Andrew's discount proposal? If you're not a number cruncher and don't have a number cruncher on staff, hire the services of one. See an accountant before jumping to conclusions—conclusions that could be disastrous.

The cat box lesson

Regardless of the size of your small business, if you use an accountant for financial record and tax return preparation, ensure that the paperwork you hand over is complete and orderly. Establish how your accountant prefers to receive your material and then comply with this preferred format. Not only is this good business manners, but you'll also save money if the accountant doesn't have to spend time locating documents and generally making something orderly out of a disorderly mess.

During my public practice days I dealt with numerous clients whose accounting and auditing bills were much higher than they should have been simply because they were, quite frankly, paperwork slobs. The aversion to administrative and accounting matters that so many small business owners seem to have is no excuse for being a paperwork slob. I learned this lesson early in my career.

It's often said that you don't forget your first time for anything. I've never forgotten my first accounting client. One day the partner to whom

I was assigned in the accounting firm to which I was articled, announced that he was going to introduce me to my first very own client. For a first-year articled clerk this was a milestone in the process of being educated as a CA.

As we drove up to the client's store, my excitement dissipated. If you think about a five-year-old expecting a puppy as a birthday gift and receiving a hamster instead, you'll know how I felt.

The partner pushed open the heavy blue wood-framed glass door with a well-worn brass doorknob. A jingling bell announced our arrival. It was a small confectionary store straight out of a Dickens novel. On a bare plank floor stood ceiling-high wooden shelving units crammed with loaves of bread and bags of buns. An assortment of small items were on display in the glass-fronted counter that nearly filled half of the cramped space, leaving room for only four or five customers at a time. From the ceiling hung a previously coiled length of sticky brown flycatcher paper almost covered in victims.

"Michael will be doing your books and tax return for last year," said the partner, introducing me to Mrs. Taljaard.

"Okay," said Mrs. Taljaard, "the stuff is all in the box in the office." She gestured in the direction of the doorway behind and to the right of the glass counter. "And please just move Caesar."

On the desk in the tiny, dingy, windowless office sat the cardboard box of accounting documents for the past year. Comfortably curled up in a deep sleep on top of the documents was a grey tabby cat.

"Sorry, Caesar," said the partner as he lifted the cat out of the box and set him down alongside it on the desk. If you can imagine being lifted out of your bed in the middle of the night and left standing beside it, unsteady, disoriented, and groggy, you'll have a good idea of what Caesar looked like as we left with his bed and my first accounting assignment.

Back at the office I dropped the cardboard box next to my desk and a mushroom cloud of cat hair rose as it hit the floor. In addition to endless evidence of Caesar's shedding, the box contained a year's collection of unopened bank statements and an assortment of business documents, all of which had been randomly dropped into the box. Adding to my challenge in what amounted to a forensic accounting exercise rather than a simple annual accounting job for a very small business was the fact that many of Mrs. Taljaard's delivery documents from various bakeries were printed on NCR paper. NCR paper is treated with chemicals to produce copies without the use of carbon paper. Caesar apparently had an appetite for NCR paper. Many of these documents were chewed so badly that they were useless as accounting vouchers.

Mrs. Taljaard and Caesar unwittingly contributed to my accounting education by demonstrating that being a paperwork slob can increase your annual accounting fees exponentially. Taking a little care to sort paperwork in a tidy and logical fashion will not only save you from spending hours of time searching for needed documents, but it will save you a lot in accounting fees too—more than enough to buy a cat a proper bed.

Selecting an accountant

The title of "accountant" is quite often misused nowadays. There was a time when it was widely understood to mean someone who had completed academic requirements (usually a business or commerce degree) and a period of articles (it was once five years in some countries) before passing an exacting entrance examination set by a board established by a parliamentary charter. Depending upon the country in question, such a qualified accountant could attach the title CA or CPA to his or her name and perform audits of corporations' financial reports.

In more recent times, other accounting bodies have become established in some countries, and although they might not be certified to conduct audits, their members still carry the title "accountant." In addition, "accountant" is a common job title in many companies, even though the incumbent might not be a qualified accountant. I have also known people who would be more accurately described as bookkeepers, by virtue of exposure to the practice of accounting. They have no academic background in the topic but generously refer to themselves as "accountants" when questioned about their occupation.

I don't mean to imply that a small business owner should seek accounting and consulting services only from a certified accountant. If the ability and experience of the "accountant" suits the needs of the small business owner, then it could be a good match. At a minimum though, check references and write an engagement letter spelling out the nature and timing of the services to be provided and the fees to be charged for those services before hiring someone to provide accounting and bookkeeping services.

Be aware that accounting software packages have made it possible for people with no background in theoretical accounting and only a minimum of even basic practical accounting experience to claim to be accountants. These are what I refer to as button-pushers. When it comes to very basic, day-to-day accounting entries, the software can disguise a button-pusher's lack of knowledge, but these people run into trouble and actually cause damage when something unusual arises that can be resolved only with an understanding of accounting theory.

Select your accounting and consulting services according to your needs, but I would avoid placing any undue reliance on button-pushers posing as accountants. Aim to establish a long-term relationship. The better your accountant knows and understands your business, the better the service is likely to be.

Limitations of an Accountant

Chances are, you're a small business owner and not an accountant because of your temperament. For one thing, you're probably not particularly risk averse because being entrepreneurial and owning and running a business necessitates undertaking risks. Most accountants tend to be risk averse by nature, which is partly why they are accountants and not entrepreneurs. In addition, they are not usually intimately familiar with the down-in-the-trenches day-to-day struggles and risk taking of business ownership.

You need to understand this so as to not have unrealistic expectations of your accountant when consulting on business matters. You might have to temper any advice knowing that the two of you will see risk from different perspectives. This doesn't render the accountant's conservative, low-risk perspective any less relevant; just expect to weigh it against your entrepreneurial instincts and make a rational decision.

CHARACTER 4: LAWYER

YOU NEED A GOOD ONE

We've all heard the uncomplimentary jokes about lawyers, but love them or loathe them, we can't do without them. In our complex, litigious society, even small business owners will need a good lawyer from time to time, and when it comes to choosing one, it's best to go top drawer. I am emphatic about this and hope to convince you too by recounting some of my own experiences with lawyers.

You may have heard the expression "Talk is cheap until you hire a lawyer." While it's difficult to argue with this sentiment, I nevertheless steadfastly maintain that when it comes to legal services, taking a chance with "cheap" is definitely not smart—the stakes are usually too high. Consider another popular saying: "You get what you pay for." So, if you can, pay for it and get the best.

A good lawyer with whom you can maintain a cordial, professional relationship can be an invaluable resource for your small business. Aside from reliably providing you with routine legal services, your lawyer will be your avenue to specialized legal resources in his or her firm when something extraordinary arises (and it will). Being an established client will give you an advantage and will save you time and angst when you need the specialized help. For my business, a national firm with offices in most main centres proved invaluable.

First order of business with your lawyer

I mentioned the all-important partnership and shareholders' agreements in the Partner chapter. These essential documents should be prepared by a good lawyer. A properly-prepared, comprehensive agreement, once signed, can be placed in secure storage until needed. You can then proceed to run your business with peace of mind knowing that, if necessary, you can fall back on a clearly defined mechanism that will give effect to any ownership changes. It could be a business saver.

I say that with the conviction of someone who could so easily have lost his business after just one year, when my partnership had to be terminated. Without a clear, concise, and water-tight shareholders' agreement, there almost certainly would have been a dispute that could have smothered the business at a very delicate stage of its young life.

Ongoing routine business with your lawyer

Throughout your small business's existence, refer to your lawyer for certain routine matters that will arise. In addition to the most obvious examples of lease agreements, supplier agreements, joint venture agreements, and franchise agreements, a variety of other business contracts and agreements could have adverse implications for your business should disputes occur in matters governed by these documents.

Quite often landlords, suppliers, and others will present agreements as a fait accompli, giving you the impression it's all a matter of routine and you really have no choice but to accept them as presented. I know of many small business owners who were coerced into signing such agreements believing they were powerless to question or negotiate. Never acquiesce in this way. See your lawyer, particularly if you are disinclined to personally engage in confrontation.

Have your lawyer do what a good and experienced lawyer does well: go over the agreement or contract with a fine-tooth comb and identify those clauses that could haunt you later. Then, if necessary, engage your lawyer in the negotiations to arrive at a fair agreement. Never assume there is no room for manoeuvring or negotiating—there invariably is, regardless of how it's initially presented.

The other guy's lawyer

Lawyers are advocates for their clients. It's what they're paid to do, period. If you're in a legal situation and the other guy's lawyer contacts you, don't expect him or her to see your point of view, no matter how reasonable it may be and how unreasonable the other guy's might be. Of course it's unfair, infuriating, and distressing, but the only way to counter such a situation is to turn to your own lawyer, who will duly be an advocate for you, no matter how reasonable or unreasonable your position might be. That, regrettably, is how the system works.

The consequence of such a system is that quite often it seems the primary beneficiaries in a dispute are the lawyers. As unfair as it might be, when forced to defend against a spurious challenge, you will still likely need to incur the expense of a good lawyer in your corner. This is because not having legal advice, or receiving bad legal advice, can not only be costly but, in a worst case scenario, break your small business.

You shouldn't be surprised if at some point an interaction with the other guy's lawyer leaves you incredulous. Consider the following story. I had a customer with an overdue invoice. This was a common occurrence but more of a concern than usual in this case because the customer was big. We tried all the usual collection procedures until the accumulated overdue account amounted to about $17,000. At that point we ceased deliveries and stepped up our collection efforts, all without result, until we finally told the customer that unless we received payment in full or a proposed payment schedule, we would have to take legal action.

Instead of payment or a payment schedule, I received an aggressive letter from the customer's lawyer saying we would receive payment "in due course" but, in the meantime, if we didn't cease harassing the customer's bookkeeper, they would "take appropriate action." Within days, before I had an opportunity to respond to this outrageous letter, the bookkeeper had absconded, allegedly with funds. Not long after that our customer filed for bankruptcy and we lost the entire $17,000. I am still waiting for his lawyer's apology.

Spurious suits

Over the years I have been astounded by how often small businesses are the targets of spurious lawsuits. My business was no exception.

The first time your small business is the target of a lawsuit, particularly a spurious one, the legal process can be both disconcerting and maddening. The key, I learned, is to stay calm, engage your lawyer, and trust that the truth will prevail. I realize it's easier said than done, but it really is the only way to go about it if you're to avoid unnecessary stress and sleepless nights. The first time we were targeted by a spurious lawsuit, we spent a few sleepless nights courtesy of an associate in our industry we'll call Screen Systems.

We had been in conversation with Screen Systems about representing our products in their region of the country in exchange for representing their products in our region of the country. After extensive discussions failed to resolve some key issues, we received a tersely worded fax from the principal of Screen Systems saying if we didn't conclude a deal within twenty-four hours, he was going to cancel the negotiations. Ironing out the remaining outstanding matters in twenty-four hours was not going to be possible, and I therefore agreed to cancel negotiations.

Almost a year later I received a telephone call from a whistle-blower. He had seen a falsified backdated letter being prepared to claim that I had assured printers in Screen Systems' region of the country that we had concluded a deal whereby they would be able to buy our product from Screen Systems. The purpose of the letter was to support a claim that terminating negotiations with Screen Systems had caused them loss of potential business. The whistle-blower told us the letter had been typed on a screen-printing company's letterhead from a draft in the handwriting of Screen Systems' principal.

The anticipated letter from Screen Systems' lawyer arrived by FedEx within days. They were claiming seventy-five thousand dollars in damages for breach of contract. And, as you might have guessed, the falsified letter was offered as proof.

My lawyer arranged for one of his partners, a trial lawyer, to meet with us. I explained the circumstances, including the fact that the whistle-blower was willing to swear an affidavit concerning the falsified letter. The lawyers were almost salivating in anticipation of confronting the plaintiff in discovery and hoisting him by his own petard. That strategy quickly derailed however when I asked who would be paying for the spectacle.

As tempting as such a hoisting was, I was reluctant to fund it, and we settled instead on a much less costly yet very effective solution we dubbed the "Sword of Damocles" defence. My lawyer replied to Screen Systems' lawyer saying that we had reason to believe the letter upon which they were basing their claim was questionable. He added that if they didn't withdraw their claim in writing within a specified period (I think it was just a few days), we would allege fraud and file a civil suit for damages. Dangling a metaphorical sword secured by the thinnest of threads had the desired effect.

Within very short order my lawyer received a letter stating the claim had been withdrawn. I still ascribe the swift resolution of the Screen Systems matter to the value of having access to the resources of a partner in a large, national law firm with an impressive letterhead. Unfortunately, we needed those resources again a few years later, when I was forced to defend myself against someone I'll call David Brookes.

Mr. Brookes drags me into court

David Brookes was a principal in a company that manufactured screen printing equipment. We'd enjoyed a friendly business relationship for a number of years.

It's amazing though how quickly the tone of a business relationship can deteriorate in the event of a dispute over money—in this case, about fifteen thousand dollars.

We had sold a Calgary screen printer a set of Brookes' screen printing equipment with a value of about forty thousand dollars. One of the pieces of equipment, a conveyer dryer used to cure the prints on T-shirts, malfunctioned immediately. The temperature couldn't be controlled, and as a result it overheated, scorching garments. Over a period of two weeks, David sent replacement parts every few days, and I hired an electrician to fit them, all to no avail.

The customer finally ran out of patience when we came close to setting his shop alight as we were conducting a test passing a printed garment through the dryer. Obviously the problem hadn't been solved because as the garment emerged on the conveyor belt, it burst into flames.

A naked flame in a textile screen printing shop is good reason to panic. Fortunately, right behind me a door opened onto a sidewalk and just as the flaming T-shirt was about to drop off the end of the belt, I flung it out the door. After furiously stamping out the flames, I looked up to see a school bus parked a short distance from me with bemused faces in every window. One can only imagine how many dinnertime conversations that night included a story about a man dancing on flames.

The dryer was returned to our warehouse and the frustrated customer, who couldn't afford to hold up production any longer, sourced a different brand of dryer and within a day or two was back to full production. We paid the Brookes invoice after deducting the charge for the dryer and asked David to arrange to have a shipper pick it up. He refused and sued us for the value of the dryer.

The suit was filed in David's home province, which has an interesting pre-trial hearing process designed to alleviate pressure on the court system—a judge hears suits such as David's before they enter the formal court process. The court set a date for the hearing, during which both parties would have the benefit of a judge's nonbinding opinion and an opportunity to reach a settlement with the judge's assistance.

Our lawyer in Calgary referred me to one of his trial lawyer partners who pointed out that these informal hearings were often more effective if the judge heard directly from the parties involved. I took his advice and represented myself.

On the day of the hearing David and I were seated in awkward silence in a courtroom awaiting the judge's arrival. The judge entered, introduced herself, settled down behind an elevated bench and stared down at us over the top of reading glasses perched on the tip of her nose. She explained how she would listen to our respective positions and then give us each a frank opinion as to the strengths and weaknesses of our cases.

David told her that I had refused to pay for a piece of equipment that was in perfect working order when it was shipped from his factory. He said I had claimed the equipment was malfunctioning but that he had fulfilled his obligation under the terms of his warranty by sending replacement parts.

The judge questioned him about the terms of his warranty and then asked if he had documentation to offer as evidence. He handed her a manila folder that appeared to contain nothing more than copies of invoices—two or three pages.

She briefly looked at his documents and then turned her attention to me, asking for any documentation I could offer in evidence.

I handed over a three-ring binder about an inch and a half thick containing a copy of every document relevant to the transaction: all rough notes, transcripts of telephone conversations, letters, fax documents, emails, bills from the electrician, shipping bills, photographs of burnt-out dryer parts, and, most importantly, all the documents to and from my lawyers. Every document was filed by date and was numbered and recorded and indexed at the front of the binder. I was not the most attentive accounting student the University of Cape Town had ever seen, but one piece of advice from an auditing professor has always stuck with me: "Prepare your files in a manner a judge will understand."

As I explained how my customer and I had been inconvenienced by the malfunctioning dryer and how it had caused expenses and loss of revenue, she leafed through my binder. Eventually she again turned her attention to David. What is it about a judge's gown and glasses perched on the tip of a nose that is so intimidating?

"Mr. Brookes," she said, "I don't believe your warranty has any relevance in this matter." She went on to explain that it was a case of not fulfilling a contractual obligation to deliver a properly-functioning piece of equipment. She said that she believed that if he chose to go ahead with the suit he would be doing so with a very weak case. She suggested that he settle right away and avoid the almost certain possibility of incurring heavy costs. "As I leaf through Mr. Best's binder I repeatedly see the name of one of the most expensive law firms in the country. I don't think you'll want to pay their trial bills."

David decided to take the judge's advice and agreed to a settlement that included undertakings to withdraw his claim, arrange to ship the dryer back to his factory at his expense, refund me for the electrician's bills, and refund the travel and accommodation expenses I had incurred for flying halfway across the country to attend the hearing.

The fourfold lesson for any small business owner caught up in a similar situation is simply this: don't launch spurious lawsuits, fight back vigorously if you're the victim of a spurious lawsuit, prepare properly, and work with a good lawyer in a good firm.

Outgunned

While I advocate that small business owners should fight their legal battles with vigour, there may be times when you're simply outgunned and without the resources to sustain a lengthy battle against an opponent capable of dragging out the legal process almost ad infinitum. Credit card companies are among these opponents.

One of my customers, a textile screen printing shop, was the victim of a scam involving orders paid by credit card over the phone. It turned out the card numbers had been stolen from customers at a gas station. The credit card company billed the screen shop for the twenty-seven thousand dollars lost to the scammer. The screen shop owner saw his lawyer about suing the credit card company for restitution and was told that although he had a strong case, he was unlikely to be able to stay the course long enough to win against the big opponent, given its superior resources. To illustrate the point, the lawyer said, “If this represents the extent of your resources”—he held his thumb and index finger about two inches apart—“then this” —he stretched his arms out as if preparing to fly—“represents the credit card company’s resources.”

Some lawyers may have allowed the business owner to proceed with the suit with a view to reaping a fee. Fortunately though, it seems the owner had a good lawyer who acted in his best interests and kept him from throwing good money after bad. A good lawyer isn’t just one who knows how to battle effectively on behalf of your small business, but also one who knows when not to battle at all.

Money Pit Alert

Even if you’re working with a reputable lawyer whom you’ve known for a long time and in whom you have the utmost faith because he or she has done well for you in the past, you shouldn’t forget you are the primary guardian of your small business’s budget. A lawsuit is like a home renovation. It can be well considered, carefully planned, and meticulously budgeted, and then it can drag on much longer than anticipated and hit snags you would never have expected. It can become a bottomless money pit.

I know of lawsuits involving small businesses that, in spite of the best of intentions, dragged on and on, way beyond what seemed reasonable by any measure. These quintessential money-pit lawsuits should have been terminated, and would likely have been terminated in favour of a negotiated settlement if there had been a predetermined limit on costs.

Unfortunately, as far as I know, there is no blanket formula for anticipating the costs and benefits of a law suit—it comes down to both the lawyer's and the client's good judgement. This is just another reason to have a concerned lawyer who views you more as a long-term client than a one-off fee opportunity.

You Get What You Pay For

I can't resist reiterating my experience-based advice: be very careful when selecting a lawyer for your small business. In the cases where my opponents received inadequate legal advice, they were relying on small local practices. I'm not suggesting there aren't any good sole-practitioner generalists, but frankly, I would have reservations about one with an office above Amy's Massage Parlour in an industrial-area strip mall desperately in need of a coat of paint and with a parking lot as potholed as the surface of the moon.

May your small business avoid spurious suits such as those with which I had to deal, but if you ever need legal assistance, know that you'll be pleased when your small business lawyer is a partner in a national firm able to access a smorgasbord of talent. It will almost certainly cost more than engaging a small-firm generalist, but the odds are your business will stand a much better chance of success in its legal trials and tribulations.

CHARACTER 5: FINANCIER

A BARRIER TO ENTRY

"This Wednesday's Lotto 6/49 jackpot is twelve million dollars. What would *you* do with twelve million dollars?" asks a smarmy male voice. An animated female voice replies, "Maybe I'll open my own business ..."

I reach for the car radio's Off button. Sheer nonsense. I don't know a single small business owner who would endure the daily grind if he or she were sitting on twelve million dollars. In any case, I need silence to contemplate the concept of lotteries as a source of business funding. It's something that hadn't crossed my mind until a moment ago. I'm intrigued—not because I'd consider the proposition seriously (the odds of winning this particular jackpot are about 1 in 14 million), but because of what this lottery commercial seems to confirm about the financing of small businesses.

It's safe to assume that the lottery organization's advertising agency did its homework. And it's also safe to assume advertisers don't record the first dialogue that comes to mind; surely they conduct research and then write the commercial's script for the widest appeal? And I'll bet the research confirmed what a lot of small business owners and would-be owners have known for a long time—many people dream of running their own businesses but lack the cash. In accounting and financial circles it's more formally known as "capital," but we'll call it "cash."

The cash conundrum

It takes cash to launch a business. And once it's launched, it takes cash to sustain it for the rest of its life. If the cash isn't generated from within—by profits earned—then it has to be topped up by external sources.

Cash is to a business what blood is to a body. If a body's blood level drops below a critical level (based on its size) or stops flowing—even for a short while—it's game over. This may sound cold, but you won't find a better metaphor for what cash flow means to your small business's survival.

The blood metaphor also helps make another important and often-overlooked point about business growth and cash. For a body to survive, its blood supply must increase proportionately to meet the demands of its growth. In the same way, a business needs additional cash to fund growth. Rapid business growth often inflates overhead expenses. And in almost all cases, it will require additional investment in items such as inventory, equipment, vehicles, premises, and receivables. If there's a lag between the cash that's flowing out to fund the rapid growth and the cash that's flowing in from the growth, the result is negative cash flow. And unchecked negative cash flow is to a business what an unchecked hemorrhage is to a body. In either case, if you can't arrange a transfusion to see it through what may be a temporary shortfall, death is inevitable. There's no way to sugar-coat it—a body with insufficient blood flow and a small business with insufficient cash flow are both destined to die.

With that cleared up, we can address the other conundrum: how you're going to raise cash. And unless you're in a more fortunate position than most small business owners (i.e., you have deep pockets), you will have to confront this conundrum almost certainly at start-up, and possibly at points during your business's life, particularly if it grows rapidly. To repeat: (because it's important and not readily appreciated) one of the great ironies of rapid business growth is that it can result in business failure due to insufficient cash flow.

Ultimately, the answer will lie with a financier of some sort—an investor, lender, or donor. But before seeking a financier, you have homework to do. Consider the advice of Martin Zwilling, who wrote the following for entrepreneur.com in October 2015: "... you need to learn what investment terms make sense for your start-up and craft your own term sheet, rather than rely on one being presented to you. Start with some legal advice from a source you trust. Do your homework and networking, but don't chase investors like a one-night stand and expect it to lead to a mutually beneficial long-term relationship."

In short, carefully consider and execute your cash-raising strategy.

Cash-raising strategy

The purpose of a cash-raising strategy is to identify the right target and select the right ammunition. It comes down to presenting a persuasive argument for why a targeted investor, lender, or donor should turn money over to your small business. For instance, you'll have to persuade an investor or lender that the deal will be financially beneficial for him or her, and you'll have to persuade a donor (not usually expecting any financial benefit) that his or her donation is going to a just cause. This takes work. Be prepared to make the effort. There is a lazy person's alternative involving a mask and a gun, but I wouldn't recommend it!

I know many small business owners who would prefer almost anything to drafting a cash-raising strategy. It's the all-too-common aversion to "number crunching" and "paperwork." So while I recommend preparing a cash-raising strategy, if you feel disinclined or underqualified to do it, get some help. But you mustn't avoid it. You stand a much better chance of raising cash with a well-thought-out approach to the right people. Plus, you'll gain insight from the intense examination of your business's current situation and future prospects. And if you do get help, you must participate in the exercise. Work with a knowledgeable person who can put your ideas, projections, and cash needs through the wringer. I have to emphasize this: *this isn't something you delegate*. It's an opportunity to pause and closely examine what makes your business tick. The hamster wheel on which most small business owners spend their days seldom affords an opportunity to pause, examine, and reflect. Preparing a cash-raising strategy will force you to. This is a good thing.

So what's involved in designing a cash-raising strategy? There are four steps. The first step is to figure out how much cash you're going to need and when. This should be the easy part. It's a product of the cash-flow projection of your budget package. If this sounds like Greek to you, visit or revisit the Accountant chapter and hire the help you need.

The second step is to determine which of the various types of financiers are best suited to your small business (more about this shortly).

The third step is to prepare the pitch. You may have a lot of persuasive material about the outlook of your business and the industry, but remember that most people don't relish wading through lengthy proposals and reports, at least not initially. All they're going to want is enough information to understand the gist of what you're proposing. Frame your initial pitch like a story. Everyone likes stories, even hard-nosed investors, lenders, and donors. If your target expresses interest and further discussions follow, then expect to bring out the detailed narrative and spreadsheets.

The fourth step is to make the pitch (tell your story) to the targeted prospect. Make it informative and eye-catching but keep it brief. If you use visual aids such as flip charts or a laptop and projector—yes, cloud-dwelling big business refugees, we still use these "Stone-Age" tools in small business—support them with something that can be taken away. A one-page document or flyer with simple illustrations should be enough. Information presented graphically is generally more readily absorbed than text. I like to use graphic artists for this type of material (see the Graphic Artist chapter). Some might argue that people don't pay attention to flyers or pamphlets and that they'll end up in the closest garbage bin.

But I believe it's worth the minor risk and expense to ensure that an interested prospect has something tangible as a reminder of your pitch.

It's a little different if you're dealing with a bureaucracy, such as a bank, with rigid procedures and reams of forms. You probably wouldn't drag a flip chart or your computer and projector down to the bank. But I'd still recommend presenting a flyer or pamphlet with graphics to summarize the purpose of your loan application—a picture speaking a thousand words helps bureaucrats understand, too.

Now, what type of financier should you be targeting?

Financier

For the purposes of our discussion, a "financier" is a person (or institution) who controls a large amount of money and can give or lend it to businesses. I'm using this character to represent individuals or institutions that may favour a small business with an equity investment, loan financing, or donated funds. Let's look at each of the three options.

Equity investment

Heidi Scrimgeour's *Telegraph* article "How to finance a growing business" provides a good thumbnail explanation of equity investment: "Equity funding entails giving up a slice of your business in return for investment. Venture capital and angel investment networks are the two main equity funding routes open to small businesses, but require a clear plan for delivering a return to investors within an agreed time frame."

Note the part about "... giving up a slice of your business in return for investment." It's the key difference between equity investments and loan financing and donations.

How do you find a venture capitalist or an angel investor? As you start researching equity investments, you'll discover articles explaining how investors can be found through networking events, community organizations, professional associations, trade organizations, business conferences, Internet networking platforms such as LinkedIn, and mutual contacts.

A source not included in the list is likely coming to mind for many of you: reality shows such as *Dragons' Den* and *Shark Tank*. These shows aren't worth considering for most small business owners. They're not about small business—they're about show business. They're about entertainment, syndication, ratings, and advertising dollars. If the shows were truly about investments in small businesses, the Dragons and Sharks would humiliate and reward applicants in a private setting. So, back to the real world, where most small businesses live.

Of course it's true that most of the small business-morphed-into-big-business success stories we hear from time to time would never have happened without the backing of investors such as venture capitalists or angel investors. You know the script by now: "Small business owner has an idea for a brilliant online application, relocates to Silicon Valley, raises a couple of million dollars from investors, develops the idea, and sells it to one of the tech giants for a few billion dollars." I don't mean to pour cold water on ambition or dreams, but this is the script for only a tiny fraction of the small business community.

If you (and your advisors) determine that an equity investor is the best option for your small business, then select your target and make your pitch (i.e., tell your story). But this won't be the financing route for most of the hundreds of thousands of run-of-the-mill small businesses. These businesses won't likely arouse any interest among venture capitalists or angel investors. They won't play in the major leagues of hot products, multimillion-dollar risks, and billion-dollar paydays.

I'm referring to those typical small businesses that most people will be familiar with: restaurants; dry cleaners; coffee shops; neighbourhood pubs; small clothing boutiques; bookstores; antique stores; beauty salons; specialty hardware stores; and so on and so on. Then there are the small businesses tucked away in industrial parks where most people don't go: machine shops; furniture restorers; plumbers; sign shops; screen printers; pool-chemical distributers; wholesale bakeries; stationery printers; flooring suppliers; electrical contractors; and kitchen-cabinet manufacturers, to name just a few. There are thousands more. Holding little interest for venture capitalists and angel investors, these are the types of small businesses that rely on loan financing.

Loan financing

What else drives many small business owners to favour loan financing over equity financing (aside from failure to interest venture capitalists and angel investors)? An independent spirit. Equity financing requires giving up at least some ownership. And quite often, it also involves sharing management control. This doesn't sit well with many small business owners.

Information on the various types of lenders and their lending methods could be a complete book on its own, so I'm just going to touch on the more common options that small business owners utilize. But again, there's an important caveat—you must consult with your accountant or another qualified independent resource about any borrowing facility you're considering. The costs of borrowing, repayment commitments, and exposure of personal assets differ greatly, depending on the lender; you need to be well advised. The more common lenders include financial institutions, private lenders, business incubators, factors, and family and friends. You should understand the differences between these lenders, and the implications of dealing with them, before making any approaches. The following is a brief breakdown.

- Financial institutions are the most common source of loans for small businesses. They offer financing options such as short-term debt; long-term debt; lines of credit; and credit cards. Financial institutions also offer specifically tailored forms of financing, such as commercial mortgages (for acquiring buildings) and lease financing (for vehicles and equipment).

- A private lender is usually a wealthy individual who will lend your small business money for a higher rate of interest than he or she could expect from a lower-risk conventional investment in, say, a financial institution or blue-chip stock. Sometimes the individual will be a successful business person willing to offer advice, expertise, and useful contacts, similar to a mentor.

- Business incubators offer support in many aspects of small business management—everything from business-plan development to locating resources to general business advice. Some provide funding.

- Factors can address immediate cash-flow needs by providing cash in exchange for uncollectible accounts. Generally, they'll buy your accounts for about 90 percent of their face value and assume the risk of collecting them.

- Family and friends are tempting sources, but I don't recommend borrowing cash from them. I'll explain why shortly.

Your choice will depend on what best suits your particular small business. You'll determine this while developing your cash-raising strategy.

Donated funds

"Donation" might conjure up an image of someone handing over a bag of cash to a small business with no expectation of repayment and no strings attached. This would of course be the ultimate in cash-raising, but it's the stuff of fantasies. In a discussion on raising cash for a small business, "donation" takes on a broader meaning to include any payment that doesn't have to be repaid—for instance, government grants and subsidies.

Grants and subsidies for small businesses have been around for many years. These are usually sums of money granted by governments for specific purposes (research and development, attendance at trade shows and conferences, marketing expenses, etc.). The nature and amount of these grants will vary from jurisdiction to jurisdiction, but they will inevitably be conditional on compliance with government priorities, such as creating jobs or developing a particular industry. It's a potential source of funds worth exploring. In some jurisdictions you'll find consultants who specialize in identifying grants for which your business may qualify. However, if you choose this route, seek out reputable, recommended consultants and be wary about laying out cash up front for "fees" without safeguards and assurances. As we know, charlatans abound.

Another form of donation is crowdfunding. In 1997 a rock band successfully appealed to fans to fund their reunion tour. The concept grew more popular after that. As the term implies, crowdfunding involves appealing to the population at large for cash. In return, participants are usually offered rewards (based on a tiered system) and the satisfaction of funding something worthwhile or, as one writer put it, "… [connecting] to the greater purpose of the campaign." Nevertheless, it's a donation, no matter how you slice it.

These campaigns are controlled by rules and standards. Be clear on them. There's a lot of research material on the topic. Review as much of the literature as possible before even thinking of conducting a campaign. In the meantime, here's a brief overview of the concept, which is quite simple. You prepare a description of what you're raising cash for, state how much you're aiming to raise by a stipulated date, and offer rewards based on level of participation. That's about it.

Two popular crowdfunding sites for business-related campaigns are Kickstarter and Indiegogo. In principle they are similar but they differ in how they charge and some other key aspects. Kickstarter requires a fixed campaign target and a fixed termination date. If the target isn't reached by the termination date, the campaign is deemed to have been unsuccessful and the backers' credit cards aren't charged.

With Indiegogo, you don't have to reach a specific dollar target in order for the campaign to succeed and the backers' money to be accepted.

Though the concept is simple enough, don't assume that a crowdfunding campaign will be a slam dunk. According to a 2015 article by David Freedman and Matthew Nutting, about 36 percent of Kickstarter campaigns were fully funded in the period from their launch in 2009 to 2015. Some of the successful campaigns were spectacularly successful, however. For instance, the Pebble smartwatch campaign set out to raise $100,000 to develop a watch from which you could download sports and fitness apps and connect to iPhone or Android smartphones. It raised $10,266,845.

It's difficult to anticipate whether a campaign will be successful. I've read of unlikely campaigns succeeding (such as the joke campaign to raise $10 to make a potato salad that raised $55,492 from 6,911 backers).

And campaigns that I thought were particularly worthwhile with a good chance of success ended up failing. But if your small business has an invention or product in need of funding, it might be an avenue to explore, particularly for females. Dan Wang, in his article "The Ultimate Guide to Crowdfunding," (on the Shopify blog) noted that while only 5 percent of venture capital goes to female founders, 37 percent of successful crowdfunding campaigns are run by females. This is encouraging, though one does wonder why it's not at least 50 percent.

Unconventional funding sources

So far, we've discussed conventional cash sources. But there are certainly creative, unconventional ways to finance small businesses. The nature of a creative, unconventional funding scheme will depend on the type of business or industry—what's feasible in one business or industry may not be in another.

Here's a personal story about a creative funding scheme in the textile screen printing industry. One of my company's early objectives was to capture the ink business of the bigger Canadian textile printers. But there was a big stumbling block: delivering screen printing ink to all points of Canada in a timely manner. Textile screen printing is a quick-turnaround business with more than its fair share of bad production planners. To them, "timely" delivery quite often means "immediate" delivery. This is impossible with just one stocking point from which to serve about a dozen main centres spaced out over five thousand kilometres from east to west. To make matters worse, the product is bulky, thus making delivery by air prohibitively expensive. The economically feasible alternative is trucking, which can take a week (and quite often longer with the likelihood of blizzards, ice storms, or avalanches en route).

Our solution was to offer the larger companies we were targeting an Ink On Tap (IOT) program. It was a standard consignment concept dressed up with some fancy graphics in an attractively bound booklet and presented as a brilliant new concept. Essentially, we placed an inventory of ink on the customer's floor and monitored it monthly. Most of our targeted printers bought in mainly because it solved one of their biggest headaches—anticipating ink requirements.

IOT was simple to implement and administer. We devised controls to minimize cheating, kept track of inventories, and administered the program by means of a custom-designed consignment accounting system. At the end of each month, we billed the client for the containers opened during the month and replaced them.

The concept worked so well that my small business almost became a victim of its success—the IOT inventories and receivables required funding over and above our regular business. My start-up needed to raise additional cash to fund about twelve IOT programs.

The solution was an investment program whereby investors could joint venture with my business on individual IOT programs. The invested amount (usually about twenty to thirty thousand) and a return based on a share of the profit was repaid according to a predetermined schedule. The investors benefitted from a good rate of return and my business benefitted from capturing a share of the market it would otherwise have been hard-pressed to finance.

The IOT program is an example of the old "necessity is the mother of invention" wisdom. If you're faced with necessity, some creative thinking might turn up unconventional but feasible ways to raise cash in your particular industry. Keep in mind that all the cautions applicable to raising cash through conventional sources apply to unconventional sources too, particularly the cautions regarding qualified assistance and proper documentation.

Sources to avoid

Even when it proves difficult to raise cash, there are sources you should avoid, despite temptation. Some are obvious, such as Three-Toes Tony with his beige raincoat, cauliflower ears, disfigured nose, black-and-white brogues, and violin case. Some are less obvious, and may even seem like good sources, such as family and friends.

While I've never seen Three-Toes Tony recommended, I have seen business authors recommend friends and family as sources for start-up cash. Don't do it! No matter how tempting it might be, don't do it.

It's high risk. And the potential victim is family peace. Few things can destroy family ties and friendships as a dispute over money, particularly if it's been lost. I'll bet you know or have heard of families in this situation. I know of many. Families are torn apart, friendships are destroyed, and don't get me started on expensive court cases! This is why I believe in third-party, arm's-length funding for small businesses. Keep family members' cash out of it. Long after a business has failed and disappeared, the family will still exist. And it's so much better if at reunions, weddings, and funerals, everyone is on talking terms.

I've also seen credit cards recommended as a source of borrowing for small business start-ups. I caution against this as well. A credit card can be a siren call for a cash-strapped small business—convenient and tempting at the time but a long-term trap. Not only is it an expensive form of borrowing, but also, the outstanding balance can quickly accumulate until it becomes difficult to repay. My business had small business customers who would call in a credit card number to pay for an order, and when one was declined, would give us two or three more until one cleared. Maxing out credit cards is not a sensible way to finance a business.

Mark Zwilling lists eight other types of investors to avoid in his entrepreneur.com article (his wisdom can be applied when considering lenders and donors, too). I encourage you to read it in full as part of your research in preparing your cash-raising strategy. I've only quoted enough on each type to serve as a heads-up.

- Investment sharks: "... there are investors who prey on entrepreneurs who have little financial experience ..."
- Investors who love to litigate: "We all know that start-ups don't have money to fight in court, so it's easy for a few unscrupulous investors to jump to the conclusion that intimidation and lawsuit threats can improve their returns and control ..."
- Imperial investors: "These are investors with such massive egos that they expect to dictate both the terms of the investment as well as all future strategic decisions ..."

- Legal eagle investors: "Negotiating terms is normal before the investment, but once the check is cashed, you don't want to be second-guessed on every action."

- Academic coach investors: "Coaching should be expected and appreciated, but you don't have time for constant tutorials on how to run a business."

- Pretend investors: "They always have one more issue to investigate or another set of questions, but never bring the chequebook."

- Investors without a clue: "Many great real-estate people and doctors fall into this category. A synergistic long-term relationship in your business is unlikely."

- Investors for a fee: "These are people who rarely invest their own funds, but promise to find the perfect match and live off a percentage of the action and preparation fees."

And if all of that isn't enough, there are frogs, too.

Kissing frogs

We've all heard the expression "You have to kiss a lot of frogs to find your prince." It means you'll experience repeated failure before enjoying success—that persistence pays off. In the context of raising cash for your business, it quite correctly suggests you may have to interact with a number of lenders, investors, or donors before finding one with whom you can conclude a deal.

But I'd be remiss if I didn't caution female small business owners in particular that "kissing frogs" might not be just a metaphor. It can also have sinister undertones. In June 2016 the *New York Times* reported that a female entrepreneur had been propositioned by a Silicon Valley venture capitalist. Another female entrepreneur showed the *Times* suggestive messages she'd received from a start-up investor. Then the floodgates opened. More than two dozen women entrepreneurs spoke to the *Times* about being sexually harassed while seeking finance for their businesses.

One woman explained that at a meeting about her fitness start-up, the venture capitalist attempted to kiss and grope her. "I felt like I had to tolerate it," she said, "because this is the cost of being a non-white female founder." If this doesn't make you wince, not much will.

Other news media outlets report similar accounts from time to time. Readers' reactions are enlightening—they run the gamut, from outrage and disgust to dismissive "boys will be boys" comments. It's discouraging that these incidents still occur in this day and age, but it's doubly discouraging that some people see no harm in them.

My message for female small business owners seeking cash? Be on your guard. You don't have to tolerate sexual abuse to fund your entrepreneurial dreams. Shut the conversation down at the first sign of an ominous turn and deal with honourable financiers who don't have ulterior motives.

"Kissing frogs" was never meant to be taken literally.

Research and perseverance

Small business financing is a vast topic. You must research it thoroughly, and never lose sight of the importance of cash in the survival of your small business. Keep the blood metaphor in mind. When a transfusion is needed, set about raising cash with a carefully considered strategy.

If you're turned down, it's normal to feel discouraged briefly. But get over it and don't give up. Believe in your business and its prospects, keep refining your strategy, and keep knocking on doors until you find the right financier for your small business. In my office is a handwritten poster of unknown origin; its wonderful message seems appropriate here: "Your value does not decrease based on someone's inability to see your worth."

CHARACTER 6: FAMILY MEMBER

They should have behaved better

In her TED Talk on writing, best-selling author Anne Lamott articulates exactly why I dreaded tackling this character: "Families are hard, hard, hard, no matter how cherished and astonishing they may also be."

One hesitates to write about a family member in the way one hesitates to prod a bear with a pointed stick—neither is going to like it and both will let you know this in no uncertain terms. Family-member business relationships are common in the small business community, though. They cannot be omitted from a book about the characters who can make or break your business. I knew that I wanted to share my own experiences while addressing this topic—I've attempted going into business with both my brother and brother-in-law. But I hesitated to write about it (think bear and pointed stick). Then Ms. Lamott gave me the green light. She told her TED audience: "If you don't know where to start, remember that every single thing that happened to you is yours, and you get to tell it. If people wanted you to write more warmly about them, they should've behaved better."

Now, if everyone in your extended family is an angel, if no one ever behaves badly, if never a terse word passes between you and your family members, if your siblings' spouses encourage them to help you run your business in spite of the late hours and meagre and sporadic pay ("Don't worry, sweetheart, we'll get by somehow—you help your brother, he needs you"), then you may skip this chapter. However, if you have a "normal" family, the rest of the chapter is for you.

It's complicated

Family relationships can be complicated. When they overlap with business relationships, the potential for complications increases exponentially. And I'm not just talking about the relationship between you and the family member involved in your business. Often, business relationships draw in family members not directly involved in the business. Some family members may feel their opinions should be heard simply by virtue of their "family" status—and this belief often overrides the tact, discretion, and prudence generally exercised between non-family business associates.

Even if at first you can run your business in harmony with a family member, there's no guarantee this peace will last. All it takes is another family member with an axe to grind—most families have at least one axe grinder. He or she may be openly confrontational about your business, but a nagging, passive-aggressive, behind-the-scenes axe grinder can be just as disruptive. Persistent grinding at home will inevitably affect your business partner's mood and outlook. This will become evident at work where it will manifest itself as an attitude problem which will of course have an adverse impact on your business.

Confronting the problem in a frank discussion with all parties involved may result in a resolution, but it's best to have a discussion before entering into a business relationship with a family member. Potentially contentious confrontations may be avoided if everyone is apprised of typical small business challenges before they arise—i.e., long hours and circumstances that might necessitate belt-tightening at home. This information might clear up any misconceptions that could otherwise erupt later, but it could just as easily not sit well with some people (the spouse of the family member about to join your business, for example). If distrust and animosity have accumulated over years of family interactions—and I don't know too many families completely devoid of these issues—you may have an uphill battle establishing conditions for a harmonious, long-term business relationship.

If the business relationship proceeds after all the cards have been laid on the table, it will do so with a better chance of success. If it doesn't proceed, this may be disappointing, but it will still be a good result inasmuch as you will likely have avoided a long-drawn-out acrimonious and damaging relationship that could permanently wreck a small business and a family.

Learning the Hard Way

My suggestions on how to handle family members in business relationships are born out of unfortunate experiences. I discussed undertaking joint business opportunities with my brother and brother-in-law on separate occasions, about ten years apart. You're perfectly entitled to wonder why I'd repeat a mistake. I have no excuse, but it goes to show how easily one can slip into these situations.

In both cases, we focussed on the benefits and neglected to properly explore the challenges and pitfalls. Most importantly, we didn't have a roundtable discussion with everyone involved directly or peripherally (particularly spouses). I now know that this discussion is essential.

From the outset, both ventures encountered difficulties. Disapproving, interfering spouses played a part, and to cut a long story short, both relationships succumbed to a burden of tension, finger-pointing, and baggage dragged in from the family arena. And, I'm sad to say, both ventures resulted in permanent family disruption.

Most of us are brought up to believe that extended family is important and that whenever possible we should be considerate of family members. And perhaps this "consideration" includes finding ways to accommodate them in business ventures. But I'm older and wiser now. Subject family members to the same scrutiny and careful consideration as any other would-be employee or business partner. In fact, you should probably subject them to more—remember, you're not just getting the family member in question. You're also getting the family members holding axes they won't hesitate to grind at the first sign that not everything is coming up roses.

Who's in the family tree?

The family tree from which you'll pick your family-member employee or partner includes spouses, siblings, parents, children, and extended family members. Each has different implications when it comes to your business. Let's look at the family members most commonly engaged in family businesses.

Spouse

Spouses commonly own small businesses together. Perhaps the (often disingenuously referred to) mom-and-pop store springs to mind. But spousal co-ownership goes way beyond this. Larger small businesses are quite often run successfully by a spousal team.

While I've known a number of successful spousal business partnerships, including my own, I've also known a number that ended badly—both the business relationship and the personal relationship. I don't know whether the spousal relationships would have failed anyway, but it's difficult to imagine the failure of one of the relationships not undermining the other.

This is why it's important for a couple to thoroughly explore all the pros and cons of working together before taking the plunge. At first blush, working together might seem like a romantic extension of your personal relationship. But don't be surprised if upon closer examination it no longer looks that way. The worst thing you can do is allow romance to eclipse reason. And don't be dismayed if you decide that you're not suited to working together—it's not a reflection on your personal relationship. Not at all. On the contrary, your personal relationship might be dodging a bullet.

And if you decide against working together, you won't be alone. Numerous couples have told me that for the sake of their personal relationship there's no way they'd even consider a business relationship. Also, there's a financial aspect to consider—you'll be putting all your eggs in one basket. If you're both working in the business and it splutters or fails, this could be very hard on the family budget. For those couples yet to establish themselves financially, it might make sense for one person to take on the risk of business ownership while the other holds down a job with a steady income—at least until the business is established and turning a maintainable profit.

If you do decide to work together, know that irritation and tension arising from incidents at home are invariably carried to the office, and vice versa. I know this from personal experience. And until my wife and I met a remarkable couple who had undertaken two driving adventures—from Cape Town to Cairo and from Alaska to the southern tip of Argentina—I didn't come across a good solution to the problem of carrying irritations back and forth between the office and home.

Janet and Tom were cooped up with only each other for company in the confined space of a vehicle all day every day for months at a time. Irritation and disputes inevitably came up, and for both the sake of their marriage and the sake of the adventure, they needed to find a way to manage them. They devised the "twenty-minute solution": either or both parties had twenty minutes after an "incident" to sulk, blow off steam, or do whatever was necessary to restore peace. Apparently it worked very well for them—they're still together and Janet is writing a book about their experience.

If you're involved in a dual business and spousal relationship and want to keep tension from dragging on for too long or from spilling over from one relationship into the other, the "twenty-minute solution" or some variation thereof is worth considering. There were certainly times when my wife and I could have used it.

Sibling

A business relationship with a sibling must comply with all the criteria required for a business partnership. But more importantly, the sibling relationship itself must to be sound. Sibling relationships can bring with them years of accumulated baggage not conducive to a peaceful, productive business relationship. You need to assess the nature of the personal relationship before entering into a business one. Any fractiousness is bound to journey back and forth from the business relationship to the personal one, to the detriment of both.

That said, a number of sibling partnerships go about their businesses quite cordially. I talked with some of them while writing this book, and all parties said that if their personal relationship hadn't been sound, they wouldn't have been able to conduct a business relationship. All also confirmed that it was necessary to distinctly divide duties and responsibilities to minimize conflict.

Further encouragement and advice is offered by Judith Lowry, who owns Argosy Book Store in New York City with her two sisters. In the November–December 2016 issue of *Family Business* magazine, she said: "When we took over, we made a pact that we wouldn't argue about little things. We get along because the business is more important than who's right and who's wrong."

Parent–Child

I know of many cases where the children wanted nothing to do with the parents' business and took off to pursue careers in entirely different fields. I've seen parent–child business relationships that couldn't be sustained amid persistent clashes and tension. However, I also know of a few successful parent–child business relationships. But, importantly, the individuals involved in them all stipulated one prerequisite for success: a solid personal relationship.

Each pointed out that a generation gap with potentially significant implications should be anticipated, and that it must be managed carefully to avoid conflict. The younger generation is typically less experienced but more current when it comes to certain aspects of the business (e.g., fashion trends, customer demands, and technological developments). They also tend to be more energetic, more adventurous, and less risk averse. Given what we already know about generational differences in society at large, none of this should come as a surprise. The important point is that anyone contemplating a parent–child business relationship ignores generational differences at their peril.

So, you've hired family members. Now what about getting rid of them?

You're fired!

My friend Mac ran a successful business for many years, and at various times, he employed a number of family members.

Unlike some other small businesses owners I've known with similar family member involvement, Mac told me that his level of tolerance was the same for all employees. Being family didn't guarantee tenure in Mac's business. He fired at least two family members that I know of—a son and a nephew. I'm not sure how much family discord it generated, but his business continued to thrive.

In terms of business, Mac was right in his approach. No partner or employee should expect tenure just because he or she is family. Most small businesses can't afford to carry underperformers. Unlike big organizations, small businesses have neither the resources to carry them nor the back pages on bulky organization charts to hide them in.

For the sake of your small business's survival, hold family members to the same performance standards as every other employee. If they aren't meeting these standards, tell them what every other employee would hear: "You're fired!"

Non-family fallout

The presence of family members in your business can create difficult working conditions for your non-family employees and partners. If you haven't considered the situation from their perspective, you'll likely want to do so once you read what I've been told by non-family employees in family businesses. Nobody I talked to cited any particular advantages of being a non-family employee in a family business, but there was no holding back on the disadvantages. Two disadvantages in particular came up every time.

The first was that while non-family employees understood that every family has its drama, they wished that family members would leave it at home. Realistically, I think it's expecting too much. How do you have a bun-fight on Sunday afternoon at a family event and pretend it didn't happen on Monday morning at work? I don't know many people who can compartmentalize their emotions this way. At any rate, non-family employees wished it were possible because they inevitably found themselves drawn into the family drama, and they didn't like it. If your business is suffering from poor morale or high staff turnover, consider whether this could be the reason.

The second disadvantage that came up repeatedly was the insubordination of family members in junior positions. This is bound to happen unless the owner makes a point of ensuring that the family member is clear that he or she has no special privileges and that insubordination won't be tolerated. But this is difficult to enforce if an owner confers unusual privileges on family members. For example, one person told me that she resigned from a company not long after the owner employed his young daughter as a trainee (the daughter knew nothing of the business or industry) and gave her a company car and gas allowance. No other employee received these benefits—not even the girl's supervisor. A case can be made that a business owner is entitled to favour family members any way he or she wishes, but it shouldn't come as a surprise if it emboldens the family members and rubs non-family employees the wrong way.

The lesson here is to view the involvement of family members in your business from a non-family employee's perspective. Otherwise, you may see poor morale or even lose valuable, contributing employees. And of course, both of these things can harm your small business.

Careful contemplation and management

If you're considering entering a business relationship with a family member, or you're in one already, just remember Anne Lamott's observation: "Families are hard, hard, hard, no matter how cherished and astonishing they may also be."

Think carefully about this relationship before entering it, and once you're in, manage it carefully. In that regard, consider a strong advisor or outside director to mediate intrafamily conflict and provide objective advice.

CHARACTER 7: SIGNIFICANT OTHER

"Have a great day. I hope that meeting doesn't drag on too long this evening, but if it does, don't sweat it. Lemme know when you're on your way and I'll order pizza or something. Oh, and where's your laundry slip? I'll pick it up on my way home from work."

The front door is being held open for you. With key fob in hand and both arms embracing the paperwork that kept you up until two this morning, you step out into the cool pre-dawn air. It's barely 6:30. Most of the houses on the street are still in darkness, as usual.

As your thumb feels for the unlock button on the fob you suddenly remember that thing you'd stored in the back of your mind. You've been trying to recall it since you dragged yourself out of bed. Even as you gulped down the coffee and devoured the bacon and eggs that had been cooked for you it was lurking out of reach …

"Oh damn! I'm out of gas!"

"It's okay, I filled up last night," says the person at the door.

With this kind of understanding and support you're able to tackle the day without worrying about how irregular hours and other typically unanticipated business issues are affecting the home front.

This person at the door is your significant other—a significant other not engaged in your business.

In the previous chapter we discussed family members engaged in your small business, including significant others. But an *unengaged* significant other is quite a different character from an *engaged* significant other—the former's impact isn't readily obvious. This person is a presence beyond the spotlight, rather like a ghost hovering in the shadows. Unfortunately, this ghost is not always a supportive one. In some cases it may even be a poltergeist, but more on this shortly.

The unengaged significant other's absence in the business is probably why this person's influence is commonly overlooked by small business writers and commentators. It's a classic out-of-sight-out-of-mind oversight. Just as children watching a puppet show conveniently overlook that the character on stage is behaving in a particular way because someone out of sight is pulling the strings, we tend to overlook that a small business owner can behave in a particular way because an out-of-sight significant other is pulling strings.

The impact of an unengaged significant other's string-pulling depends upon his or her attitude to your business, which can range from supportive to hostile. It's not hard to see which significant other (supportive significant other or hostile significant other) is an asset to your business and which is a liability.

I can best illustrate this by sharing the compelling stories of two small business owners. Both are cautionary tales, not because I want to be negative but because they make a point: a less-than-supportive significant other can wreak havoc in both your business and your relationship.

Rory's story

Rory (not his real name) founded a textile screen printing business with his father and brother. Dedication and hard work got the business off to a good start and boosted it into a steady growth pattern. After some time, they moved to larger premises and increased their output capacity by investing in a state-of-the-art automated garment press capable of churning out six hundred to a thousand T-shirts an hour.

Rory was on a sales call when he met Angela (not her real name). A relationship developed and, to cut a long story short, Margaret and I were guests at their wedding. I remember the happy day well. Two young, energetic small business owners had found each other through business. This relationship had all the makings of an entrepreneurial match made in heaven.

Sadly, it didn't last. After seven years they were divorced. Ironically, rather than entrepreneurship being the tie that bound, it was exactly the opposite.

This is why now, about eight years later, I'm sitting opposite Rory in a Vietnamese restaurant in Calgary. A few days ago I traced him to a company where he's been working for the previous four years and asked if he'd be willing to be interviewed for my Significant Other chapter. Though some people are reluctant to revisit the topic of a failed relationship or business, particularly when the two were inextricably entwined, Rory agreed to provide insight into how an unengaged significant other can affect a small business.

With ordering and catch-up small talk out of the way, we get down to the matter at hand. I feel a little awkward broaching the first probing question: "Would you say there was any connection between the failure of your marriage and the failure of your business?"

Rory doesn't hesitate. "Huge! Of course there were other things as well, but the business was a big one."

"Why?"

"Probably mostly because of the hours I had to put in at the shop. It was okay at first but gradually she began complaining about my long and irregular hours."

"I'm surprised by this," I say. "You were both business owners, so I'd have thought that unlike, say, someone who had a standard nine-to-five job with a regular paycheque, she would have understood the demands of running a small business."

"You'd think, but remember she had a retail business with fixed opening and closing hours, so it was more regular than mine. She couldn't or wouldn't understand the nature of my business."

"I can see this being a problem."

"But wait, it gets worse. She was also a big spender and had money expectations the business couldn't always meet. This added to the tension between us. She accused me of being an inadequate provider."

I want to steer the conversation away from the home back to the business, which is really my main interest. "Okay, so things weren't great at home, but how did this impact the business?"

"Well, it was always on my mind. And who can concentrate at work when you're worried about your relationship and what the atmosphere is going to be like when you get home? And then it really becomes a worry when you have a big order or something else urgent and you have to work late. You just know when you get home there won't be any supper. And then there's the tension. Some nights the bedroom door would be locked and I'd have to sleep on the couch. You can't concentrate on critical business issues or put in the hours you sometimes have to with the situation at home hanging over you like a dark cloud."

The waitress arrives with our food. The interruption is timely because I think Rory's becoming emotional and the fine line between information-gathering and opening old wounds is looming.

"Number ninety-three!" says the waitress as she plonks down two big bowls of stir-fried beef, fresh lemon grass, and spring rolls on a bed of rice vermicelli. She leaves as abruptly as she arrived.

I poke at the contents of my bowl with chopsticks and take a mouthful of shredded beef and floppy, dangling noodles. I do this two or three more times before putting down the chopsticks. I'm no longer hungry. My appetite has gone. Emotionally charged conversations tend to do this to me. Rory appears to have lost his appetite as well.

I resume the conversation as I turn to a clean page in my notebook.

"It seems that an unengaged significant other's attitude to a business fits into one of three categories across a spectrum," I say. "I'm wondering if it makes any sense to you." I draw a horizontal line across the page and point with my pen. "Here on the left of the spectrum we have a 100-percent-supportive significant other. This person gets your small business and understands it can be a roller-coaster ride. He or she doesn't complain when you have to work late, volunteers to pick up your dry cleaning, lines up to renew your car licence, returns the overdue library books you haven't had time to read, and buys a birthday gift from you for your mother. If you have children, he or she will take charge of the homework, feeding, bathing, story-reading, and tucking-in and then, thoroughly exhausted, will still summon up the energy to make sure there's a glass of wine, a hot meal, and an Epsom salts bath waiting when you finally drag your weary bones home. And to crown it all, even as a good book, a favourite TV show, or much-needed sleep beckons, the supportive significant other will listen while you replay the day's events."

Rory's quizzical expression suggests skepticism. "Okay ..."

"All right, nobody is an absolute angel, but you know what I mean?"

"Sure," he says.

I point to the other end of the line. "Here at the other extreme of the spectrum we have the significant other hostile to your business. He or she sees nothing good in it, hates it with a passion, and will do nothing to lighten your burden. The attitude is that it's your bloody business and therefore your problem that you don't have time for anything. You'll be taking care of your own dry cleaning, probably forget to renew your licence until you see flashing red-and-blue lights in the rear-view mirror, run up fines at the library, and be too busy and harassed to remember to buy a birthday gift for your mother. A hostile significant other will head out with his or her friends as soon as you drag your weary body in and, if you have children, leave you to cope with the homework, feeding, bathing, story-reading, and tucking-in. You'll also make your own supper and then sit down to eat it while sharing a replay of the day's events with the dog. And if he or she doesn't go out, you'll still be doing most of this anyway, except that it will be to the background of complaints about the time you spend on the business, the money it doesn't produce, the new car you can't afford to lease, and the holidays you haven't taken."

"And you'll end up sleeping on the couch most nights," Rory reminds me.

It's my cue to slip in a somewhat-related wisecrack: "I once heard someone say you know you're in a relationship when the doghouse has carpeting, a cot, and a television." Rory barely cracks a smile. I guess when you've lived the joke, it's not a joke anymore.

I wave my pen over the middle areas of the line. "Here, between the two extremes of the spectrum we have the indifferent significant other. This is a grey area. An indifferent significant other can blow hot or cold depending upon circumstances at a particular moment. He or she may lean towards the supportive end of the spectrum when things are going well but then towards the hostile end when things aren't. The most unsettling part about an indifferent significant other is that you can't anticipate when this person will blow hot, cold, or somewhere in between."

"Exactly!" says Rory. "This situation here"—he points to the middle of the line—"is actually worse than this one here." He points to the hostile end of the spectrum. "At least you know what to expect from someone with a totally shitty attitude, but you don't know what to anticipate from someone who blows hot and cold. It's impossible."

"Okay, so imagine I'm a youngster sitting across the table from you wanting to tap into your small business experience. I tell you I'm starting a business. I've done all the number crunching, I know how much money

I'm going to need, I have premises in mind, I've researched my market, I've contacted suppliers, and I'm pretty confident I've got all the bases covered. I also tell you I know I'm going to have to work long hours to build my business and I don't expect to make a lot of money in the first few years but that's okay because my fiancée has a great job. What do you say to me?"

Rory pauses for a moment before saying, "Unless your new business turns out to be the exception to the rule, you're right about putting in long hours, at least initially. And you're quite right about the money, too. There'll probably be times when you can't pay yourself. There will also be times when the business will exhaust you, worry you, even depress you, and you won't be much fun to be around. How long before your fiancée begins to resent you for not carrying your weight financially? How long before your limited social life as a couple becomes a problem because of your long hours? How long do you think *your* fiancée will put up with this before the business causes a tide of discontent to rise up and swamp your business and your relationship?"

Maintaining my role as the eager but now puzzled young would-be small business owner, I ask, "What do you mean?"

"I know your fiancée has an entirely different career and won't be directly engaged in your business, but it doesn't mean there's a wall between your business and your fiancée. There is no wall—one *will* affect the other. So before you commit to a relationship *and* a business, you need to take a good, hard look at both. You need to decide if the one is compatible with the other. Because if they're not compatible, you run the risk of eventually losing at least one, if not both."

Before I can comment, Rory continues: "And if your fiancée and your business are to coexist then you need to be upfront about your commitment to your work. Share your calendar, be frank about finances, and say what you expect to be able to contribute to the household budget. The more transparent you are about these things, the better."

The waitress reappears and stares at the two almost untouched bowls pushed to one side. She's not pleased. She's takes an exaggerated deep breath, but before she can say anything I assure her the food is excellent, we just can't eat any more. She picks up the bowls and mutters in what I assume is Vietnamese—probably something insulting. To her, what's just happened is that two bowls of perfectly good food have been wasted. To me, what's just happened is that I've recorded a story to help alert present and potential small business owners to the tenuous relationship between an unengaged significant other and a small business—a relationship tenuous enough to make or break a small business.

If Rory's generosity in sharing his story and advice helps prevent even just one repeat of his experience, two wasted bowls of number ninety-three will have been a small price to pay.

Anne's story

Anne (not her real name) co-owned a granite countertop business with her husband. But granite countertops left Anne cold. Her passion was the hospitality industry—something she'd acquired growing up around her parents' successful restaurant. Increasingly she was missing the hustle and bustle, the guests, and the atmosphere of restaurants, cafés, and coffee shops.

Understandably, after two years of granite countertops, she decided she'd had enough and would open a coffee shop. This solved one problem but immediately created another. Her husband, resenting her decision, adopted a hostile attitude to Anne's small business.

I don't know Anne as well as I know Rory. I've not met her ex-significant other and I'm not nearly as familiar with her home life and business as I was with Rory's. But I've got to know her well enough to have heard her say her business played a significant role in the failure of her marriage. It's about four years since the failure and I'm sitting in Anne's coffee shop. She has generously taken time out from behind the counter to enlarge on how a significant other's attitude to your small business can affect the business, your home life, and eventually your relationship.

Anne is now separated and a single mum. There's no suggestion her business was the sole villain of the piece, but it did play a role, and she's about to tell me how.

"The first problem was that most days I'd have to be here to open at seven o'clock in the morning. I wouldn't go home until after I'd closed at seven in the evening. He didn't like this. It meant he had to support me by doing things like taking our daughter to school in the mornings and picking her up in the afternoons. He hated the café from the beginning and wasn't supportive at all. Even though I'd come home exhausted I still had to cook and clean."

"How did it affect your business?"

"It was very difficult, especially when he went out of his way to make life hard for me. I realized this couldn't carry on when one day a customer was talking to me and I didn't hear a word he was saying because my mind was elsewhere, worrying about whether my husband was going to pick our daughter up at school. I'd been phoning and phoning to remind him and he wasn't answering. It had become a pattern of hostile behaviour."

Anne's story is beginning to sound familiar.

She continues to explain: "Once our relationship began to deteriorate, his hate for my business grew until it seemed that closing it was the only way for me to resolve our relationship issues. But I had obligations—like five years left on the lease—and in any case, there was no guarantee that getting rid of the business would solve our problems at home. Eventually we split."

I sketch my spectrum of attitudes and ask Anne if it makes sense to her. She agrees that it does. "You can't run a small business successfully and with peace of mind if you're in a relationship with someone hostile to your business. If typical small business challenges, such as long hours and irregular cash flow, become contentious issues in your relationship, things can go downhill quickly."

What have we learned?

What Rory and Anne hope to have taught us is that an incompatible twosome—your significant other and your business—is a prescription for an unhappy existence at home and at work. It's likely also a prescription for an eventual loss of at least one, if not both.

Unfortunately, this lesson doesn't get the coverage it deserves in business literature. If you are in a relationship or own a small business and embark on the other, and unless you know somebody who had to deal with an incompatible twosome, you're unlikely to give the matter any consideration at all before plunging in. This could be disastrous.

My two pennies' worth

Although I've known other small business owners who've wrestled with an incompatible twosome, I have no first-hand experience with this challenge. I therefore don't feel qualified to offer solutions other than to urge avoidance in the first place. But if it's too late for this because you're already in a stressful, incompatible twosome situation and want to avoid the way Rory's story and Anne's unfolded, then I'd suggest relationship counselling. Considering what we invest in our relationships and our businesses, surely we should pursue whatever avenues we can for a resolution before we pull the plug on either?

Failing a workable solution—and assuming you can't see yourself in your current situation indefinitely—you could be facing an either-or choice. Either the significant other or the business has to go. I'm afraid I'm not aware of any tried-and-tested formula for resolving this dilemma. There is no silver bullet: it must be resolved by honest conversations between your heart and your brain. Even if you consult with family, friends, and professionals, it's still ultimately your decision.

This is a dilemma I wouldn't wish on my worst enemy—all the more reason for small – business owners to be aware of the risks associated with unengaged significant others. All the more reason to make wise, informed, and well-considered choices before asking an unengaged significant other and a small business to coexist.

CHARACTER 8: DIRECTOR

An outsider

If your small business is incorporated, you are probably a director. But the director we're discussing here is not you. This chapter is about a director who is not employed by your business, who has no day-to-day operational role in it, and who has no ownership in it. This is an outside director. And for the sake of convenience, I'm going to refer to a single outside director. Keep in mind there could be more than one.

Only a tiny minority of small businesses appoint outside directors, but pinning down a number is difficult. Business literature largely ignores the topic, and even sources such as the Canadian Federation of Independent Business and Statistics Canada—which can usually tell you anything you need to know about small business—offer no insight. The closest I came to a number is the 5 percent suggested by a 2014 *Forbes* article entitled "Outside Board Members Bring Needed Experience and Perspective to Your Company."

The article speculates that small business owners don't appoint outside directors because the owners think they're smart enough, they think it's too expensive, or they think it would constrain their decision-making abilities. I can buy these reasons, but I'd add that many small business owners probably haven't given the matter much thought. I didn't. Of course I now know that I should have. Twenty-twenty hindsight is cruel in its clarity. However, *you* can avoid this future frustration by not repeating my oversight. If your small business is one of the 95 percent, now might be a good time to consider whether it could benefit from the appointment of an outside director. And even if now isn't the right time, the circumstances of your business could change (e.g., as a result of growth or expansion into a new field), so you may want to keep this discussion in mind.

Anticipated benefits

Two words in the *Forbes* magazine article hint at the key contributions a small business might expect from an outside director: *experience* and *perspective*. In other words, two elements often lacking in small businesses—the first due to the owner's inexperience (especially in the case of new entrepreneurs) and the second due to the owner's immersion in day-to-day operations at the cost of neglecting the bigger picture. It's the ol' chief-cook-and-bottle-washer trap from which some small business owners never escape.

According to the *Biographical Memoirs of Fellows of the Royal Society*, Francis Arthur Freeth, a British industrial chemist, once acerbically asked about the directors of Brunner Mond Ltd., the company he worked for: "What are they doing, examining last month's costs with a microscope when they should be surveying the horizon with a telescope?"

Freeth worked for a large company, but small businesses shouldn't neglect the horizon either. They too need someone with a telescope keeping an eye on the bigger picture and choosing an appropriate direction for the business. This is where an outside director's experience and perspective can make a major contribution. So, what does this outside director look like?

Older man in a dark suit

Shut your eyes right now and picture a "company director." What do you see? Chances are it's an older man in a dark suit, right? To test my theory about the generally-held perception of company directors, I conducted an informal email survey among friends and associates:

Do you want to help me with a one-question survey? It's not a trick or IQ test or anything like that. I'm just testing a theory. Close your eyes and picture a "company director." Don't read on until you've done this.

Now, which of these eight images most closely approximated the image that immediately came to mind?

1. *An older man in a business suit*
2. *An older woman in a business suit*
3. *A young man in a business suit*
4. *A young woman in a business suit*
5. *An older man dressed casually*
6. *An older woman dressed casually*
7. *A young man dressed casually*
8. *A young woman dressed casually*

The almost-unanimous choice was the older man in a business suit. Even a self-proclaimed feminist friend admitted to thinking of an older man in a business suit first. Then she added, "I wish it had been 2."

The media seems to be the main culprit (perhaps unwittingly so) in perpetuating this stereotypical image. To be fair, it's primarily big corporations' directors who make the news, and they're almost invariably older men in dark suits. We seldom see younger folk because it takes time to earn your way into the boardrooms of big companies, and in most developed countries, women constitute fewer than 20 percent of big companies' boards. So how is this relevant to small business?

When I say you might want to consider appointing an outside director for your small business, I don't want you to think I'm advocating an older man in a dark suit. Despite the first image that comes to most people's minds, any of the eight possibilities I listed above could make a great director. It all depends on the mix of expertise and experience your small business needs. In some of today's emerging industries, the older man in a dark suit might be hopelessly out of his depth whereas a twenty-something in a T-shirt and jeans might have a wealth of expertise and experience.

Compensation

Once you've found the right outside director, there's the question of cost. If you believe that directors cost an arm and a leg, you probably got this impression from the same source that promotes the stereotypical male director. You'd be correct in the case of the Fortune 500 world. According to compensationforce.com, directors' compensation packages often include retainers, board meeting fees, committee fees, and stock options. But relax, that's the Fortune 500 world—small business directorships are an entirely different kettle of fish.

Outside directors in small businesses are compensated much more modestly than their counterparts in big corporations. But just as business literature hasn't much to say about how small businesses appoint outside directors, it has less to say about how they're compensated. Some formal studies of private companies' directors' compensation packages have been conducted, but they don't include businesses with less than $10 million annual revenue, thus excluding most small businesses. This leaves us trying to build a picture from anecdotal information and the occasional snippet gleaned from business articles, all of which allude to modest compensation packages.

How modest? Well, they may include travel and accommodation expenses for attending meetings, mobile phones or other digital devices, and limited cash stipends. How limited? According to the allbusiness.com website, very limited: "If your company can afford to provide it, offering a cash stipend based on company performance is a nice way to compensate your hardworking board members. You can make the cash stipend contingent on meeting specific company goals, or you can decide to set a specific stipend for one year of board membership, for example $2,000 to $5,000."

It's quite reasonable to question why someone would agree to a small business directorship for such modest compensation. Significant growth potential is a possibility. An outside director "getting in on the ground floor" may speculate that modest compensation now could grow into something much more significant later, when the small business hits the big time. But considering how elusive the big time is for most small businesses, I doubt it's a significant reason for serving as a small business director. The most likely explanation is therefore altruism. And if I'm right—and I do believe that I am—this altruism is particularly admirable considering not only the time commitment but also the legal obligations a director bears.

Legal obligations

Directors, regardless of whether they are owner-directors or outside directors, assume legal obligations when appointed. These obligations will differ from country to country and even from jurisdiction to jurisdiction within countries.

In some jurisdictions, directors' liability insurance is available, and it may be something you can offer as part of a compensation package. It's the least an owner can offer to recognize an outside director's altruism in accepting a small business directorship.

It may be difficult

All small business owners—particularly start-up owners—can benefit from an outside director's experience and perspective. A former investment banker, Gord Robb, told me: "I've had experience filling director positions for company IPOs. The most beneficial attributes are demonstrated success and experience in the business and the willingness to use contacts to assist profitability of the company. The usefulness of lawyers and accountants on a board goes without saying but a board member who can directly add value to revenue is golden." Unfortunately, finding an outside director of the calibre Gord envisages might be difficult for most typically cash-constrained small businesses which are forced to rely on altruism.

If it isn't feasible for your small business to appoint an outside director, fear not. Other sources of experience and expertise are out there, and one of these is a mentor. We'll discuss this character in the next chapter.

CHARACTER 9: MENTOR

WHY A MENTOR?

Picture this. It's the end of the day. Everyone has gone home. Everyone except the small business owner. This person is sitting, elbows on a desk, forehead cupped in hands, eyes closed. We see an exhausted person. We see a frustrated person. Perhaps this person is worried about survival, or how to take the business to the next level. In either case, we see a person badly in need of inspiration, badly in need of someone to talk to—someone who's seen it all before, someone with a few ideas.

It's a common sight.

What's also all too common is that many small business start-ups, or even some established small businesses, don't have the budget for directors, consultants, and coaches. In addition to the cost deterrent, these roles can be overkill for the smaller of small businesses such as sole proprietorships. But the owners of these businesses still need advice, guidance, and encouragement during those times when managing their business is reminiscent of Sisyphus's struggle.

Sisyphus was the poor guy in Greek mythology condemned to roll a bolder uphill without any help while knowing that once he reached the top of the hill, it was going roll back down—and he'd have to start all over again. Sisyphus: the personification of pointless, unrewarding labour. Sounds uncannily similar to a small business owner's lot some days, don't you think?

Fortunately, small business is not Greek mythology. No small business person has to feel like Sisyphus, who had no help. For today's small business owner, help is everywhere. One source is mentorship. And one attractive feature of mentorship is that it's budget friendly.

So what is mentorship, and where did the concept originate?

Rooted in Ancient History

In the world of small business, "mentor" describes an experienced and knowledgeable business person willing to share his or her experience and expertise with a less-experienced and less-knowledgeable business person, the mentee. The mentee is often a relatively new owner who needs help tackling isolation, bewilderment, and the desperation that can accompany small business ownership.

Mentorship is a potentially business-saving concept with an interesting history. It's about sharing knowledge informally—and mentoring is such an instinctive human behaviour that it's fair to assume it's as old as humankind. Perhaps it's deeply imbedded in our DNA.

The descriptor "mentor" (adopted as a business term as recently as the last quarter of the last century) is thought to have originated with the character Mentor, in Homer's *The Odyssey*. Scholars tell us this was composed near the end of the eighth century BC.

Interestingly, Homer made Mentor an ineffective old man, which is exactly the opposite of how we characterize mentors today. I have no idea how the name of an ineffective old man became associated with the noble act of sharing knowledge. We'll put it down to one of those mysterious quirks of language evolution.

But it doesn't really matter if we don't understand the origin of the word. What matters is that, to small business owners, mentorship is a valuable and generously-bestowed resource. And this time-honoured, knowledge-sharing ritual is expressed in small business through three essential qualities.

A Mentor's Three Essential Qualities

The first two of three essential qualities a small business mentor must have are obvious: knowledge and experience. They're so obvious we don't need to explore them here. The third is not so obvious, but it's certainly essential.

The third quality stems from a presumption that small business mentoring is free of charge—a presumption I wholeheartedly endorse. Those who are experienced must share knowledge with those who are inexperienced. This is how civilization advances. If the sharing can be done without charge, so much the better.

I'm of course referring to one-on-one, informal knowledge sharing, not to institutionalized mass education (schools, colleges and universities). I'm also not referring to directors, consultants, and coaches, who share knowledge as a full-time profession. I'm referring to no-charge small business mentoring, which is not a profession but a commitment. It's a commitment that necessitates the third essential quality of a mentor: generosity.

Generosity

Mentorship is an exercise in altruism, and altruism isn't possible without generosity. Obviously you'll pick your mentor for his or her perceived knowledge and experience, but if genuine, heartfelt generosity isn't an integral part of the potential mentor's personality, I doubt that the mentoring process will be truly fulfilling and productive.

Imagine sitting down with your mentor for a scheduled monthly discussion. Perhaps you're feeling a little sensitive about receiving expert consulting for no charge in a world—the business world—where this is definitely not the norm. If this person gives you the slightest impression that you're an imposition, or displays a let's-get-on-with-it-you're-getting-this-for-free-you-know attitude, it's bound to taint the relationship. It's bound to inhibit your participation.

But selecting a mentor isn't as onerous as it might seem. You're not likely to pick a mentor by stabbing at a business directory with a pin. A potential mentor is likely (a) someone you know personally, (b) someone to whom you're referred, or (c) someone to whom you're introduced by a mutual acquaintance. You probably already know that the potential mentor has the knowledge and experience you'd like to tap into. And this person likely has a reputation as an involved and caring mentor. You may already know that the potential mentor is generous for truly altruistic reasons. But if not, I'd venture that it won't take you long to establish this.

If you discover that your mentor isn't genuinely generous with his or her knowledge, experience, and time, terminate the relationship and find another.

The mentor-mentee relationship

Different mentors will adopt different approaches. A mentor with the appropriate knowledge and experience will quickly assess your business and adapt his or her mentoring emphasis accordingly. Whatever the emphasis in a particular small business mentoring situation may be, in general, the mentor's role is to listen and offer options—a smorgasbord from which the mentee is free to pick and choose.

Small business mentoring works best when the mentor-mentee relationship is power free. Your mentor shouldn't portray an authoritative attitude, regardless of status. Displays of power have no place in the small business mentoring arena. Your mentor should be a facilitator, a teacher who allows you to discover your own direction. You don't want to feel star struck and bossed around, even if you're lucky enough to have as your mentor, say, Richard Branson or Marissa Mayer. Hence the smorgasbord concept—the mentor lays it out and the mentee picks and chooses.

I'm not particularly interested in mentoring millionaire business owners who want to become multimillionaires—they can afford to pay for coaches, consultants, and Tony Robbins retreats. My interest lies in working with the vast numbers of small business owners who don't have the budget for coaches, consultants, or retreats. I prefer situations where some pertinent advice can make the difference between failing and surviving, and perhaps surviving and thriving.

So, here's how you can expect a mentor-mentee relationship to unfold.

The mentee approaches (in writing, by phone, or in person) with a brief explanation of why he or she is seeking a mentor. Unsurprisingly, the mentee is often that frustrated person we saw at the opening to this chapter. And usually, this person is motivated to find a mentor by a single, over-arching "how" challenge: "How do I survive?" "How do I grow?" "How do I restructure?" In short, "How do I stop being a Sisyphus?"

The mentor may have an initial discussion with the mentee to better understand the nature and circumstances of his or her business and to explain how much and what to expect of the mentor. This is the approach I favour. I suppose you could consider this to be an interview, though it's not nearly as intense as an interview for a job or a consulting assignment because the potential relationship isn't going to be nearly as comprehensive as either of those.

Typically, the mentee drives the relationship—that is, the mentee poses questions and the mentor responds. A mentor should make this clear by pointing out that his or her role is not to dictate how to run the business. Mentoring is not a hand-holding exercise. If the mentee needs hand-holding rather than occasional suggested course corrections, he or she probably isn't ready for the journey.

And while a mentor should typically be passive and reactive, if the mentee appears to be taking a route unlikely to lead to the desired destination, it's incumbent upon the mentor to be more proactive. But even then, it's the mentee's prerogative to alter course or not.

The mentor should commit to a schedule of regular discussions (usually monthly). Hour-long discussions should be enough but don't be surprised if they become two-hour or longer discussions when the topic is particularly interesting. Some mentor-mentee meetings take place over dinner or coffee, but I prefer privacy, out of the earshot of strangers. After-hours exchanges tend to be more relaxed and productive. Few things are as annoying as having to hurry a stimulating discussion or even end it to rush off to another meeting or deal with a typical business-day interruption.

The mentor should also be available for occasional unscheduled meetings about urgent matters that cannot wait for the next scheduled discussion.

If I agree to serve as a mentor, I confirm it by email. In the email, I also reiterate the important points mentioned during the initial meeting (especially those that pertain to what's expected of me) and clarify that our mentor-mentee relationship may be ended at any time by either party.

While I prefer face-to-face discussions, I'm not averse to Facetime or Skype. In fact, I've had productive Facetime discussions with small business owners as far afield as Australia. There's no reason why fourteen thousand kilometres of ocean should get in the way of a productive business discussion.

How I was semi-mentored

I didn't have a formal mentoring arrangement when I launched my small business, partly because I was under the impression that, as a chartered accountant, I knew all there was to know about business. I was wrong, of course. And I sorely regret it now.

I did, however, have access to advice on an informal, occasional-discussion basis from a retired drilling company owner. He'd been very successful during the boom years in the Alberta oil patch. He gave me various useful snippets of advice and helped me realize that I had to terminate my ill-considered partnership before it was even a year old. And he actually offered to facilitate it with a short-term loan.

In the early days of my small business, I also organized a small business owners' discussion group. I modelled it after the Executive Committee (TEC), a Canadian-based organization for business owners and executives. Among other services, TEC engages experts in various fields to address its members at monthly meetings. But many small business owners cannot afford to join organizations like TEC. Our group met every month for about two years until it became apparent that far from serving as a mentor substitute, each meeting was really a process of the blind leading the blind.

And therein lies a question for small business owners invited to join discussion or industry groups—are you being offered more than what amounts to a class of students without a teacher? As a small business owner you'll almost certainly get more mileage out of a mentor or two than a group of similarly inexperienced peers.

Not an either-or solution

By no means am I implying that a mentor is the sole, or even the best, solution to a small business owner's search for advice, guidance, shared experience, and encouragement. In the previous chapter I discussed directors, and I've mentioned consultants and coaches as well—they can all be good resources.

And please understand that none of these need be stand-alone, either-or solutions (they could be, but they don't have to be). The solution could be a combination of these resources. It all depends on what's appropriate and feasible for your small business. The important takeaway is that there *are* solutions.

Peeking behind the scenes

Finally, a behind-the-scenes peek into your mentor's world ...

When you arrange to meet with your mentor once or twice a month for an hour or two, this is not the limit of his or her contribution. What you're not seeing is that every hour spent with you is matched by as much as another hour spent thinking about your situation, crunching numbers, bouncing an idea for you off a colleague or two, arranging introductions, digging up helpful reference material, noting questions to challenge you with, and even lying awake at night mulling over the ins and outs of an issue you may have raised.

Why would your mentor do this? Because mentors are also entrepreneurs, and entrepreneurs are stimulated by business challenges. Overcoming challenges gives them a buzz. Contributing to a mentee's success also gives them a buzz.

Perhaps since the dawn of humankind mentorship has always been about the buzz. Regardless, a good mentor is a powerful, budget-friendly resource that can help make your small business.

CHARACTER 10: BUSINESS AUTHOR

AN OFFER YOU CAN'T REFUSE

What if a stranger suddenly popped up out of nowhere and made you an offer almost too good to be true?

"I can share a ton of wisdom and experience you can use to improve your business in every respect. I can promise you big ideas, small ideas, exciting ideas—stuff you'd likely never even think about. And the best part is that I'm willing to share this treasure trove of invaluable information for virtually no cost. All you have to do is give me some of the time you currently waste watching TV and surfing the Internet."

As a scam-wary small business owner, you'd probably be skeptical: "Oh yeah? Who are you and where's the catch?"

The stranger, not at all deterred by your skepticism, replies, "There's no catch. I'm the composite of every business author who has ever written, and will ever write, a business book or article. The gift I'm offering is guaranteed to benefit you and your business. You just have to make the effort to become a habitual reader of business books, articles, and posts."

Would you accept the mysterious stranger's gift? Would you believe the promise of "big ideas, small ideas, and exciting ideas"? You should, because the stranger's assurance about the benefits of reading business literature would be absolutely correct. And he or she would be in the good company of many well-known and often-quoted luminaries such as Charles William Eliot, president of Harvard University for forty years, who said: "Books are the quietest and most constant of friends; they are the most accessible and wisest of counselors, and the most patient of teachers."

What to read?

There are more business books, articles, and posts than you have time to read in a lifetime. So what do you read and what do you pass over? While you'll come across "must-read" lists, favourable reviews, and colleague recommendations from time to time, ultimately you must read what piques *your* interest—what seems applicable to *your* business and personal development.

Some of the best advice and ideas I found were in books you wouldn't see on any recommended reading lists. It's amazing what you can find exploring the business sections of both new and used book stores. Search beyond the critically-acclaimed and bestsellers.

Bestsellers about business "celebrities" starting up in their dorm room or mother's garage and going on to become billionaires might be entertaining, but they're hardly helpful to the vast majority of small business owners and would-be owners whose more immediate concern is day-to-day small business management.

I prefer to scan the index and flip through the pages of a book (or any other piece of writing) rather than blindly follow a recommendation. Doing this gives me a good idea of whether it deserves more of *my* time. If nothing catches my attention or arouses my curiosity, I put it aside, pick up the next one, and keep doing that until I find something promising.

A conversation

From an early age I was taught to revere books, handle them carefully, and treat them with respect. I can remember how we made brown paper covers for our school textbooks to preserve them in good-as-new condition. We were also prohibited from marking the pages in any way. This was all with a view to getting a better price for the books on the thriving used textbook market at the beginning of the next academic year. To this day, I ensure all my books remain in pristine condition with one exception—business books.

I'm not sure when I first committed what amounted to heresy and scribbled a note in a business book. But for a long time I've been a firm advocate of conversing with business books rather than just reading them.

A business book is a working book and shouldn't be treated as something sterile if it's to fulfill its purpose. If you had a conversation with the author, wouldn't you jot down notes, offer comments, make counterarguments, and perhaps take issue with something? Well, converse with his or her book in exactly the same way. In fact, I don't see how anyone can get the most out of a business book without highlighting or underlining passages, recording thoughts and comments in the margins and other open spaces, and marking pages with little 3M flags or paper clips.

Do this, and when you get to the end of the book (and periodically for years after), you can go back over the flagged pages and extract ideas, revisit concepts, or remember the thoughts you noted the first time.

The only disadvantage of working with business books in this way is that you have to own them. You can't, for instance, scribble in the local library's books—they would definitely take exception to your "defacing" their books, no matter how enlightening your notes and comments might be.

Sources other than books

Books may be the primary source of business ideas and concepts but they're by no means the only one. In addition to articles in business magazines, social media platforms can be gold mines of information. I've found LinkedIn to be particularly useful in this regard—by following certain authors and joining LinkedIn groups specifically with your business in mind, you can enjoy a steady stream of business articles or posts. Blogs and online newsletters are also good sources of information, and Google is helpful when it comes to finding writing on specific business topics.

Print and file online articles that you'd like to keep (I find three-ring binders work best for this). Just as you would with a book, highlight and underline information, record comments and notes, and revisit these articles later.

Audio books are useful for times such as the slow drive to and from the office. You obviously cannot interact with them the same way, but that doesn't mean that they can't supplement the written edition. You may have certain favourite books that you like to read from time to time, so reinforce the message with the audio versions when the less-productive alternative is listening to music or mindless chatter on the car radio.

I've also found it useful to listen to audio books—while doing other activities (driving, walking, gardening, etc.)—as a screening process before deciding whether or not to work through the printed version.

Filter

Regardless of the source—book, audio book, magazine article, or online post—all content must be passed through your business's suitability filter. Some of it might be suitable for your business exactly as presented, some of it might be suitable only once adapted to your business, and some of it might not be suitable at all.

Even though I diligently select books, it doesn't follow that they've all been great. While none have ever applied completely to my circumstances and industry, from every one (and there have been about a hundred), I've gleaned something useful or stimulating.

It's not about the big "Wow!"

If you read only in search of the single big idea that's going to propel your small business up into the business stratosphere where you'll orbit with

Amazon, Apple, and Microsoft, you're going to overlook a lot of smaller ideas and concepts that, when taken together, can improve your business significantly. This doesn't mean that you won't stumble across the single big idea; you may be lucky enough to hit the business-idea jackpot. In the meantime though, you'll encounter many smaller, business-boosting ideas to make your small business more fun and more profitable. One example from my business illustrates the point.

Tom Peters, the business author and speaker who rose to prominence with *In Search of Excellence*, coauthored by Robert Waterman, included a story that led to a twenty-year tradition in my business. The now-famous story, "The Case of the Two-Cent Candy," is about a retail store handing out candy as a parting gesture at its checkouts. It struck a chord with me because early in my career, I came to realize that people prefer to do business with people they like, and people like people who offer them friendly gestures, and offering someone even something as simple as a candy is a friendly gesture.

My business's customers were spread all over Canada—I'd estimate that fewer than 5 percent ever visited either of the branches. I was, however, determined to use the candy idea and therefore had to adapt it. One idea led to another that ultimately led to the twenty-year tradition of including candy bars or cookies in every parcel we delivered. I had small plastic bags printed with a thank-you-for-doing-business-with-us message, and into them we sealed the candy bars or individually wrapped cookies (food hygiene is important).

I had no way of proving whether this gained us any business, but it certainly did a lot for customer relations—many positive messages from customers over the years confirmed this. It was also nice to often hear that our parcels were opened immediately after they were delivered and that sometimes there would be a scramble among a customer's employees to get to our parcels first. The only occasional "complaints" were about preferring one kind of chocolate bar or cookie to another.

Business authors have a lot of creative ideas to share; the key, though, is to read them.

Your business book library

If you don't already have a business book library (i.e., at least one well-scribbled-in, dog-eared, frequently-visited business book), you will shortly if you're persuaded by this chapter. And when you do, you must keep in mind a very important piece of advice I had to learn the hard way.

Keep your library in a place where it'll be safe from loss by flooding, fire, or some other disaster. Also, keep a detailed list of all the books in your library in case you have to replace them or file an insurance claim. A time-saving alternative to a list is to take a digital image of each book and then at some future date use the images to compile a list, should the need arise. It goes without saying of course that the record (images, list, or both) must be stored off-site.

I lost a library of over a hundred business books during the Calgary flood of 2013. I didn't have a list and had to compile one as well as I could from memory and with the aid of digital images taken in the aftermath of the flood. A list or digital images taken before the flood would have made preparing the insurance claim a lot easier.

An alternative to physically keeping a list is to subscribe to one of the online cloud-based library catalogue services. They have many useful features to help keep your library organized. How often have you looked for a book only to realize that you loaned it someone but can't remember who? Well, scratch your head no more, these services include a feature to keep track of loans.

The cost of these library catalogue services is minimal, in fact, some are free. A Google search will provide you with a selection.

The reading advantage

If he were still with us today, I feel sure that he'd say "man or woman" and not just "man," and would agree that by "good books" he also means digital books and articles. With that assumption, let's allow Mark Twain the last word: "The man who does not read good books has no advantage over the man who cannot read them."

CHARACTER 11: LANDLORD

The tenant's lament

The landlord is one character most small business owners would prefer to exclude from their business equation. Many—home-based business owners and those who own their business premises—are able to do so but a large number are destined to be tenants.

This chapter deals with the question of ownership versus leasing and the cautionary notes attached to each. Home-based business owners might want to bail out here, unless you're considering premises ownership or tenancy, in which case you need to hear the tenant's lament. Forewarned is forearmed.

Proceed with caution

"Drink is the curse of the land. It makes you shoot at your landlord and makes you miss him." This Irish proverb echoes a common sentiment about landlords in the small business community. I don't mean to imply all landlords are two-headed monsters, but there is enough anecdotal evidence to suggest that a small business owner should be very circumspect about the landlord–tenant relationship.

The traditionally unfavourable view of landlords may stem from a perceived imbalance of power favouring the landlord. It's to be expected that one would walk on eggshells around the landlord when he or she accounts for a major monthly overhead and can trigger a disruptive relocation of your business.

Lease or own?

Most small business premises are leased rather than owned. The reasons for this range from limited capital to force of circumstance. For instance, a business owner may have the capital to invest in a premises, but leasing may be the only option if the business is location dependent. Professional services required to locate in city core tower blocks, retail outlets in large malls, and light industrial businesses in industrial business parks, are among many examples.

Just as leasing may be the only option for a small business in one circumstance, owning may be the only option in another. If you locate in a small village or town with a shortage of rental properties, buying or building premises might be your only choices.

In either case, you would be well advised to involve expert assistance from one or more sources, such as an accountant, a lawyer, or a realtor. The risks and pitfalls associated with both leasing and buying should be carefully weighed before making what is a big decision for a small business.

Implications of owning

Advocates of business premises ownership point to the commonly-accepted advantages of investing in real estate, most particularly, capital appreciation—and there is much to be said for that. I've known a number of small business owners who owned the building from which they operated and eventually stood to make more from the sale of the building than from that of the business.

Opponents of ownership will point out that if you outgrow your premises and have to move, the real estate market might not be favourable for a sale at that time and you could end up having to decide between curtailing your business's expansion and taking a loss on the building's sale. It's a reasonable point of course, assuming you can't find an alternative solution such as renting out your building and renting elsewhere or, where space permits, expanding the existing building.

Something else that opponents of ownership will question is the wisdom of tying up money needed for working capital. The relevance of this argument depends very much on individual circumstances such as working capital requirements and the availability of investment or loan capital that could be secured against the building. This might take care of a working capital requirement while at the same time accommodating building ownership and capital appreciation.

Ultimately, regardless of enticing reasons to own one's business premises, most small business owners choose or are forced by circumstances to lease rather than buy.

Implications of leasing

Assuming you are among the vast majority of small business owners and lease your premises, or are planning to lease your premises, you should be aware that there are implications for your business, some of them adverse enough to break it.

The first risk is the possibility of good judgement being overshadowed by a state of euphoria—the rush you experience as a new small business owner when you think you're about to clear one of the big hurdles many of us encounter when starting out: finding premises. It's an exciting development, particularly if it's your first start-up. *Finally!* you think, as you picture the name of your business above the door. *Where do I sign?* But not so fast. Caution needs to be the watchword.

Important issues must be considered before you sign a lease and get into bed with a landlord. It's always possible that you could enter into a lease agreement with little caution and be fine for the duration of the tenancy. A much wiser tack though is to protect yourself and your small business as well as you can against all eventualities that can befall a tenant. For instance, consider Graham's experience.

Graham's tenancy

The tenant in this story is a very good baker. Let's call him Graham. He worked for a number of large bakeries before he launched his own small business, a bakery and restaurant. He leased premises already fitted out as a restaurant in a large building of light industrial bays.

The variety of freshly baked goods and nutritious meat-and-two-veg type of lunch meals on offer became popular with the factory and office workers in the surrounding industrial area and Graham soon built up a loyal clientele.

From the day he opened, he and his wife worked hard in the restaurant while simultaneously raising a family. Similar to that of the thousands upon thousands of small business owners, their existence was not easy. Yet, they successfully established a business that for five years provided for the family while simultaneously providing a valuable service to many customers.

As was customary, a few months before the lease renewal date, the landlord presented Graham with an offer to renew. It contained a shock. The new rent reflected an increase of approximately 50 percent. Graham's accountant determined that he couldn't accommodate this increase in one of his major overheads that was already relatively high. A realtor with sound knowledge of the prevailing market rates for rentals was engaged to negotiate on Graham's behalf, but the landlord wouldn't budge.

In order to retain his clientele and keep operating, Graham looked for other premises in the immediate area. He was unsuccessful in his search and consequently had to fold his small business.

More than five years have passed, and Graham's former premises are still unoccupied. Since the landlord's representative declined my request to discuss the matter, one can only speculate that the property manager noticed how busy Graham's business was and, knowing he couldn't easily relocate and retain his customer base, assumed he could be squeezed for a much higher rent. If that was the strategy, it failed miserably. Everybody lost.

Graham's tenancy experience highlights a risk of renting—the impact a seemingly irrational landlord can have on a small business. It was a similar story for someone we'll call Andrea, except that she devised a plan B.

Andrea's Plan B

Andrea owns an art supply store. She bought the business in 2002, reorganized it, and by hard work has grown it every year since. It was originally one of a number of stores in a premises on a busy boutique shopping street.

Like Graham's, Andrea's landlord offered to renew her lease in 2013 but with a 40 percent rent increase. Unlike Graham, however, Andrea was able to relocate. She found much larger premises in a newer building with more than enough free parking for customers—a vast improvement over her previous location. And, in addition to doubled retail space, she had enough extra room to build two large studios for art lessons and exhibitions. The landlord's apparent gamble, though distressing to Andrea at first, worked to Andrea's advantage by forcing her to seek alternatives. She now occupies a better location for approximately the same rent and her business is doing better than it did in the old location.

Andrea was able to find alternative premises without much difficulty, but in another city it might not have been so easy. Her experience emphasizes the need to have a plan B. Without a plan B, the fate of your small business could lie in the hands of an unscrupulous landlord.

Leanne (also not her real name) had a plan B too, but she developed it well before the end of her lease.

Contrasting landlords

Unlike Graham or Andrea, Leanne planned to terminate her relationship with one landlord while actively pursuing another. Hers is a story of perseverance and contrasting landlords.

Leanne owns and manages a franchise health food store for pets. When she selected her first location, she did so with what she believed at the time was all due care. She met with the landlord's representative who showed her drawings and an artist's impression of how the new mall would look when it was fully occupied by small retail stores. She remembers the impressive drawings and how excited she was about the prospect of being part of the mall.

A few days later, Leanne met again with the landlord's representative, this time accompanied by her business partner and franchisor's representative. At the meeting she signed a ten-year lease. Leanne and her partner were the first to move in and were followed in short order by another retail tenant. Then, instead of the remaining retail spaces filling up, something unexpected happened. The remaining spaces were converted into a single larger space and a community health centre moved in, changing the appearance and nature of what was supposed to be a retail mall.

At the time she agreed to commit to a promised retail-only mall, it hadn't occurred to Leanne to request an inclusion in the lease with a no-penalty termination provision that would apply if the retail mall promise wasn't met. Having signed a ten-year lease with no recourse for addressing broken promises about the nature of the mall, Leanne had no choice but to keep the store operating at a level somewhat below what would have been its full potential in the originally promised retail mall.

With about three years left on her lease, Leanne set about searching for a more suitable location. She found one in a small retail strip mall on a busy intersection not far from her existing store. It was an ideal location with only one problem—it was occupied by a tenant with a month-to-month lease. Every month for two years she called the landlord to maintain contact, build rapport, and check on the status of the premises.

Eventually the existing tenant gave notice, and Leanne's persistence had paid off. Not only did she negotiate a rental cost similar to that of her first location, but the landlord also agreed to a rent-free period for the first six months of the ten-year lease. This was particularly helpful in view of the fact she still had a year left on the lease for the original premises that the landlord wouldn't forgive.

It all worked out well. Not only was the new location conveniently close enough to the old location to retain the existing customer base, but also, as anticipated, the exposure to passing traffic boosted business immediately. Of the second landlord she says, "[He] has been completely open, honest, caring and helpful with us so far."

Her experience with the first landlord emphasizes the need for caution. As she puts it, "So, there is a lesson learned—don't trust anybody! Sad as that sounds."

Scout the Location and Ask, Ask, Ask

Not far from where I lived in Calgary is a popular street of boutiques, restaurants, art galleries, spas, and coffee shops about eight city blocks long. Most of these small businesses are in rented street-level space in office and condo buildings. A number have been operating for many years, but one building has always had a noticeably higher tenant turnover.

It's a fashionable building with good curb appeal and six street-level rental spaces seemingly ideal for the high-end retailers it has attracted over the years. "What accounts for the high turnover of small businesses in this building then?" you might be wondering. The answer lies in a popular realtors' expression: "Location, location, location!"

The building is situated at the end of the street, where there is less foot traffic. There is no adjacent parking and all the parking lots within sight are reserved for other businesses. Anyone wanting to visit one of the businesses in this building would have to park at least three or four blocks away. To the detriment of the small businesses in question, in our car-centric society, busing or walking are often not options, particularly in winter.

One can't help but wonder why new tenants would think they can succeed in a location in which many others before them, with similar businesses, have failed. The assumption has to be that they don't do their homework on the location. It's not always easy to find and question previous tenants, but the search is surely worth the trouble it if saves a business owner from committing to a bad location. A brief discussion with neighbouring businesses' owners on the street would also likely alert him or her to the building's long-standing parking disadvantage and high tenant turnover. Puzzling as it may seem, potential tenants tend not to conduct inquiries of this type.

While scouting the prospective location, take note of the neighbours too because they can have a significant effect on your business. If you were considering opening a children's book or toy store, would you really want the neighbouring business to be an adult entertainment store? On the other hand, having a children's clothing store as a neighbour could be very good for your book or toy store. And don't just be satisfied to take what you see at face value: establish whether or not the landlord has documented restrictions on the types of tenant businesses he or she will allow and whether that safeguard can be included in your lease. You wouldn't want to be left with no recourse after signing a multi-year lease only to watch the children's clothing store move out and an adult entertainment store move in. Based on Leanne's experience, assurances included in the lease agreement with a no-penalty termination clause could be a business saver.

A less-obvious issue that must be considered when selecting a lease location often rears its ugly head only after the business has moved in. Crime and vandalism is an ever-present threat to businesses, so it's wise to inquire about the extent of it in any area in which you're thinking of locating. If the area is targeted more than others, you should know about this and factor it into your location choice.

Drive-by observations

Once you have your eye on a particular rental space, visit it frequently at various times on different days of the week, even if you just do drive-bys. You need to know about daily and weekly occurrences, favourable and unfavourable, that might affect your business.

Traffic patterns, parking availability, foot traffic, and even something as apparently obscure as how the sun falls on the building, may matter to your business.

Location and proximity

Ample customer parking and proximity to public transit is important to some businesses. But even if parking and public transit are not important to your small business, there may be other location considerations such as proximity to trucking routes, suppliers, or customers. These considerations should be taken into account during the location selection process.

Check inside and out

If you're working with a good agent, he or she should alert you to any potential structural concerns with a building you might be considering. However, don't rely on the agent. Check the important aspects of the building yourself. If you can live with any shortcomings, fine, but at least be aware of them before you commit to a lease.

Clues that the landlord may be less than diligent about the property's upkeep might be the need for a fresh coat of paint, potholes in the parking lot, cracked or broken windows, graffiti, unkempt landscaping, and an untidy or unsanitary garbage collection area. A poorly maintained building with a shabby appearance could be detrimental to your business.

Inside the building, check for signs of water damage. Water-stained ceilings or walls could indicate leaking pipes or a leaking roof. If your small business needs a greater than usual supply of power, ensure that the building is wired to provide it. If lighting is important, check to see if it's adequate. It's often easier to persuade a landlord to address these things when he or she is trying to get your signature on a lease than when you've already signed.

Due diligence on the landlord

As is apparent through Graham's, Andrea's, and Leanne's leasing experiences, part of the decision-making process should include finding out as much as you can about the landlord.

"Landlord" in this context means the person or company that will interact with you over your tenancy. If the building is owned and managed by an individual, then find out what you can about that person's management style. If the landlord is a bigger organization and you'll be dealing with one or more of its employees, such as a property manager, find out what you can about these individuals. Advanced knowledge is usually advantageous.

If prospective tenants had asked for my opinion on the landlord in one of the buildings in which we rented premises, I would have explained that when the well-liked landlord passed away, management of the property development company was assumed by his four disinterested and aggressive children. Sadly, those tenants who didn't inquire before moving in could later be heard complaining about various aspects of the property's management.

The lease and the lawyer

Any small business owner should have a good lawyer review a lease before signing it, particularly if it's the first lease he or she has ever signed. Landlords are inclined to present leases as "standard" and the signing process as a "formality" to be handled as expeditiously as possible. Don't fall for it. Leases are binding legal documents. They require careful scrutiny.

A good lawyer will spot unusual or prejudicial clauses as well as omissions. The cost of having a lease reviewed is minimal when measured against the potential cost of the consequences of not taking legal advice.

Buildings do change hands

There is an ever-present possibility that the building in which you are a tenant will change ownership. You can't do much about it other than be aware it can happen and ensure you negotiate a lease immune to an adverse ownership change. We had it happen to us twice in one of our two locations. The first time it worked out to our advantage whereas the second time it did not.

We went from tenancy bliss with a small family-owned development company landlord that was all one would want a landlord to be, to a large bureaucratic property developer.

When your landlord changes from an accommodating, responsive, and caring individual to a large company of bureaucrats and confrontational nitpickers, you want to be able to pat yourself on the back for having a watertight, lawyer-reviewed lease tucked away in your safe. If nothing else, it will provide your small business with security of tenancy under unalterable terms until the renewal date.

A GAME OF POKER

When the time comes to negotiate or renew a lease, not all landlords will approach it with the take-it-or-leave-it attitude Graham and Andrea experienced. Much depends upon circumstances such as prevailing vacancy rates in the area and the general economic outlook, among a host of other influencing factors.

I was about to sit down to negotiate the renewal of our main office lease with the property manager of the building. I'd heard that the landlord was aiming for an increase I considered to be higher than market value, and certainly higher than I anticipated accepting.

A lease negotiation can be like a game of poker, with each party trying to guess at the other's cards before showing its own. I had minimised the guessing by advanced knowledge of the proposed rent increase. I also knew we were regarded as a desirable tenant and guessed that the landlord wouldn't want to add to the existing unleased bays in the complex.

About ten minutes before he was due to arrive for the meeting, I had an idea that, in retrospect, and in all modesty, was not only fun but a stroke of genius. I found a manila folder and filled it with an assortment of colourful brochures, price lists, and sundry promotional material we had lying about the office. I then wrote "PREMISES SEARCH" on the cover of the folder in black marker pen and placed it on the far end of the meeting room table, where it was out of reach but close enough for the title to be read.

By the end of the meeting during which there were many furtive glances at the manila folder, we had agreed on a very modest rent increase in line with what I regarded as fair. In addition, my request for new carpeting at no charge was agreed to. Amusing, stroke of genius, or manipulative, call it what you will—the manila folder of assorted screen printing pamphlets did its job.

Be a good tenant

If you become a tenant, be a good one. Pay the rent on time, keep the premises clean and meet all your obligations under the terms of the lease. Landlords are more inclined to cooperate with trouble-free tenants—and there will be times when you need cooperation.

Worth repeating

And again, always, but always, ensure that you have a properly-executed, lawyer-reviewed lease agreement and a plan B to help minimise the possibility of a landlord breaking your small business.

CHARACTER 12: INSURANCE BROKER

Your insurance broker as a buffer

From a small business owner's perspective, an insurance company has just two departments——Premiums and Claims. The former's function is to maximize cash inflow and the latter's is to minimize cash outflow.

In reality, an insurance company is more complex. Behind the scenes exists a huge bureaucracy consisting of lawyers, accountants, actuaries, assessors, underwriters, investment analysts, consultants, administrators, clerks, and in some cases, offshore head office executives whose annual bonuses exceed what the average worker will earn in a lifetime. Insurance is a big industry with big players.

This is where your insurance broker enters the picture. He or she is essentially the buffer between you—the small business owner—and the insurance companies. Well, at least at the policy-purchasing stage. The claims stage is a different matter, and I'll address that later in this chapter.

Selecting a broker

You should take as much care in selecting an insurance broker as you would in selecting any resource that can make or break your small business. If your business was so unfortunate as to suffer an insurable event, the claim-filing process would not be a good juncture at which to discover that your insurance coverage is deficient because of an ill-advised broker selection.

I found that the best way to find a reliable broker is by personal recommendation. Ask fellow business owners not only about how much effort their brokers put into understanding their business risks and how they handled the policy-purchasing process, but also about the contribution their brokers made to any claims experiences their small businesses might have had.

Depending where your business is located, you may be able to purchase business insurance from sources other than brokers. In some jurisdictions, financial institutions such as banks have agreements with insurance companies to sell their policies. You may also encounter tied agents operating under a specific insurance company's banner and writing policies for just that company.

After earmarking potential candidates (broker, financial institution, or agent), meet with them to discuss your insurance needs. Based on their input and responses to your questions, select the one in whose hands you are most comfortable placing the onerous responsibility of your insurance coverage. Whether you're considering an institution, agency, or broker, exercise the same degree of due diligence in the selection process. Keep in mind though that with financial institutions and agents, you'll probably forego the advantage of comparative shopping that independent brokers offer.

Your broker's job

In theory, an insurance broker (let's assume this includes financial institutions and agents) is an expert who identifies your particular insurable business risks and then sells you the most appropriate and cost-effective coverage.

Usually the broker's service doesn't cost you a penny—he or she is remunerated by the insurance company with whom your business is placed. But therein lies a potential conflict of interest and further reason to select carefully. You want to trust that your broker will not put his or her commission before your risks when recommending an insurer. In any case, even after a very careful selection process, you should still assume full responsibility for your insurance portfolio. Make sure that you understand every aspect of it and ask questions when you don't.

Review your policies annually as a matter of routine. In my experience, some brokers left to their own devices can be less than diligent about monitoring your file, particularly if you're a small pony in his or her client stable of big, valuable thoroughbreds. I've known some to simply renew an existing policy without even a cursory review, year after year. Typically, a policy is written, the monthly debit order is set up for the premium, and then it tends to become one of those out-of-sight-out-of-mind matters that you never get around to visiting. The problem is that a small business's circumstances can change over time and insurance coverage can be found wanting when disaster strikes.

Assist your broker

It would pay to do some homework before meeting with your broker to determine the various forms of coverage your small business should have. Although your broker should include all the risks common to most business insurance policies, not all businesses carry the same risks.

It's a worthwhile exercise to take a pad of paper and a pen to a quiet location where, without interruption, you can list all the insurable losses your business could possibly incur. Not only will this assist your broker in the event that he or she has overlooked any, but it will also raise your awareness and deepen your understanding of the risks attached to your small business.

An Internet search for various types of insurable business risks yields a long list, and some of the items on this list will be irrelevant, some even amusing. For instance, just because coverage for alien abduction or kidnapping and ransom is available, it doesn't follow that your small business needs it. The following coverage would be more pertinent to most small businesses: key person insurance, life insurance, disability insurance, partnership insurance, critical illness insurance, business interruption insurance, vehicle insurance, liability insurance, property insurance, product liability insurance, accounts receivable insurance, and employee dishonesty insurance, among others.

Preparing for the Possibility of Claiming

Once you've purchased your policy, contrary to what is typically done next—namely nothing—prepare for a possible claim. This is not a particularly onerous undertaking but a particularly important one.

An insurance claim quite often follows a traumatic event such as a fire, a flood, an accident, a storm, or a social upheaval, to name but a few. When the dust settles after one of these events and the insurance claim has to be prepared, recollecting events and details of items lost can be difficult in a stressed state of mind. In addition, few of us have faultless memories even under ideal circumstances.

I was working in Tehran during the Iranian Revolution of 1978–1979 and just hours before being evacuated took the precaution of photographing all possessions, both at the office and at the apartment. My concerns about the fate of our possessions were well founded. Everything we left behind was reportedly looted during the period of anarchy that followed the fall of the Shah's regime. Later, when a claim had to be filed, the photographs proved invaluable, not only as a reminder of what had been lost, but also as proof of possession.

If you do not have a photographic or video record of all possessions when disaster strikes though, all may not be lost. After a burglary or fire, recalling lost items might be difficult but something like a flood may afford you a second chance to prepare a record. Following the Calgary flood of 2013, we took digital images of every item as it emerged from the water and mud before it was tossed into a dumpster. I cannot overemphasize the value of this simple procedure.

Your broker and claims

Don't assume that your broker is going to be an advocate for you or a buffer between your small business and the insurance company if you are unfortunate enough to have to file a claim.

I'm not sure why I assumed that my broker would shepherd my claim through the maze of paperwork and the hostile to-and-fro claims process just because she guided me though the policy-purchasing process. I suppose one tends to think of brokers as the contact point for all insurance matters, but they are not remunerated by the claims process and some are therefore understandably reluctant to immerse themselves in it.

Perhaps expect your broker to provide contact information for your insurance company's claims department and to advise that department of an imminent claim; don't expect much more than that.

Claiming can be like a brutal wrestling match

The policy-purchasing experience is quite different from the claims experience, and it's easy to understand why. The policy-purchasing experience is about you doing the paying whereas the claims experience is about the insurance company doing the paying—two diametrically opposed actions bound to elicit two diametrically opposed attitudes.

Regardless of who calls the insurance company's claims department, it has to be done expeditiously—they prefer immediately. This is the trigger for the claim-filing process, and with the broker out of the picture, it's now the small business against the insurance company or, in many cases, a tough assessor acting for the insurance company. If this sounds adversarial, it's because it is adversarial. The interaction might be quite civil, but that doesn't change the fact that your interest lies in maximizing the claim and theirs in minimizing it. It's a business wrestling match of sorts between mismatched opponents.

In one corner we have a big brute of an insurance company and in the other a shrimp of a small business about to wrestle for a purse. Even though Little Shrimp battles valiantly, it's not long before Big Brute's size and stamina begins to tell. Just as Shrimp begins to run out of ideas on how to battle Brute and starts to wonder how much longer he can keep wrestling, Brute offers Shrimp a draw. But in exchange for the draw, Shrimp has to accept less than the purse he was expecting. An exhausted and frustrated Shrimp accepts the less-than-anticipated purse just to end the fight and get out of the ring.

Anyone inclined to doubt that a wrestling mismatch is an appropriate metaphor for the claims process following a disaster, probably didn't have a small business or home in the flooded areas of Calgary in 2013.

A RARE SPOTLIGHT ON THE INSURANCE INDUSTRY

A newsworthy disaster giving rise to a large number of insurance claims involving a large number of insurance companies and their reinsurers is a rare opportunity to witness the insurance industry in the spotlight.

The Calgary flood was just such a disaster—the downtown core, twenty-six neighbourhoods, and seventy-five thousand people were affected. In my neighbourhood some main floors were under eight to ten feet of muddy water. Major losses were incurred, particularly in the flooded basements of houses and businesses. Restaurants lost the contents of their wine cellars. Inventory and equipment stored in business's basements also accounted for significant losses.

Within hours, insurance company representatives were saying that claims would be denied because the disaster was the consequence of overland flooding—an uninsurable risk at the time in Canada. If this had been a single claim involving just one small business not worthy of even a couple of column inches on the inside pages of the local newspaper, the matter might have been laid to rest right there. But this was not a single claim involving just one small business.

Spectacular images, videos, and reports of widespread damage flooded the mainstream and digital media worldwide. Within days, politicians—municipal, provincial, and federal—were involved, outraged policy holders were forming action groups, and news conferences were called by some of the policy-holder action groups to vent indignation at the insurance industry. Everywhere in the public eye graphic images of the disaster were juxtaposed with the insurance industry's claim-denial position.

In less than a week the outpouring of demands by policy holders for a revision of the insurance companies' claim-denial stance, apparently bolstered by behind-the-scenes government intervention and powerful offshore reinsurers urging avoidance of a public relations calamity for the industry, began to force a change of heart. I received an email from my insurance company's assessors asking that I ignore a letter that had been mailed denying any liability on their part due to the cause of the damage being overland flooding. They said they had changed their position and would settle a claim under the sewer backup clause of my policy.

So, is there a lesson in this for small business owners? Well, public relations departments and advertising agencies working for insurance companies will have you believe that they are your best friend in times of disaster. Take this with a grain of salt. That an insurance company's first reaction to a claim is to determine how they can minimize the payout is old news; seeing it so blatantly exposed in Calgary was merely confirmation. The lesson? Prepare your claim properly and, providing the sum at stake is significant, invoke influential help. In some jurisdictions an arbitration service might be available to assist in the event of a dispute between a small business and its insurance company.

Preparing a claim properly

By "properly" I mean prepare it so completely and in so much detail that it leaves very little room for questioning or criticism. Your aim should be to minimize the usual to-and-fro claims process and effect timely settlement. A properly-completed claim should help accomplish this by conveying a high degree of credibility and facilitating the insurance company's claim-checking procedure.

When submitting a claim, first and foremost, be completely honest about the circumstances of the event and the extent of the damage and losses. Then, depending upon the nature of your coverage, provide all the details that could reasonably be required to assess your claim. For example, my 2013 claim was for the replacement value of all property lost in the flood. I submitted a spreadsheet that for every item listed provided a replacement value with a reference to the source of that value—websites, catalogues, and, in some cases, manufacturer and supplier quotations.

In cases where the exact replacement could not be found, I identified a close match, priced it, and explained by a footnote. For more nebulous items such as my hundred-book business library, I estimated a total value by applying the average price of a typical business book and then supported it by a full explanation of the method used.

Every item on the spreadsheet was cross-referenced to images on a memory card included with the claim. Admittedly, I should have had an updated photographic record before the flood. In the event of a fire or burglary, I would have had a much more difficult time properly preparing a claim—hence the importance of a regularly updated photographic or video record.

Once more: you and your broker

Insurance peace of mind for your small business starts with cautious selection of a broker, but it doesn't end there. You too have a role to play in ensuring that your coverage remains appropriate as time passes—meet with your broker at least annually.

Neglecting your business insurance either through a poor choice of broker or failure to ensure your coverage is current could break your small business. It's not worth the risk.

CHARACTER 13: ALARM TECHNICIAN

Before the Horse Bolts

If ever a proverb applied to small businesses and alarm systems, it's the one about the futility of shutting the stable door after the horse has bolted. To invoke another old expression, I wish I had a dollar for every time I heard about a small business calling an alarm technician for the first time the day after a burglary.

An alarm system is a necessity rather than a luxury unless, unlike most small businesses, your business is located in a crime-free area. Not only can it provide an immediate response to a break and enter, but also, merely having it is often enough to discourage break and enter attempts.

I had alarms installed in both our branches and not once in more than twenty years did we have a break and enter, whereas neighbouring small businesses without alarm systems were burglarized a number of times.

Is an alarm enough at your location?

While an alarm alone was sufficient in the areas where my branches were located, it's often necessary to supplement an alarm with other security measures. I have visited businesses in high-crime areas where alarms were just part of overall security systems that included iron bars over all accessible windows; steel doors; security gates over doors; steel shutters; barbed – and razor-wire fences; electrified fences; closed-circuit television cameras; and guard dogs. On a visit to South Africa, I saw attached to a gate a large photograph of an angry German shepherd with glaring eyes and exposed canines above a caption that read, "He can make it to the gate in three seconds. Can you?" In a burglar's shoes I would be inclined to move on.

Also while in South Africa, I noticed most alarm companies offer "armed response." I was told that should an alarm be activated, one or more armed alarm company guards would attend the scene—often ahead of the police. If this were the case in Calgary a number of years ago, a surprise party at a business associate's office might not have been possible.

The alarm company sportingly agreed to participate in a prank by calling the victim on the night of his fiftieth birthday to say that the alarm at his business was indicating an unauthorized entry. In under ten minutes he arrived at the building in a dimly lit and deserted industrial park. Opening the front door cautiously, he took a half step into the reception area, straining to see in the darkness. But a split second later, he was disappearing back through the doorway as if hit by a shotgun blast before about forty of us could even yell "Surprise!" Later, sheepishly explaining the hasty retreat, he said that as he stepped in and suddenly realized that there were multiple body shapes in the darkness, it flashed through his mind that he was dealing not with a single intruder but a gang.

In retrospect, this alarm prank could have gone wrong in so many ways; thankfully he wasn't armed and had a sturdy heart.

Cheap at the Price

An alarm system is a sound investment for a small business, particularly when the cost of the alarm is weighed against the cost and inconvenience of burglaries. Cost will of course vary according to the system's complexity and size but, after checking prices in a number of countries, I believe it's fair to say that in most places alarm systems are inexpensive relative to the benefits.

There is of course no guarantee that an alarm system will prevent burglaries, but an ear-piercing siren and the knowledge that alarm company guards or the police are on their way should limit the burglar's "work" to minutes rather than hours. Even this is worth the price of a system.

In Canada, a wireless small business alarm system in a three-thousand-square-foot premises consisting of two motion detectors, detectors on each of three doors, and a two-way voice response unit, all controlled by a keypad, cost my small business just under fifty dollars a month on a thirty-six-month contract. In addition, the alarm system earned us a discount on our insurance premiums.

Faking It

If truth be known, an alarm system's most effective items just might be the alarm company stickers, which can be placed on windows and doors. I once saw a television commercial in which burglars avoided a place with an alarm sticker in favour of one without. I think the premise is plausible but I remember wondering whether the commercial might encourage prospective customers to simply acquire stickers somehow and forego the alarm system.

I've also known some small businesses to have installed faux alarms. While burglars are certainly senseless enough to commit burglary, I wouldn't bank on their being senseless enough to be fooled by bogus alarms. Trying to save a few dollars this way is surely an example of how you could "spoil the ship for a ha'penny's worth o' tar."

Install a good alarm system—messing about with faux alarms and stickers is gambling with the security of your small business.

Selecting an alarm service

There are three important aspects to an alarm service: set-up (the alarm must be configured for the premises), maintenance and rapid repair, and rapid response in the event of an intrusion.

Alarm companies, as with most resources small business owners access, come in varying degrees of competence. Recommendations from fellow small business owners are always a good way to locate two or three possibilities to consider. However, I wouldn't even consider a service that didn't offer twenty-four-hour monitoring and rapid response. An alarm without dedicated response is almost as ineffective as no alarm at all. How often have you heard an alarm and done absolutely nothing because you assumed that someone else or the "authorities" would attend to it?

False alarms

Once the alarm system is installed, it's entirely likely that you'll experience equipment failures and false alarms from time to time. When these things happen and the equipment needs immediate attention, it pays to be associated with a reputable alarm company with capable technicians.

My business experienced two false alarms. On the first occasion, a motion detector raised the alarm for no apparent reason. Our puzzled alarm technician couldn't find evidence of equipment failure, nothing had fallen or moved, and none of the sensors at the entry points had triggered the alarm. Then, while re-examining the motion detector, he found a spider web attached to the cover and concluded that a spider could have walked across the lens. If there were anything at all amusing about an alarm causing a business owner, two police officers, and an alarm company guard to mobilize, then it would have to be that it was accomplished by a tiny spider. But there is nothing amusing at all about leaving a warm bed in the early hours of the morning to go out into sub-zero temperatures in a snowstorm to attend to a false alarm caused by a spider.

On the second occasion I was in a restaurant about three thousand kilometres away when the alarm company called to ask how soon I could be at the premises. Everyone on their contact list was out of town and we had forgotten to advise them and nominate an alternative. Fortunately, the police determined that there had been no forced entry and chalked it up to a false alarm. That brings me to the question of availability in the event of an alarm emergency.

Current contact information

It's an important, but often neglected, aspect of alarm management that you can get away with until an incident occurs. In the event of an incident, your alarm company needs current information as they will quite often ask the contact to attend the premises to meet their patrol and the police to give them access. A list of contacts that includes people who are out of town and ex-employees is not helpful in an emergency.

If forced entry occurs, the contact needs to be there to take care of whatever damage has occurred as neither the police nor the alarm company will likely be willing to safeguard the premises until regular opening hours.

Alarm system control

For obvious practical reasons, a number of employees and perhaps even contractors such as janitors must be trusted with the code for the alarm system. Control over the code should therefore be strict, and just as locks, computer passwords, and website and systems access codes are changed when an employee's or contractor's services are terminated, the alarm code should be changed as well.

The alarm technician and the bolting horse

With a good alarm system installed by a good alarm technician, you will be in a better position to prevent the horse from bolting—an event that could break your small business.

And don't forget an alarm system needs managing. You can't just consign it to the out-of-sight-out-of-mind category once the technician has completed the installation.

CHARACTER 14: JANITOR

First impressions

There is no truer adage than "First impressions are lasting impressions," and one of the characters in your business that helps contribute to a good first impression is your janitor.

Tom Peters, business consultant and author, once said that a coffee-cup stain on the flip-down tray in an aircraft raises questions in his mind about the airline's overall commitment to excellence, including excellence in maintaining the aircraft's engines. I initially thought this sounded a bit harsh, perhaps even a bit eccentric. But, with experience comes wisdom, and I have since been convinced there is indeed a direct correlation between attention to cleanliness and tidiness and attention to product quality and customer service.

Think about this for a moment. When you walk into a business for the first time and it's clean and tidy, doesn't that create a favourable impression?

Don't you think to yourself, *Looks like they run a sharp operation here*? But if you walked in and the air smelled like the half-eaten tuna sandwich on the receptionist's desk, the floor had obviously not been swept for some time, the waste basket was overflowing, paperwork littered every flat surface, and there was a layer of dust thick enough to write your name in a dozen places, would you still think they ran a sharp operation? Wouldn't you be inclined to have doubts about the product quality and customer service or, worse still, be inclined to consider a competitor?

A CASE IN POINT

In the early days of my business, I visited an ink factory in Toronto for a meeting about the possibility of distributing their product. A receptionist showed me into the conference room, pointed to one of six chairs, and asked me to wait while she rounded up the people with whom I was scheduled to meet. I thanked her but then selected one of the other chairs—the one with the fewest ink and greasy food stains imbedded in the fabric seat.

The conference room resembled a poorly-maintained storeroom. Filing boxes, some spewing their contents onto the floor, appeared to have been carelessly dropped along one wall. Three or four coffee cups containing cold, partially-drunk coffee shared the table with a scattering of paperwork, colour charts, a stapler, a three-hole punch, and a selection of pens. Three of the six recessed ceiling lamps were not working, leaving the remaining three to produce what amounted to inappropriately subdued lighting better suited to a theatre than a conference room.

Unfortunately for this company, a benchmark for screen printing ink manufacturers had been established in my mind just months before when I attended a similar meeting at an ink factory near Atlanta. The contrast couldn't have been starker. There were no ink stains on the carpet in the reception area, and the brightly-lit conference room with its highly-polished table and black leather boardroom chairs resembled that of a high-end law firm or a Fortune 500 head office. Everything about the company spoke of professionalism and quality. And it should come as no surprise that as time went by, I found the quality of their products and business style matched my favourable impression of their premises.

Back in Toronto, as you might have anticipated, the meeting did not go well. Their products lacked quality and their business conduct lacked finesse as much as their premises lacked a janitor. Any possibility of our doing business together perished right there in that janitor-free zone.

I can further underscore the correlation between a clean and orderly premises and an excellent company through twenty-three years of regular dealings with a few hundred customers. Of course this is just anecdotal evidence but nevertheless, I observed a population large enough and over a period long enough to convince me of how important a janitor is to a well-managed small business.

Beyond your four walls

A good impression can extend beyond the four walls of your premises. For instance, if you have delivery vehicles or are in the transport industry, unless your vehicles are unmarked, they're effectively billboards on wheels. It always amazes me when I see an unwashed commercial vehicle—the impression it creates is exactly the same as a dirty and untidy premises would.

I find unwashed food industry vehicles particularly troublesome. Just as poor maintenance of the flip-down tray in an aircraft makes Tom Peters wonder about the maintenance of the rest of the aircraft, a filthy food industry vehicle makes me wonder about the business's commitment to good food management practices. I don't know about you, but I can't imagine how unloading food from a dirty vehicle can create a good impression.

Kurtz Trucking of Breslau, Ontario, understands that the impression their vehicles create extends to the impression of their business overall. For many years Kurtz, a privately-owned family business, hauled weekly shipments for my company from Atlanta to Cambridge, Ontario. I was always pleased to point out the spotless Kurtz eighteen-wheeler big rigs as "Our shipper"—I think we all know that we (and our businesses) are judged by the company we keep, and it therefore doesn't hurt to be associated with impressive businesses.

Until I visited Kurtz's premises I wondered how they managed to keep their big tractors and fifty-three-foot box trailers clean and shiny when so many competitive truckers clearly either had trouble doing so or just couldn't be bothered. What I found was a process implemented by Brian Kurtz, the founder of the company, and now maintained by his four sons. Brian had a wash bay built and insisted that trucks go through it before leaving the yard. Big brush rollers that were easy for the truck drivers to operate cleaned the entire rig—a simple process that made a huge difference to the business's overall image. But cleanliness doesn't just happen; it takes conscious enforcement by an owner who understands that first impressions are lasting impressions and that good impressions generate good business.

Who is the janitor?

Depending upon the size of the small business, the janitor could be an individual or service contracted to attend regularly, or it could be a full-time staff member. In many small businesses, particularly small start-ups, the owner is quite often the janitor (among a number of other roles) until circumstances permit otherwise.

Regardless of who fills the janitorial role, cleanliness must be everyone's obsession, most particularly the owner's, since he or she sets the standards for the rest of the organization. The role of assistant janitor should be an assumed part of every employee's job description.

Sensitive situations

The pursuit of cleanliness can involve sensitive and potentially embarrassing situations but, as a small business owner, you just have to gird your loins and deal with it.

We certainly had our share of sensitive situations, and although we laugh about some of them now, most were more awkward than funny at the time. One such situation was the result of our decision to have two unisex washrooms rather than designated male and female washrooms. Both were kept in mostly spotless condition except for one aspect that drove Margaret crazy—urine spots on the floor around the toilet bowl. Not only did she find it offensive, but she was also concerned about the impression this would give visitors.

By a discreet process of elimination, she identified the culprit. She and I discussed the issue, and I remember being concerned about the sensitive nature of the situation. I tried to defuse what I feared might become an explosive incident with a little levity—a story about my grandmother complaining about the same thing in her household of four males and two females. My grandfather's response was that it was more likely to be the women missing the bowl because "they had nothing to aim with." Margaret was neither amused by my story nor sympathetic to my sensitivity concerns. Instead, being a no-nonsense wife and business partner, she took the bull by the horns, convened a meeting in the washroom with the offender, pointed out the spots, and commanded that there would never again be urine spots on the floor.

If the spotted-floor incident led to any behind-the-scenes whispering among the staff members—a certainty you can bet on—my ban on tuna sandwiches and other fishy lunches must have also sent tongues wagging. My single biggest turnoff in a place of business is the nauseating aroma of canned tuna or some other smelly seafood wafting through the workspace. I reasoned that the janitor's work would be all but wasted if the premises smelled like a fishmonger's. I expect most small business owners would agree, except, of course, the fishmongers among them.

The Janitor as a Morale Booster

In addition to the impact that a clean and orderly small business premises has on outsiders, we can't lose sight of the impact it has on most employees. Few things will chip away at staff morale as much as a dirty and disorderly work environment. The janitor therefore plays a key role in maintaining staff morale.

Recognition

I am proud to have been able to lay claim to three indicators that our business had a clean, orderly, janitor-assisted environment. One was that employees had no hesitation showing family members where they worked. A second was that customers and other visitors often offered unsolicited compliments, and a third was that other small business owners brought their employees for tours of our premises to impress upon them how they wanted their own premises to be organized and maintained.

A concluding thought

I can't think of a single circumstance in which janitor-free premises would boost staff morale or give a small business an edge over the competition. I wouldn't have thought that anyone else could think of one either, but unfortunately cleanliness and orderliness remain concepts not fully grasped by many small business owners, who may never know the positive effects a janitor can have on their businesses.

CHARACTER 15: NEIGHBOUR

Three categories of neighbours

Business neighbours are either neutral, beneficial, or problematic.

Depending into which of these classifications they fit, neighbours can have a make-or-break impact on your small business, and therefore, whether you are renting or buying, you must choose your location carefully.

Neutral neighbours

Neutral neighbouring businesses, the most common type you'll encounter, will have no particular impact on the well-being of your business.

They are engaged in non-competitive activities or different industries. In matters involving the typical lightning rods for conflict, such as customer parking, staff parking, noise, and garbage management, they are as considerate of your needs as you are of theirs. There are no bones of contention, mostly just peaceful coexistence.

Beneficial neighbours

These neighbours are ideal. A beneficial neighbour is one who is useful in some way. For example, this neighbour might provide your business with advantages such as cooperative bulk buying, shared services, and customer sharing.

My earliest awareness of beneficial small business neighbours dates back to my childhood, when I was living near Cape Town. Friday was payday for many of the trades and farms. In those days, weekly wages were paid in cash and by Friday evening, crowds of workers would be wandering the streets with pockets full of money looking for a slap-up meal and a couple of bottles of wine. Not far from where I grew up was such a reveller's one-stop bliss—a fish and chip shop and a liquor store, side by side. On Friday evenings both were busier than Grand Central Station. A long distance apart, they still might have done quite well individually, but side by side, each "made" the other or, as I remember my father often pointing out, each turned the other into a gold mine.

Beneficial neighbours are not usually a necessity, but they are certainly nice to have.

Problematic neighbours

A problematic neighbour is of course the opposite of a beneficial neighbour and can be detrimental to your small business.

The degree to which this type of business neighbour can be detrimental ranges from merely irritating to seriously destructive. Such neighbours could break your small business if, in a worst-case scenario, by their presence or behavior, they discouraged customers from visiting your premises or doing business with you.

Here's an extreme example. Close your eyes. Picture a strip mall with a children's toy store wedged between two adult entertainment stores with titivating window displays. Do you see any minivans packed to the gills with wide-eyed youngsters and their parents or grandparents driving up? No, I don't either.

A less extreme but real example is a small flooring company I know, which is located alongside a convenience store. For about an hour every afternoon on school days, flooring company customers have to pick their way through a hoard of unruly high school students blocking the entrance to the company's showroom. The students are convenience store customers and, typical of that age group, they like to "hang out."

To make matters worse, after the crowd disperses, the flooring company staff have to pick up food wrappers and other litter dropped in front of the showroom. The convenience store owner is sympathetic enough but he, personally, is not the problem. The problem is that the nature of his business is problematic to his neighbour. All the solutions tried so far have focused on eliciting cooperation from the students but, not surprisingly, all have failed. And nobody could reasonably expect the convenience store owner to discourage what amounts to a daily business boon.

Some irritants arising between business neighbours might seem minor and therefore bearable—some might even consider the flooring company owner's situation to be bearable—but just as minor irritants can grow into major irritants that over time lead to "irreconcilable differences" in personal relationships, they can do the same in business neighbour relationships. Both types of relationship breakdowns, after all, often have the same catalyst at their roots: irrational human nature. Sometimes too—and I regret admitting that my gender is a particular problem in this regard—the irrationality is exacerbated by substantial doses of testosterone that summon forth machismo and banish all reason. You'd think that by now we'd have evolved to the point of realizing that chest thumping is best left to gorillas, but we haven't. The other guy, also infused with testosterone, responds with his own chest thumping and once we start down that road, there's no turning back. What began as perhaps a minor irritation pretty soon escalates into a battle. Then the first responders arrive: the lawyers.

Quite often all of this can be avoided by careful location selection. But, unfortunately, even that doesn't guarantee you will avoid a problematic neighbour detrimental to your business. A solution may be required—preferably one that avoids the costly and disruptive step of relocation.

Reforming a problematic neighbour

If the nature of the neighbouring business is the cause of the problem, a solution other than relocation is hard to envisage—it's hardly reasonable to expect a neighbour to change the nature of his or her business because it is problematic to yours. But if it's a behavioural problem, consider other solutions before relocating.

For example, if discussions, negotiations, and the landlord fail to resolve the problem, it might be worth consulting with your lawyer or engaging an arbiter. But whichever of the three most common solutions is considered—doing nothing, relocating, or engaging professional help—the cost should be weighed in both financial and emotional currency. All three can be both financially and emotionally draining. It's a question of which solution, on balance, will be the least draining in your particular circumstance.

We can all become a bit indignant when confronted by someone doggedly wrong, particularly if we just know that we are right. But even then it might be more advisable to walk away rather than provoke a confrontation. As a grizzled old veteran of the tough international engineering–construction industry once advised me, "Don't get into a pissing contest with a skunk—you're bound to lose."

If lawyers, arbiters, and other professionals become involved, costs could quite conceivably escalate beyond those associated with doing nothing or relocating—not smart in the final analysis if the sensible solution was walking away but machismo required a "win." Many a Jack Russell terrier can confirm that you might win by killing the skunk, but you will stink for a long time.

Pick your neighbours

I firmly believe that careful location selection is not only potentially beneficial to your business, but also the solution to a number of problems that can beset a small business—one being the problematic neighbour. However, I also caution that there are no guarantees because neighbours come and go, things change. If they change for the worse and you find yourself with a problematic neighbour, you will almost certainly have to take action. Remember, the sole focus of your actions should be your welfare and that of your small business. If necessary, be a smart Jack Russell—overrule your instinct and walk away rather than tackle the skunk.

My wish for you though is that your small business will thrive in the company of neutral or beneficial neighbours and that you will never be forced into action over the threat of a problematic neighbour breaking your business.

CHARACTER 16: BURGLAR

Your business is a target

This character is a regrettable reality with whom a small business owner is bound to cross paths—in some cases, repeatedly.

I've chosen a burglar to represent an entire class of characters with the same objective in mind: ill-gotten gain at the expense of a small business.

Unpleasant as it is to contemplate that your business is a target for unsavoury characters lurking out there with evil intent, you cannot afford to stick your head in the sand. You absolutely need to understand the extent and potential sources of the threats, and then you must take the appropriate countermeasures.

Shapes, sizes and disguises

The burglar's gang of cohorts includes a wide range of characters in various shapes, sizes and disguises, from brainless and desperate shoplifters to technically sophisticated and ruthless hackers, and an assortment of characters in between. And all are intent on victimizing your small business.

They might be employees, customers or strangers; they might be dressed in three-piece business suits or ragged jeans and T-shirts; they might intrude in person, by phone, or online; they might be beautiful, ugly or faceless; they might be rude, crude, or charming; they might be armed or disarming; and they might brazenly appear in broad daylight or skulk about after dark. There is neither a stereotypical burglar nor a prerequisite for this occupation other than perhaps a sociopathic personality.

Everything your small business owns is fair game

It's an exhaustive list. Every asset of your small business is a sitting duck—your petty-cash box, cash register, bank account, inventory, computers, equipment, company vehicle, website, and a host of other items you could probably think of without too much effort.

I know of a recent instance where, ironically, the burglar's haul from a screen printing supply company included its closed-circuit television recorder. If the CCTV had been installed as a deterrent, or to help identify burglars, then, in failing, it illustrated an important point—deterrents must be properly planned and executed.

Deterrents

The potential threats and the events that could lead to these threats being executed must be identified before a deterrent is adopted. For instance, you should consider your circumstances and location and determine if you are vulnerable to break and enters, holdups, vehicle jacking, employee fraud, hacking, or any other event.

Once you have identified all the potential threats, you must consider which assets would be vulnerable should one of these events occur. With that information at hand, you can develop deterrents, which fall into two categories: tangible and intangible. Common tangible deterrents are alarms, lighting, and impediments to physical entry such as locks and steel shutters. Intangible deterrents include internal accounting controls and digital elements such as passwords, codes, and software.

You should expect to consult experts about some of the various deterrents your small business will need. You can quite easily source assistance for everything from securing your premises against physical intrusion to securing your online facilities against hackers. But—and here's my cautionary note repeated throughout this book—select your advisors carefully and obtain multiple references whenever possible.

Common tangible deterrents

For most people, an indoor alarm is probably the first measure that comes to mind in the tangible deterrents category. I've already addressed the details of indoor alarms in the Alarm Technician chapter.

In an ideal situation, outer deterrents would discourage a breach, but much depends upon the nature and quality of these deterrents. Fences, window bars, doors, shutters, locks, outdoor alarms, security cameras, and guard services are available in varying configurations and quality but, given enough time, incentive, and determination, just about any deterrent can be breached. For this reason, an expert can prove useful in striking a balance between cost and an appropriate level of deterrent for your circumstances.

The fact that there are no guarantees of absolute security even in seemingly impregnable locations was amply illustrated by a jewelry heist in London over the 2015 Easter weekend. The thieves broke into a building, climbed down an elevator shaft, passed by closed-circuit security cameras, and drilled through a two-meter-thick concrete wall to enter a vault, where they broke open about seventy safety deposit boxes. Even when the deterrents are designed to match the incentive, the incentive might be enough to mount a determined attempt to overcome the deterrents.

Common intangible deterrents

Today, intangible deterrents are as important as their tangible counterparts. That's not to say that intangible deterrents are particularly new. For instance, internal accounting controls prominent in the public accounting and auditing profession since the early 1900s have apparently been used for over two thousand years for preventative and detective measures in accounting systems.

But the digital age has given rise to a whole new range of intangible deterrents necessitated by a growing constituency of digital burglars. These frighteningly accomplished burglars are able to find their way into previously secured files, steal personal information, misappropriate cash, and generally create digital havoc all from a secret location almost anywhere on earth well beyond the hitherto long arm of the law.

Off-the-shelf and downloadable software packages designed to address viruses, malware, and other online threats now abound. A good computer technician should be able to advise and assist in selecting packages appropriate to your particular computer or network. I've found that contrary to popular belief reinforced by advertising, it's often not as simple as downloading an item of software and then believing you're protected from all threats. A few dollars spent on good advice during the selection process can save thousands of dollars and a lot of grief later.

Your small business website, particularly an e-commerce site, poses some serious security challenges because, among other things, customers need to trust the security of the site enough to use their credit cards on it. Even if you take an expert's advice and believe, as I did, that your e-commerce site is secure, you can still encounter very unpleasant surprises.

Shortly after transferring my company's e-commerce site to a new firm of website developers for the express purpose of effecting certain upgrades, it was hacked.

One morning we attempted to log on to the administrative pages of the site, as was our daily routine, and found that we were unable to do so. The site's host had detected unusual activity on the site and promptly shut it down. It turned out that the hacker was unable to access any customer information but was able to destroy or damage over two hundred files. I suppose it was the digital equivalent of a burglar breaking into a building, finding the valuable items securely locked away, and then, in anger or spite, committing vandalism.

To restore the damaged files cost my small business eight thousand dollars and two months of lost online sales. Adding to my frustration was the fact that we had no way of identifying the vandal. I was also advised that even if we were able to locate the culprit, the cost of doing so would be wasted because restitution or any other resolution would, in all probability, be next to impossible.

The hack was possible because the latest security upgrades for our shopping cart program we were using hadn't been downloaded. When the previous and the new website developers indulged in finger pointing, each blaming the other and neither willing to assume responsibility for the oversight, I had to bear the cost of what amounted to a costly lesson in e-commerce website security awareness. Now I tell any small business owner who'll listen that you simply must obtain assurances in writing from your website developer that your e-commerce site is protected as well as can be expected and they will undertake to download all security updates as soon as they become available.

Small businesses are also targets for telephone and online scammers attempting all manner of fraudulent activity. In these cases, the small business owner's Achilles heel is ill-informed or naive employees. An effective deterrent for this type of despicable crime is employee training.

Instructing new employees on and periodically reminding existing employees how to spot and deal with telephone and online scams is essential. Also essential is sharing every new article, email, text, or tweet on the topic with your employees. It will help ensure that they are better equipped to protect your small business from telephone and online fraud.

Creative and unusual deterrents

In addition to the more common measures that businesses take to protect their assets against theft, small businesses have been known to exercise considerable creativity in devising unusual deterrents.

Occasionally you'll see a sign in a small business's window pointing out that no cash is kept on the premises. I've seen similar signs that mention the absence of narcotics, cigarettes, and other commodities that might be of interest to potential burglars.

A coffee shop I knew placed an empty cash drawer from the cash register in the window each night presumably to suggest that no cash would be found on site.

At one time, burglars were targeting computers in the industrial area where my business was located. Some businesses were alarmed, but it only takes seconds to smash open a door, grab a computer, and flee before anyone responds to the alarm. To counter this possibility, I bought steel cable kits and locks to secure the computers to desks or bolts in the floor. I reasoned that one could struggle with a steel cable and lock while an alarm blared for only a short time before giving up. The same measure could be used for other easily snatched items as well.

Insurance—for when deterrents fail

Deterrents do fail. Insurance is not an ideal solution to an asset loss because restitution is seldom 100 percent. Effective deterrence is a much better option. But when a loss occurs, failing recovery of the lost assets intact and in full, insurance is usually the next best option.

The downside of insurance becomes apparent if the value of the claim renders it uneconomical because (1) the deductible, (2) the premium hike following the claim, (3) a reduction in future coverage, or (4) a combination of these considerations exceeds the loss.

In the Insurance Broker chapter, you'll find more detailed information about small business insurance.

Violent confrontations are not recommended

You've probably seen the occasional video on YouTube of an irate shop owner disarming a robber, or a passerby pursuing a fleeing shoplifter, apprehending the fugitive, and pinning him to the sidewalk to await store security or the police. These events are proffered as examples of heroics, but what about the events we don't see—the ones that end tragically?

A gas station owner I knew kept a hammer at hand under the counter for the express purpose of threatening self-service drive-aways. Where I live, the profit for a gas retailer amounts to, at best, a mere $0.06 per dollar, which means that it takes just over $1,300 in additional gas sales to recover the loss of an $80 tank of gas. The anger is therefore understandable.

This particular small business owner was once able to catch up to and confront a drive-away while he waited for a break in the traffic to make his escape. She was so incensed that she smashed the hammer right through the car's back window. And who could blame her? However, excusable as her response might have been, intervening personally in a confrontational and perhaps violent manner can have tragic consequences. In similar circumstances, a female employee of a gas station had been on the job for only two weeks in Calgary in May 2015 when she attempted to confront a drive-away. She was struck and killed by the fleeing vehicle.

In another instance of ill-advised intervention, twin brothers who ran a textile screen printing shop were working overtime on a rush order. In the wee hours of the morning they noticed a car parked across the street with a single occupant. It caught their attention not only because it was an unusual occurrence in a dark and deserted industrial park, but also because there had been a spate of burglaries in the area. When the car was still there some time later, they decided to confront the occupant.

Armed with a baseball bat, I believe, they demanded to know what the driver was up to. They were told that there was nothing nefarious taking place and that they should go away. Well that wasn't good enough for these two, who by now believed that there was indeed something nefarious going on and that they might be about to "make a bust." When it became apparent that rather than going away, the brothers were becoming more belligerent, the occupant of the car produced a badge and explained that he was a plainclothes police officer on a stakeout. *Then* they heeded the advice to go away, sheepishly.

On another occasion that could have led to a confrontation, the police poured cold water on a plan to thwart an anticipated burglary. A business neighbour of mine ran a vending machine company. His warehouse had been burgled and thousands of dollars in cigarettes had been loaded into his delivery van and driven away. The empty van was later recovered, but the much more valuable inventory was of course lost.

The police warned him that a second visit from the burglars was possible because they would expect him to replace the stolen inventory and, since the first burglary was successful, they would fancy their chances of pulling it off again. The police might have been urging him to improve his security, but his preferred solution was to sleep in the warehouse with a shotgun loaded with salt pellets.

Fortunately, a severe word from the police changed his mind. Instead of the shotgun solution, he opted to install a big safe, in which the new inventory of cigarettes was locked by the time the predicted burglary attempt occurred a few weeks later. I suspect that a backside full of salt pellets would have thwarted the burglary too, but in the end, the deterrence of a safe was just as effective and, very importantly, legal.

In most circumstances a small business owner or employee is best advised to leave confronting the culprits to the appropriate authorities. Usually the police are only a phone call away, and it makes no sense to unnecessarily risk one's life, or perhaps even commit a crime, by retaliating. No matter how infuriating an attempted crime may be, attempted heroics can easily turn to foolishness.

A sobering calculation

If you still have any doubt about the effect the villains I've lumped together under the burglar character can have on your small business, do this quick calculation: Take the replacement value of a selection of assets you could conceivably lose to crime and deduct what you might recover from sources such as insurance to arrive at a net loss for each item. Then, using your average gross margin percentage, calculate how much additional business you'll have to do to recover the loss.

It can be a very sobering calculation, and I hope it spurs any doubters into immediately reviewing their deterrents and insurance coverage.

CHARACTER 17: EMPLOYEE

An Acquired Skill

When you hear former small business owners say that this is the character they miss the least, what they're really saying is that employee management is not a walk in the park.

Employees are idiosyncratic creatures, and when we pour all those idiosyncrasies into a small business like ingredients into a blender, most of the time we cross our fingers and hope for the best. Well, therein lies the average small business owner's problem. It requires more than luck to select the right ingredients and blend them the right way to produce a palatable mixture—it requires skill.

Show me a small business owner complaining about employee problems, as many incessantly do, and I'll show you a small business owner lacking employee management skills. Many owners gamble with this important aspect of their businesses by settling for seat-of-the-pants employee management rather than acquiring the skills or help to properly hire, train, manage, and fire. Successful employee management is a critical aspect of managing for success. Consider the existence of human resource departments in big companies, usually led by a highly-paid VP—clear recognition of the complexity and importance of employee management.

So what is a small business owner with limited resources to do? For most, a full-time human resource specialist is out of the question. Therefore, the owner must often fill the role ordinarily performed by an entire HR department in a big company, from recruiter to VP. And there's not much choice in the matter because I don't believe it's possible to manage a small business's staff effectively without a reasonable level of employee management skills. The question is, where do you gain that skill?

One source is business literature. Employee management is a popular topic for business writers—in addition to numerous articles in business magazines, there are a veritable ton of books on the many aspects of the topic. How to hire, how to manage, how to motivate, how to train, how to remunerate, how to reward, how to deploy, and how to fire: it's all there and it's not difficult to find.

If you don't have time to read—a common claim among busy small business owners—buy or borrow audio books and listen to them while spending time on otherwise unproductive activities like crawling along in rush-hour traffic.

A CLEAR STRATEGY

I can't possibly cover every aspect of this character in one chapter—that's what the vast body of literature on the topic is for. However, I can give you some insight into my experience managing small business employees and hope that it will convince you to supplement your current level of employee-management expertise and intuition with reading and, if necessary, a consultant or two.

Your small business's long-term success may rely more on this complex character than any other. It therefore only makes sense that your employee-management strategy should be carefully formulated and executed.

WHAT KIND OF EMPLOYER DO YOU WANT TO BE?

Ideally, before hiring your first employee, you should establish what kind of employer you want to be. It didn't occur to me to do this and instead, like many small business owners, I drifted into my small business's employer role without much planning or forethought. Consequently, I made mistakes. Huge mistakes.

Reflect on the kind of employer you want to be and the work environment you'd like to create. It's a necessary first step to formulating an employee-management strategy that best suits the objectives and circumstances of your particular small business.

One way to determine the kind of employer you want to be is to determine the kind of employer you don't want to be. For instance, you might not want to lose your temper as a customer of mine routinely did. On one occasion, after the third costly error in his textile screen printing shop in the space of a couple of weeks, he made a general announcement to about twenty employees. In an expletive-ridden tirade, he claimed that he was losing money because of their shoddy workmanship. He then added that he'd lose less money if they all stayed home and he mailed them their cheques every two weeks. I was there to witness the employees' cringing under the verbal onslaught. It was very unpleasant.

You also might not want any of your employees to experience the humiliation to which an employee in the same textile screen shop was once subjected. The employee in question was sharing lunch with colleagues in the staff kitchen when the owner appeared in the doorway. He held up a sweatshirt for everyone to see: the image had been printed on the stomach area instead of the chest.

"Who printed this?" he demanded.

"*I* did," said the hapless employee as he raised his hand.

"Well, you're a fucking idiot!" blurted the owner before turning and stomping off.

Someone once reminded me that every employee is somebody's doting lover, the apple of a mother's eye, or the hero of a little child. His words struck a chord. These are the threads woven into the fabric of a person's self-esteem and dignity and, as the employer, you have no right to soil or tear that fabric. There are ways of handling reprimands and other inevitable employee-related problems without humiliating people or undermining their self-esteem and dignity.

Leaping out of bed

I'd always hoped to create a business that would have employees leaping out of bed every morning hardly able to conceal their excitement at the prospect of another day at work. Naive? Perhaps. For most small business owners, a more realistic goal would probably be to have employees who are not reluctant to get out of bed at the prospect of another day at work.

Nobody should be reluctant to get out of bed and go to work for fear of verbal abuse, embarrassment in the presence of colleagues, sexual harassment, shoddy or dirty surroundings, or any number of other bad situations found in some workplaces. Alarmingly, it seems to escape some small business owners' understanding that it's not just about basic human decency—an abused, unhappy workforce is also unproductive.

But basic human decency and productivity considerations aside, surely spending eight hours or more a day like a warden in a place where everyone yearns to be someplace else will eventually affect an owner's demeanour and possibly his or her mental health? Many a small business owner would be well advised to remember Richard Branson and his contention that one of the reasons for being at work is the fun.

The budget is not an excuse

Small businesses are quite often constrained in what they can do for their employees, particularly in the early days when budgets tend to be tight. However, the budget is no excuse for below-par working conditions. Tidiness and cleanliness, primarily, require commitment and effort, not a big budget.

Much has been written about the fact that while money is a factor in job satisfaction, nonmonetary elements are at least as important. This is particularly crucial for small business owners to understand. Create a happy environment for employees—it's not only the decent thing to do, but it also contributes to higher productivity.

In my small business's two branches, I ensured that the premises created a favourable impression of the company. We put a lot of effort into the colour selections, wall decorations, and furnishings to maximize appeal, comfort, and efficiency, in both the offices and the warehouses. I wanted employees to feel proud enough of their work environment to not hesitate to show it to family members.

All of this can be accomplished without breaking the bank. The landlord usually has as much interest in enhancing the appearance of his or her building as you have in a suitable workplace and can therefore often be badgered into providing carpeting of your choice and perhaps even a fresh coat of paint. Inexpensive used or unfinished furniture can be, with a bit of effort and ingenuity, turned into attractive office and showroom furniture.

Small business owners should also be mindful of the fact that if employees are expected to do a good job, they must be given the tools with which to do it. This might sound obvious, but I've heard many small business employees complain about old computers, outdated software, and broken or poorly maintained equipment. What their bosses might not realize is that what they think they're saving by being thrifty, they might be more than losing in poor productivity.

Nonmonetary and low-cost benefits

Certain nonmonetary and low-cost benefits can mean a lot to a small business employee and make the difference between just another place to work and a great place to work. We used a number of them. For instance, birthdays were a paid day off in my business, and not only did the employees appreciate it, but they also told me how impressed their friends were, which of course made them feel good about where they worked. These types of gestures garner so much goodwill for such a low cost that I can't understand why more small businesses don't offer them.

I accommodated preferred vacation dates even though most of them were in the summer months during our busiest season. Upsetting an employee's entire family by messing with their vacation plans will do nothing for morale in the long term. This is especially true in a business like ours where we believed that family came before work.

We also closed the business every year between Christmas and New Year's Day and treated this time as an extra paid vacation. Again, not as expensive as it might sound because this was a very slow time of the year in our industry.

I introduced a few monetary benefits not common in the small business community. To encourage continual learning, I offered up to five hundred dollars per year towards any career-related course fees. Again, a modest expenditure equivalent to just over forty dollars a month per participating employee but potentially a helpful personal development boost and a reinforcement of the message that we valued and encouraged ongoing education.

I had hoped that it would be used for any of the myriad of courses offered by various educational institutions, but this was the least popular of the benefits we offered. Interestingly, it was the few employees who already had post-secondary education who took advantage of the money to attend computer and business management courses. A common excuse among the majority who declined was that studying would eat into their leisure time. At times like this I had to restrain myself and remember that I was their employer, not their parent.

Expert hiring assistance

It's a conversation conducted between small business owners probably thousands of times daily all over the world—the one about how difficult it is to hire the right people. I had such a conversation over dinner at a trade show with the owner of an engineering firm who enjoyed a fiercely loyal and long-serving group of employees.

He explained that his secret was a consultant with many years of experience using sophisticated employee assessment tools to help companies acquire and deploy talent. Let's call him Dr. Gordon. He said that for a number of years Dr. Gordon had been assisting with his hiring process and that the result was a spectacular drop in employee turnover.

We arranged a telephone introduction and from that moment, our hiring results improved dramatically. In addition to matching the character traits of prospective hires to the job description, Dr. Gordon helped me select employees best suited to the personalities of the principals and other employees—an important consideration in a small business.

When people work in close proximity on a small staff day in and day out, compatibility is essential. He helped accomplish this by first establishing the principals' personality types. He then had a benchmark against which to test prospective employees' compatibility.

When we'd selected a short list of three or four applicants for a particular position, he would send us a multiple choice questionnaire for each applicant to complete. We then sent the completed questionnaires back to him. After he reviewed them, he would call us to discuss his assessments.

In every instance, the assessment of the character traits and behaviour patterns of the employees we hired with his help proved to be astoundingly accurate. In some cases we shared the assessments with the applicants, and I can't recall one who thought his or her assessment was inaccurate. My post-Gordon appointments were vastly better matches to the job than my pre-Gordon appointments.

To demonstrate the value of Dr. Gordon's assistance, I often refer to the instance where I was absolutely convinced that I had found the perfect candidate to establish and grow our new e-commerce venture. Confirmation of my choice would be a mere formality—she was the consummate dynamic sales professional who had just sold me a new phone system. She was a great catch for my small business.

Dr. Gordon disagreed. He told me that I would drive her crazy with boredom. He said that she was not suited to the position because she needed the challenge of the face-to-face cold call; face-to-computer was not for her.

When the applicant and I reviewed the assessment together, she agreed. She said that Dr. Gordon had accurately identified her key character traits and, on reflection, his assessment of her need for the challenge of cold-calling was correct.

It was the first time I'd seen someone who'd failed to secure a job leave with a spring in her step. Not long after that she landed a sales position cold-calling doctors for a large pharmaceutical company for much more money that I would have been able to pay her. Some months later she called around to thank me for having her assessed and added that she was happy and doing very well at the pharmaceutical company.

Without Dr. Gordon's input, I would have committed a costly error that probably would have ended badly for both me and my supposedly perfect candidate. I've often wondered how many bad and costly hiring decisions are made daily in the small business community—decisions that a consulting fee of a few hundred dollars could remedy.

Employees Do the Darndest Things

For the most part, I believe that small business employees take their jobs seriously.

Most mean well.

However, they are human. And regardless of how well you hire, create as close to an ideal work environment as possible, and manage your employees according to the best advice available, things will go off the rails from time to time.

There can be any number of reasons for out-of-character behaviour, but lapses in judgement seem to have been at the root of most of the darndest things a few of my employees did and said.

Some of their star turns left me variously speechless, angry, and amused. When you experience moments like these with your employees (notice *when*, not *if*), you'll find yourself wondering if this is normal. Don't sweat it—it's normal and all part and parcel of being a small business owner. Sometimes you'll have to say something and other times you'll just think it.

Here I am on some of those occasions:

- *How can you possibly be surprised that she wants to bite your head off? You drummed on the washroom door calling her name and yelling that she had a phone call. Why didn't you just take a message? Would you want the whole building to know when you're in the washroom? Why didn't you just get on the intercom and announce that Margaret's in the washroom? Where the hell did we find you?*

- "Listen, I don't care how busy you are or how mad you are that he brought the container of ink back to have the colour adjusted for the third time. And yes, he's a pain in the neck. But you can't stand in the reception area and tell a customer to eff off because you're too busy to eff around with his effing colour!"

- *Wow, that's one of the loudest and most embarrassing things I've heard in a meeting! Joan's trying to pretend she didn't hear it and Margaret looks horrified. Must have been air trying to escape from the rubber cup of his prosthetic leg when he stood up.*

- "You can't exchange 566 gossipy, sexually-explicit, personal emails with a friend in just under a month on company time using your company email account and expect to keep your job." *And particularly after what you wrote about me!*

- "Yes, I know it's not fair to accuse you of ruining his brand new Nikes. And yes, if he spills black ink all over himself he can't say it's because you made the ink too runny. But you've got to watch your temper. Throwing a full ladle of ink across the warehouse is not acceptable. Now please clean it up! I'll tell Mary you weren't aiming at her."

- *You're taking a day of compassionate leave because your parents' geriatric dog had to be put down?*
- "So you're telling me that my computer maintenance budget is blown because she was putting in service calls and asking you, my computer consultant, to come around, not because there was a problem, but because she was trying to get you into her Jacuzzi? Why didn't you tell me when she was still here?"
- *You've just come in complaining bitterly about smoke from the forest fire polluting the air and now you're going back out for a smoke break?*
- *So you don't think we know that you flew your boyfriend in to surreptitiously share your hotel room while we're all at this trade show with a full program of exhibit visits, supplier and customer meetings, and social events?*
- *This is a bit awkward. How am I going to explain that the computer technician told me the system crashed because you were spending time on inappropriate sites?*
- "Mary, listen, no matter how busy we are, you can't tell a frantic customer looking for advice on a Friday afternoon to call back on Monday about his printed bandannas bursting into flames in the dryer!"
- *What? She wants time off to have a Brazilian wax in preparation for her clubbing trip to Vegas?*

Taken together, these incidents might suggest I was producing a tacky reality show rather than running a well-managed small business but, in my defence, please understand they accumulated over a long time.

Every small business owner I know has tales of outrageous employee behaviour. These things are bound to happen—what matters is how they're handled. Some can be ignored while others have to be addressed firmly. Unfortunately, I'm not aware of any formularized response to these situations. I can only suggest patience, tact, and good judgement.

Though tempting at times, the medicinal-whiskey-in-the-bottom-drawer alternative only offers temporary relief.

Familiarity breeds contempt

The relaxed atmosphere characteristic of most small businesses should not be construed as an invitation to anything other than a cordial but professional employer-employee relationship based on mutual respect. It's a business relationship that amounts to nothing more than money changing hands for time and expertise rendered—to view it any other way is to court trouble.

If that sounds a bit cold, consider for a moment how awkward routine employee-management activities such as performance reviews, salary negotiations, promotions, demotions, and terminations might be if the employer has a personal relationship with the employee.

The employees' private lives are none of the employer's business. Conversations not related to work should be polite, brief, and superficial. Intimate topics such as relationships, finances, and relatives have no place in the employer-employee relationship. Sentiment should not enter into the equation. And I shouldn't need to mention this: sleeping with employees is bad business practice. It's a sure way to discover the wisdom in the old adage about familiarity breeding contempt—a slow-acting but deadly poison in a business relationship.

It's just business

In the small business community we are sometimes inclined to think of our friendly employer-employee relationships as sustainable, but don't be disappointed if you never again hear from a former employee, promises to the contrary notwithstanding. It might happen occasionally, but it's not common. A departing employee's "I'll stay in touch" means about as much as a shop assistant's mechanical "Have a nice day."

A small business employer–employee relationship might be intellectually stimulating, intriguing, pleasant, personable, and productive—but, in the end, it's still just a business arrangement.

CHARACTER 18: COMPANY PET

Part of the fun

This is a character you're unlikely to find in most business books, but for many years pets have been a presence in small businesses of all types—that is, when they can reasonably be accommodated without running afoul of regulations or common sense. If your small business is in the food or health industries, a company pet is not likely to be appropriate.

But if your business can accommodate at-work pets, I'm all for it. I favour a "fun and productivity" small business philosophy—something to which a well-managed pet can make a contribution.

Not something new

In the last few years, I've read numerous articles in business publications about at-work pets. It amuses me that some portray the concept as a recent phenomenon introduced by creative leaders in business management, such as the big .com companies. The rest of us are encouraged to reap the benefits of this newly discovered stress reducer, productivity tool, and all round cool idea.

Well, more diligent research might have revealed that at-work pets were quite common in small businesses at least three decades ago, well before the .coms seemingly became the trendsetters in everything cool in business. However, after twenty years of being accompanied to the office every day by one or more Jack Russell terriers, I would have to agree with those journalists in every other regard—a properly managed at-work pet program will reduce stress and contribute to a more productive workplace. Regardless of other benefits, a more fun workplace is a sufficient reason to grant the company pet a place in a book about small business characters.

Discretion around visitors

I once received a perspective adjustment from a Jack Russell breeder, who pointed out that dogs are not little people in fur coats. This means they cannot be trusted with the latitude or freedom of movement around the business that people have. Notwithstanding tongue-in-cheek claims that both my Jack Russells were smarter than some employees, they were capable of un-businesslike behaviour that even the most indiscreet of employees would not consider.

Ryley, my Jack Russell male, smart and affectionate but feisty by even that breed's standards, would spend a few hours every morning napping just inside the front door of the reception area. The perfectly-positioned morning sunbeam was one reason, and the other was his cookie-carrying friend, Darcy, the FedEx driver. He always wanted to be the first to greet him.

The problem was that Ryley lacked the discretion to disguise that he didn't feel about all visitors the way he felt about Darcy. For reasons we never understood, he would take an immediate dislike to any human or animal exhibiting any irregularity of form or outline. And then, by planting all four feet firmly, baring his teeth, and growling with an intensity that belied his small size, he'd leave the object of his aggression in no doubt as to his or her standing.

That is not appropriate in a place of business, particularly if it involves a customer. We therefore had to make up for Ryley's lack of discretion by swiftly removing him to a back office if we anticipated a potential problem. Fortunately this didn't happen often because most of our customers were spread across the country and we therefore had relatively few visitors. However, we never seemed quite quick enough to avoid a Ryley confrontation when it came to a few periodic visitors.

One such visitor was a consultant who occasionally tested for methane emissions in all the units in our industrial park. (There had once been a dump close by, and although the area had been reclaimed for baseball fields, there was still apparent concern about migrating methane gas.) He wore an electronic gadget on his back about the size of a day-hiker's backpack. Attached to the gadget was a rubber hose, which was in turn attached to a hollow wand about the size and length of a walking stick. At the end of the wand was a rubber cup the size of a teacup that emitted a sniffing noise as the machine drew air through it. In Ryley's defence, the consultant did look a bit abnormal, particularly when waving the sniffing wand about.

Their first encounter set the tone for all subsequent visits. Ryley was woken from a deep sleep in the sunbeam by a sniffing noise and a rubber cup inches from his nose. The rubber cup instantly suffered the same fate as a veterinarian's stethoscope that was once suddenly and unexpectedly pressed to Ryley's chest. In both cases, he did what Jack Russell's instinctively do. He shook the rubber "rodent" fiercely to break its neck while clamping down with powerful jaws until he could be persuaded it was dead. If you've ever tried to persuade a Jack Russell terrier to release something firmly clamped in its powerful jaws before it believes that the quarry is "dead", you'll know there are few endeavours more pointless.

This type of behaviour would probably not be tolerated in big companies where the pets-at-work concept has recently become fashionable. Typical of big companies, some have issued policies and procedures to govern pets at work, and while that might seem too bureaucratic for the taste of most small businesses, discretion still has to be exercised. A total laissez-faire alternative is not a good idea either.

Some visitors will be afraid of dogs, some visitors won't like cats, and some visitors will be allergic to certain animals. Few people can conduct business with a dog slobbering all over them or a cat strolling around on the meeting room table. If any of these visitors are customers or potential customers, the company pet could be bad for business.

The company pet isn't going to exercise discretion around visitors; you have to do it.

Discretion around employees

I was the boss and so pretty much had the last word on everything, including the dogs-at-the-office policy. That's how it works in a small business. But that doesn't mean you can completely disregard your employees' preferences. It's difficult enough to find and retain good staff without losing them because of poor company pet management.

The first step is to be completely open about your company pet policy at the recruiting stage, whether through an advertisement or an employment agency. State up front: "We have a pet-friendly work environment." Don't be afraid that it will undermine your hiring process—I don't believe we had even one prospective employee decline a position because of our dogs-at-work policy.

The second (and ongoing) step is to make sure that once you hire an employee, you don't overtax his or her tolerance of the company pet. Again, as with visitors, you can't leave it to the company pet to exercise discretion around employees.

If asked, I'm sure former employees would say that I didn't always practice what I preach. They'll probably mention meetings when five or six of us would be gathered around the table with both my Jack Russells dozing under it. Jack Russells seek human company, particularly a crowd; my two would never miss a meeting.

It would all have been fine if Cassie, four years older than Ryley, didn't have an occasional stomach-churning flatulence problem. She knew it, and she knew that we knew it. She also knew that shortly after an emission there would be a very unfavourable vocal reaction followed by a scrambling evacuation of the room. So, as might be expected from a dog of her intelligence, she would slink out of the room immediately after a gaseous emission and be well clear before it wafted up and caused the predictable mayhem and scorn.

This might sound like a gross encroachment on my employees' tolerance, but it really didn't happen too often, and, in any case, one learns to adapt. Ryley learned to leave the room as soon as Cassie did, and I learned to quickly adjourn a meeting if I saw the two of them sneaking out.

Stress relief

Stress relief is one of the often-cited benefits of having pets at work. There is a proviso of course that at-work animals must be well trained. Even the most ardent of proponents of pets at work will agree that a poorly-trained, rambunctious animal could be a stress inducer rather than a reliever.

Animal lovers know that just reaching out to pat a furry head or scratch a floppy ear is calming and stress relieving, albeit momentarily, in a way that's difficult to explain to someone who has never experienced it. And since stress is part of small business management—it comes with the territory—an effective drug-free antidote to stress at work is the at-work pet.

When the degree of stress calls for more than a pat or a scratch, there are walks, games of catch, or visits to the company pet next door.

A happier workplace

Aside from the stress-relief benefit, at-work pets can contribute to a happier workplace. Dogs are particularly good at this because most I've known are of a happy disposition. It takes a very determined grump to perpetuate a bad mood in the presence of an upbeat, happy, tail-wagging member of staff. And so much the better if morale is boosted and a light-hearted mood created by an at-work pet able to initiate entertaining and amusing behaviour—within reason of course, unless you plan to turn your business into a circus.

Something that always caused hilarity in our warehouse was Ryley's unwrapping shipments. When he heard a delivery truck arrive, he would dash to the loading dock and quiver with anticipation until the shipment was unloaded and he could begin tearing the plastic shrink wrap off the pallets. Jacks are ferocious and energetic little workers, and even though the pallets of boxes and pails could be packed as high as five or six feet, he would leap up and hang on the plastic wrapping until it gave way. This always amused the truck drivers and our warehouse staff alike. The only downside was that Ryley could not distinguish between incoming and outgoing shipments. When outgoing shipments were being shrink wrapped, he had to be kept out of the warehouse.

Both Cassie and Ryley could perform tricks for staff and visitors. Cassie was an accomplished performer on agility courses and would jump through hoops and over objects on command. Ryley consistently beat all two-legged comers at the old pea and shell game, which we played with three cups and a dog biscuit. His friend Darcy the FedEx driver once accused him of cheating because he sniffed the cups before making his selection. But even when given an equal opportunity to sniff the cups, Darcy still lost.

Far from being distractions and productivity killers, these interludes (and many others for which I don't have room here) contributed to a happier workplace.

PROFIT *AND* FUN

When people like Richard Branson advocate fun and profit as reasons for being in business, I'm not sure that they have the company pet in mind, but I don't think it's too much of a stretch to link the company pet with fun at work, and fun at work with the profit objective. As is often said, a happier workplace is a more productive workplace.

However, it bears repeating that discretion is the key to successfully integrating a company pet into your small business. By failing to exercise discretion, you could rapidly turn the advantage of the company pet into a disadvantage. And that would be a sad outcome for all concerned.

CHARACTER 19: COMPANY CLOWN

FUN AND PROFIT

Way back in the sixteen hundreds, Thomas Sydenham, a British physician and author of *Observationes Medicae,* a medical text book, said: "The arrival of a good clown exercises a more beneficial influence upon the health of a town than 20 asses laden with drugs."

Now, almost four hundred years later, we still discuss and study laughter, not so much to understand its impact on human health (it's generally accepted to be beneficial), but to understand why it's beneficial because neuroscientists still aren't sure what happens in our brains when we laugh.

Regardless of what scientists may or may not know about laughter, I'm an enthusiastic advocate of it in the workplace. And it's not just about occasional laughter—it's much broader than that. It's about a culture of humour; it's about creating an atmosphere in which the natural inclination to indulge in humour is encouraged; it's about balancing fun and profit.

In his 2013 book *The Humor Advantage: Why Some Businesses Are Laughing All The Way To The Bank*, Michael Kerr links humour in the workplace with profit but points out that the type and degree of humour in the workplace depend very much on an organization's culture. The question then becomes one of why a small business owner should create a culture that encourages humour.

What's in it for you?

Okay, you may be wondering, *so I create a culture that encourages humour in the workplace, but what does it do for my business? Do I want people falling about laughing instead of working? Do I want to run a business or a comedy club?*

Unless your small business is, literally, a comedy club, no, I'm not talking about running a comedy club. On the contrary, I'm talking about boosting the upside potential of your business—quite simply, employees are more productive in some work environments than they are in others. Humour, properly embraced and managed, contributes to increased productivity.

Within the literature on humour in the workplace, various commentators cite ways in which humour facilitates productivity. For instance: it creates an upbeat atmosphere; it helps to build trust because humour often reveals the authentic person; it boosts morale because people like to work with others who have a sense of humour; it puts people at ease; it's a stress buster; and it facilitates creativity because humour relaxes people, and people tend to be more creative when relaxed.

Obviously enhanced productivity is good for your small business's bottom line. But bottom-line considerations apart, who wants to spend his or her workdays in a depressing, humourless environment? Life's too short and workdays too long for that.

But as we know, much of what is put forth as humour nowadays has no place in decent company or in a decent company. Therefore, as owners of small businesses, we have to draw a line between positive, healthy humour and negative, unhealthy humour to maintain decency.

The fine line

Once humour becomes offensive, it can be disruptive, adversely affect productivity, or result in high employee turnover and even loss of business.

A small business tends to take on its owner's traits; your sense of humour is no exception. This is why you must indicate the line between healthy and unhealthy humour, between positive and negative humour. You don't need the formal dictates of the bureaucratic world of big business—rather, you can draw the line by example, by a subtle frown, or if necessary, with a word on the quiet. Most employees are astute enough to get the message about where the line lies and to then stay on the right side of it.

So what's on the wrong side of the fine line? Generally anything that specifically singles out individuals or causes embarrassment and discomfort. A study at Marshall University, West Virginia, unearthed two common sensitive subjects—age and weight. To that I would add sex, clothing, intelligence, marital status, and substance abuse. Comments involving these delicate topics, though meant to be funny, will most often be taken the wrong way and contribute to an uncomfortable, if not hostile, environment.

Bullying disguised as humour

While I was articling with a major accounting firm in Cape Town, one of the audit managers incessantly teased and tormented a few of the articled clerks. They were vulnerable not only because of their lower rank in an antiquated hierarchical system, but also because they were shy and introverted.

It was uncomfortable and at times disturbing to see. In retrospect, what was being touted as humour was actually bullying by an authority figure probably motivated by inadequacies in need of some time on a psychiatrist's couch.

Bullying "humour" must be nipped in the bud as soon as it rears its ugly head.

A RECEPTIVE ENVIRONMENT

I've found that when humour is an element of a workplace's atmosphere, it's often detected by outsiders, who will then feel comfortable enough to make their own humorous contributions. This helps to maintain the happy, relaxed, and hence productive workplace.

Neil, our IT consultant, brought the house down when he turned up one Halloween dressed as a computer geek complete with buck teeth, thick black-rimmed glasses, slicked-down hair, pants belted halfway up his chest with turn-ups hovering six inches above his black shoes, white socks, and white shirt with plastic pocket protector, and carrying an orange plastic pumpkin full of candy. The cameras came out, laughter rang through the building, and within five minutes of humorous "geekiness," the normally consummate information technology professional had enhanced his relationship with a client. A sense of humour is an admirable trait. And the incident affirmed that we had a humour-receptive work environment to which Neil felt comfortable contributing; this was gratifying for me to see.

A humour-receptive environment frees up employees to enjoy moments of spontaneity; as humans, we have an inherent need to punctuate our lives with a good therapeutic laugh now and then. Humour is particularly effective when it turns out to be just the right therapy at just the right moment, arriving unannounced and disguised as, say, a Swedish fax.

My company supplied small PVC beads appropriately named caviar beads. These beads, which are used to decorate garments, are applied to the fabric and then passed on a conveyor belt through an oven, in which they are heated to 320 degrees Fahrenheit. The heat causes them to partially melt and therefore adhere to the garment.

In a valiant attempt at written English, a Swedish screen printer tried to explain that he wished to buy a small quantity of caviar beads with which to conduct tests. He wrote: "I want caviar beads for my testes."

The fax was read aloud for all within earshot. Now, was the rowdy discussion—amid gasps for oxygen and smudged mascara—about how he would cope with adhering the beads at 325 degrees Fahrenheit a bit juvenile? Perhaps. Did it cross the line? I don't believe so. It would have been different if the Swedish inquirer had been present, but he was a faceless individual thousands of kilometres out of earshot. Did it break the tension on one of those stressful it-never-rains-but-it-pours kind of days? Absolutely!

That fax, with its therapeutic humour, delivered just what the doctor ordered at just the right time. If we hadn't had a humour-is-always-welcome culture we wouldn't have derived the mood-altering benefit from that fax. Instead, we'd likely have gone home fed up and grumpy. Humour can punt a bad mood out the door in an instant.

The type of business shouldn't matter

A humour-receptive culture is possible in every business. Have you ever wondered about the atmosphere in an operating room? Imagine lying anaesthetized on the operating table while the surgeons fiddle around in your body cavity with razor-sharp instruments. Do you, as I did, wonder if it's all very sombre? That the silence is disturbed only by occasional barked commands? "Scalpel! Clamp! Sponge!" Well wonder no more. They play music, they chat, they crack jokes, and they laugh. In short, humour helps get them through a stressful, deadly serious job. You can take my word for it—my daughter's a surgeon.

Here's another business you wouldn't associate with humour—at least I didn't. In the business and share valuation part of my career, I was assigned to determine the value of a business that ran two funeral homes. It was co-owned by two brothers, both undertakers. I had never met an undertaker nor been behind the scenes in a funeral home. Heavily influenced by stereotyping, I approached the first meeting with the brothers with a stomach full of butterflies. There was, however, no need for the butterflies. They were two of the most jovial, humorous people I'd ever met. In fact, if I'd met them without knowing that they were undertakers, I'd have assumed they were a comedy act.

I don't want to leave you with the impression that their humorous dispositions ever impinged upon their professionalism; they managed the humour appropriately in a line of business that would surely be exceedingly stressful without the release humour provides.

My early awareness of humour in the workplace

I was about six or seven when I overheard my father telling a story about "the office." At the time I had a very limited understanding of the office. All I knew was that it was where Sunlight soap came from and that it had two other names—the salt mine and Lever Brothers. I also knew it was where Dad had to go on the days I had to go to school. Each day, he'd leave at 7:30 a.m., well before I left, and would come home at 6:00 p.m., well after I'd been let out on parole. I resented the hours spent at school with the beak-faced Mrs. Jones and her slaphappy eighteen-inch wooden ruler, but I had a much worse impression of the salt mine. How was a six-year-old supposed to feel about a place that demanded the commitment of all his dad's daylight hours? That was until I overheard the story.

On a Saturday evening, my father, well known for his sense of humour, was entertaining guests who'd dropped in for sundowners. He told the story of how, one lunchtime at the office, when he'd been on the job as a junior accounting clerk with Lever Brothers for only a few months, he glued down everything on a colleague's desk. Pencil, pen, eraser, coffee cup, paper, stapler, two-hole punch, telephone, and everything else that had been left on the desk—he glued the items in situ with Jewelex (a quick-drying, solvent-based modelling adhesive commonly used for plastic model assembly at the time). The whisky-fuelled laughter was deafening as Dad demonstrated how the victim had pried everything off his desk. And it only grew louder at the explanation of how the glue had eaten into the varnish on the wooden desk, and how Lever Brothers had docked some of Dad's wages to pay for the restoration.

Suddenly, to this eavesdropping six-year-old, the salt mine sounded like a lot more fun than school. I didn't know it at the time of course, but this was my introduction to humour at work, and perhaps this early introduction made me the advocate for humour at work that I am today.

Thinking of the story also reminds me that even an advocate of workplace humour needs to understand that there's a line that's not to be crossed and, as funny as my dad's story was, he had crossed the line.

Reining in the company clown

I introduced the Company Clown as a character, not so much as an individual but rather to represent the broader topic of workplace humour, though your small business may well have a jovial employee with a well-developed sense of humour who earns the label.

A company clown can help maintain a humour-friendly workplace through observations, pranks, and spontaneity, provided his or her delivery is subtle and nonthreatening. The humour should never be overbearing or dispensed in excessive doses. There's nothing as unfunny as someone trying to be funny all the time. And if the company clown indulges in damaging pranks, cutting sarcasm, hurtful teasing, ridicule, or any of the other wrong-side-of-the-line items mentioned earlier, subtle correction may not be enough. As the owner, you must then rein in the company clown before his or her antics harm your business.

On your shoulders

Remember, it rests on your shoulders to ensure that humour is part of your small business's culture. But—and it's a big but—it must be positive, healthy humour. If you can manage this, you'll create a happier, more productive workplace.

CHARACTER 20: VIRTUAL ASSISTANT

Virtually present

While reading a book about recommended resources for small business, I encountered the term "virtual assistant" for the first time. Initially thinking it referred to computer software, I was probably influenced by the term "virtual reality"—commonly associated with computer games since the early nineties.

As I continued reading, it became apparent that "virtual assistant" referred not to an assistant that didn't really exist in the flesh, but to an assistant on a different continent on the other side of the globe.

The concept evolved out of the fact that agencies in relatively low-cost jurisdictions, such as India, could offer services in relatively high-cost jurisdictions at a much lower cost for the same quality and efficiency. All it required was a willingness to communicate digitally rather than face to face.

Initial resistance

The book mentioned one agency in particular that went by the unlikely name of Brickwork India, located in Bangalore. Bangalore—therein lay one of the major obstacles for me. I had been opposed to utilizing offshore resources for purely economic gain ever since witnessing the flight of Canadian textile industry jobs and production orders to low-wage offshore locations.

Starting in 2005, the government relaxed import–export restrictions. This unfortunate development left many casualties in its wake—garment manufacturers relocated offshore while others closed down. Within two years most of my business's large textile screen printing customers had faded away as a result of the large screen printing orders taking the same route as the garment manufacturers. The domestic Canadian textile industry has been a shadow of its former self ever since.

In addition to my concerns about the morality of using offshore resources that were available onshore, I wasn't sure that dealing with an assistant almost thirteen thousand kilometers away in a time zone eleven and a half hours ahead of mine wouldn't be fraught with difficulties. For one thing, the question of security came to mind. I wondered how much leverage I would have with the judicial system in a foreign country if my data was misappropriated.

In spite of a growing intrigue with the idea and a wavering on the morality issue, my reservations about working with an assistant I would never meet face to face prevailed. Consequently, I shelved any thoughts of engaging a virtual assistant.

And shelved they remained until almost a year later, when circumstances forced me to re-examine the virtual assistant concept.

Necessity overcomes resistance

A sudden convergence of suppliers' price increases and a significant exchange-rate adjustment necessitated an urgent price review of all our products, domestic and imported. Pricing our screen printing inks and chemicals involved a lot of variables, including the manufacturers' list prices, discounts that varied according to volumes purchased, freight costs, border clearing costs, import duties, repackaging costs, exchange rates, markups, margins, and sales discounts, to name just a few.

We used a Microsoft Excel spreadsheet to factor in all the elements of determining a suitable price for every product in our warehouse. Every size of every product type was represented on the spreadsheet. If you can picture a spreadsheet of about three thousand lines and about twenty columns, you'll appreciate how onerous a task such a pricing exercise would be for a small business with limited human resources.

The obvious answer was to call for temporary help. My experience with temporary help in the past had been less than satisfactory, but I felt I had very few options and therefore called one of the better-known local temp agencies. In spite of clearly spelling out exactly the kind of expertise we needed, after just a day it was obvious that the person we had been sent was going to do nothing to change my reservations about the locally available temporary help. She was slow to grasp instructions, displayed an indifferent attitude, and made mistakes that cost me a lot of time to correct.

Frustrated, I terminated the temp service and emailed Brickwork. Within a few hours I had paid just over a hundred dollars by credit card for ten hours of work, been assigned a specific assistant, exchanged a few emails with my assistant, and provided guidelines and input data. The work had proceeded by the time I went to bed that night.

The next morning I had an email from my virtual assistant to which was attached a sample spreadsheet for my approval. Her grasp of my instructions was as sound as the test results she had produced. The rest of the task was completed by the next day within the time allotment.

All in all, it was a pleasant, economical, and productive experience. Not only was the work completed at a much lower cost than a local temp agency would have charged me, but it was also flawless. I was immediately enamoured of my virtual assistant, but not enough to declare blind faith in the concept.

Dealing with the Security Concerns

Blind faith is not a good data-management strategy when working with a virtual assistant, particularly when the data may be sensitive. You risk exposure during transmission and after the assistant receives it.

Exposure during transmission can be addressed by digital security measures to thwart hackers and other digital miscreants. The greater risk lies in placing your sensitive data in the hands of a recipient you haven't met working in an environment you haven't seen. You may have no reason to doubt his or her integrity, just as I had no reason to doubt my virtual assistant, but even then it would still be imprudent to throw caution to the wind.

While your virtual assistant may be the paragon of integrity, what if the person in the next cubicle has a grudge against the agency or your virtual assistant and exercises it by misappropriating your sensitive data? Your pricing or other financial data might turn up in your competitors' inboxes. Far-fetched, you think? Not unless you're absolutely confident of the agency's security measures. And how are you going to know that from thirteen thousand kilometers away?

In addition to covert exposure of your sensitive data, you should be concerned about overt exposure. Haven't we all accidentally pushed the wrong button at some time or another and sent something to where we shouldn't have sent it? It's possible that your virtual assistant may have built-in measures to prevent accidental mishandling of your data, but do you want to take that chance?

So does this mean that security concerns negate the benefits of engaging a virtual assistant? Not at all! If the work involves sensitive data there are precautions you can take. For instance, the pricing spreadsheet I had my virtual assistant work on contained a lot of proprietary and sensitive information such as markup formulas, margin calculations, standard shipping costs, delivery costs, discount rates, and other information we would not want to share with competitors or customers.

However, on an Excel spreadsheet, information can easily be disguised.

I simply entered false formulas for the columns I wanted to disguise, and once I received the spreadsheet back with all the raw data entered, I reintroduced the correct formulas in a matter of minutes. If the spreadsheet had somehow fallen into the wrong hands, the data would have been totally useless to anyone with nefarious intent.

Not an Endorsement

My virtual assistant at Brickwork India completed subsequent assignments promptly, efficiently, economically, and accurately. Nevertheless, this book is not intended to endorse any particular products or services. I have been insistent throughout that, while it's a sound practice for small – business owners to solicit recommendations and referrals, you should select your products and services in terms of your own criteria.

While Brickwork India was a trailblazer in the virtual assistant concept, many others have entered the market and can be found by a simple Google search. Comparison shopping is always a good business practice.

Extracting the Best from Your Virtual Assistant

Clarity is always advisable when issuing requests or instructions. In the case of a virtual assistant, it is particularly so.

If you induce angst in the people with whom you work face to face by failing to deliver clear instructions, imagine how much worse it will be for a virtual assistant thirteen thousand kilometers away working on your assignment while you sleep. They can't just pop into your office, and you'd probably be less than impressed if your cell phone rang at three in the morning.

Urging clarification might sound like stating the obvious, but I've worked with some people who issue requests and instructions so convoluted and confusing you just know they're not going to see the results they want. Then, when the inevitable happens, they have the gall to be annoyed! I tended to exhibit this flaw early in my career until the senior partner of the accounting firm for which I was working emphatically pointed it out to me.

My hard-earned advice is to be pedantic to the extent of risking oversimplification. In fact, I have on occasion apologized in advance for potentially oversimplifying, and while I'm sure it has annoyed some people, better that than everyone being annoyed later when a lack of clarification results in less than stellar results. Allow me to pass on what a very wise accounting professor once told me—it takes five times longer to fix a mistake than it does to do it right in the first place. And therefore, he should have added, the task ends up costing five times what it should have.

Part of the reason my virtual assistant completed her assignments successfully with minimal fuss was because the instructions I sent her with the raw material were designed for someone who had never seen anything like my assignment before. For instance, for the pricing assignment, I included a scanned spreadsheet template with hand-drawn arrows and hand-written comments inserted wherever I anticipated that guidance could possibly be required.

This degree of attention to detail might sound excessive, perhaps even obsessive. On the contrary, thinking through my virtual assistant's assignments in detail not only helped her complete the job well but also helped me correct certain shortcomings and spot enhancements. She later confirmed that my detailed instructions and guidelines made the assignments much easier; there was no guesswork involved and no work to be redone.

An Assistant for Just About Anything

The range of services virtual assistants offer nowadays covers everything you might expect from an in-house assistant, and more. Services have been expanded to include accounting, human resources, web-based support, research, general administration, and even location-specific taxation.

You'll find that the engagement models include hourly projects, fixed-bid projects, and retainer arrangements. If your small business has limited human resources and needs occasional help with projects, or even regular ongoing support, a virtual assistant might be the way for you to achieve results effectively and economically.

CHARACTER 21: COMPUTER TECHNICIAN

INDISPENSABLE WHITE KNIGHT

A computer technician is an indispensable resource in most small businesses. We live in an era of inescapable reliance on technology, and it's hardly necessary to point out that most of what we do to conduct and administer a small business involves a computer. And while both hardware and software are much more reliable and user-friendly than they were even just a few years ago, sometimes your small business's computer network will need attention.

Unlike large companies with a dedicated IT staff, most small business budgets cannot accommodate a full-time computer technician. Fortunately, these professionals are not the frequent visitors to small businesses that they once were because nowadays, small business computer networks usually run smoothly between the two events that commonly require a technician: set-up and failure. However, in the case of the latter, time is often of the essence, and it's then that the small business owner needs to have a "white knight" on speed dial.

Computer failure—hardware or software— brings with it the prospect of a one-two punch of downtime and a hefty bill. It's enough to cause a small business owner to descend into a state of despair. While the bill is inevitable, whether the problem is addressed immediately or at some future date, the cost and frustration of downtime demands immediate attention. Computer failure has the uncanny knack of occurring at critical times with deadlines looming and when downtime is unthinkable. On these occasions you need the white knight to gallop to the rescue and lift your spirits by putting the broken Humpty Dumpty of technology back together again before the proverbial whiskey bottle begins to look like an attractive alternative.

Competence is key

Choose your white knight for those inevitable downtime emergencies with care. Computer technicians come in varying degrees of competence; limit your choices to the upper end of the range.

Not only will a competent technician save you when technology emergencies strike, but he or she will also help you make sense of the alternatives when new technology is being considered. They can help cut through the mind-boggling, unfathomable techno-talk that often accompanies new technology.

A not-so-competent computer technician can not only cause serious damage to your systems and computer records, but also, as the expression goes, "drive you to drink". However, the alcohol-fuelled consequence of engaging a not-so-competent computer technician is not really the point—the point is that a small business's computer network is too important to be placed at risk, so a computer technician must be engaged with a great deal of caution.

Among the computer technicians, good and bad, who attended to my business computers over the years, Sparky (I anointed him thus) stands out as the embodiment of an incompetent technician. In order to pause a power supply unit fan to confirm that it was the source of an unhealthy noise, he inserted a screwdriver through the protective grate and into the fan blades. I suppose it would have worked if he had approached the problem with the delicacy of a surgeon handling a scalpel. Instead, he handled the screwdriver with the finesse of a lumberjack wielding an axe, thrusting it through the grate, past the fan blades, and into the live wires behind the fan.

A thunderclap accompanied by a six-inch blue flame and the screen's fading to black was followed by a few moments of stunned silence during which I decided that this would be the last we saw of Sparky.

The technicians you need and how to find them

Your small business will generally have access to one of three computer technician resources, depending where you're located—there may be exceptions in some countries and small towns. The choice lies between sole practitioners, companies consisting of a staff of technicians (most are small, with ten or fewer staff), and nationwide franchises with multiple offices, marked cars, and logo-embroidered golf shirts.

The advantage of hiring multi-technician computer service companies over sole practitioners is that the former's technicians have likely been tested for competence during the hiring process. When you engage a sole practitioner, the competence checking falls on your shoulders. In the end, however, it all comes down to the individual technician's competence, regardless of whether he or she is a sole practitioner or an employee of a service.

Being able to communicate technical matters in plain language is also a welcome attribute in your computer technician. Tim was one such technician whose expertise we were fortunate to have for a few years. He had a knack for explaining complex technical issues in plain English. When we were switching our operating system from MS-DOS to Windows, programs operating on the old and the new operating systems clashed and caused each other to malfunction.

Instead of the usual techno-talk about bits, bytes, and binary numbers, Tim likened the clashing of programs to the two of us trying to leave the room by the same doorway at the same time—we'd get stuck and neither of us would be able to move. In the context of what we were experiencing, his comparison helped me understand the issue better. And sure enough, once all programs were operating on Windows, everyone came and went through the doorway in an orderly fashion, one at a time, and without further clashes.

A few years later, another technician demonstrated a similar ability to explain technical matters in plain English—perhaps plainer than I had bargained for. We were making a major upgrade to a program on the server, and it had come down to one final press of a button. Neil, the technician in question, had spent a number of hours getting us to that point and, as he stood poised for that final press, he wanted me to understand that, once done, there was no reversing the process: "You know that we can't cram the shit back in the horse?"

In addition to being a plain speaker, Neil was also a very competent technician and it turned out that there was no need to cause the horse any discomfort.

When Your Small Business Is Considered Too Small

When I sold my business and became a home-based writer and consultant, I still needed computer support, albeit somewhat scaled back. I tried to engage conventional multi-technician firms with which I had previously dealt. To my consternation, I found that since I no longer had a server and at least six workstations, I did not meet their basic criteria for customer qualification. Frustrated, I eventually engaged a sole practitioner on the recommendation of a local computer component store. And while not a Sparky, his knowledge turned out to be limited resulting in my having to change technicians midway through writing this book.

The second time, in accordance with the once-bitten-twice-shy convention, I selected a sole practitioner very carefully on the basis of a strong recommendation from a reliable source. Fortunately, my second choice turned out to be a very good one.

My advice, based on hard-earned experience, is to not engage a computer technician until you have recommendations from his or her other clients with similar requirements to your own. For me those include (1) a willingness to make home-office visits to develop trust and rapport before switching to remote access, (2) experience and formal training in the areas in which I need support, and (3) reasonable availability when I need it.

You should define your technical support requirements taking into account your particular circumstances, engage a service accordingly, and be sure to make recommendations a key part of the selection process.

Special instructions for your computer technician

If your small business has employees, the first thing to do is discuss with them the standards you've laid out for the use and care of your company computers. Make it clear that should they come across something untoward, they are to let you know.

Surreptitious use of company computers by employees happens, and the consequences can be far-reaching. I discovered this when a computer crashed at a remote location. I hired a technician over the phone, and fortunately he turned out to be a good choice. He arrived promptly, located the problem, and had the computer functioning within a few hours.

We had a follow-up conversation about the problem in which he suggested that the virus detection on the computer needed upgrading. After closer questioning, he hesitatingly, and somewhat awkwardly, suggested that the crash had occurred as a result of the computer being used to access "inappropriate" websites.

I realized then that I had been negligent in not thinking it necessary to lay out rules for the use of my company's computers. I naively assumed that employees would know that using company computers to access inappropriate websites would be, well, inappropriate.

Lay out the rules, be brutally frank about the consequences, and make it known to your employees that part of the computer technician's mandate is to let you know about potentially damaging misuse of the computers. Unfortunately, while most employees can be expected to act responsibly, just one exception can cause a lot of damage. A good technician should be able to advise you on how the possibility of such damage can be minimised.

Back up, back up, back up

I know that you probably hear "back up!" repeatedly, but it's surprising how many small businesses don't do it properly or even ignore the advice completely.

Not backing up properly can be as bad as not doing it at all. I once believed that three drives mirroring each other would safeguard against a drive crash, which is of course a perfectly reasonable assumption. After all, how often have you heard of three drives all crashing at the same time? The problem is that the number of drives is not really the issue. Even three dozen drives wouldn't mitigate loss by fire, flood, or theft. However, secure off-site backup would. The key of course is that it must be as secure as possible against natural disasters or hacking. Your technician should be able to recommend a suitable service.

Ultimately, it's about your selection

There are no guarantees that your selection will be perfect, but choose a computer technician with due care and you give yourself the best chance of enjoying a relatively failure-free computer network. If you find that you've selected a Sparky, be ruthless about dumping him. If you find a Tim or a Neil, hang onto him.

CHARACTER 22: MAINTENANCE TECHNICIAN

AN UNDERSTATED ROLE

This is the character who maintains the assets that keep your small business operating smoothly and without unscheduled and costly interruptions.

Depending on its nature, your business will rely to varying degrees on a number of operating assets—buildings, computers, equipment, vehicles, and furniture, to name the more common ones. You may rely on certain assets so completely that should they malfunction, your business will grind to a halt. A severe case of business interruption could result in business failure.

In spite of the obvious importance of keeping assets in good working order, I've often seen small businesses neglect maintenance. A breakdown of an essential income-producing asset will usually cost a lot more in lost business and repairs than the price of preventative maintenance. And when a breakdown happens, it's sure to be at the least opportune time.

I was reminded of this when a coffee shop I frequented shut down for a few days. The thirty-thousand-dollar coffee maker couldn't make coffee because of an inexpensive part that could have been replaced during routine maintenance.

This is why the maintenance person (who is usually a third party but could be you or your employees) has an important role to play in the life of a small business. Sadly though, many small business owners don't appreciate how important this role is.

The maintenance person's role

This character's role is to keep the workplace—its facilities, equipment, computers, and furniture—operating efficiently and safely by inspecting, testing, servicing, repairing, and replacing.

The role is carried out in three main ways: by conducting preventative maintenance (often referred to as scheduled or routine maintenance), emergency maintenance, and cosmetic maintenance.

Preventative maintenance

Preventative maintenance forestalls breakdowns and keeps the income-producing assets in good operating condition—a sensible management practice but an often neglected one.

A common cause of neglected maintenance is money. In accordance with Murphy's Law, preventative maintenance schedules can clash with cash-flow troughs and be delayed or even cancelled. At these times it's wise to keep in mind the old adage about spoiling the ship for a ha'penny's worth of tar.

Emergency maintenance

Emergency maintenance is required when a malfunctioning asset threatens to cause costly damage or impede operations. One good example is a restaurant freezer malfunctioning while stocked with expensive food. Another is something that happened to my business late one winter's night in Calgary, when the outside temperature hovered around minus thirty-five degrees Celsius. We had to momentarily open the loading dock's big overhead door, and then it jammed and wouldn't shut when a spring snapped. Cold air began swirling into the warehouse packed with expensive freeze-sensitive emulsions.

Equipment failures like these happen in spite of routine maintenance programs—it's just a fact of life that there are no guarantees. However, the impact of an event requiring emergency maintenance can be minimized by a simple measure: a list of emergency contact numbers. Fortunately we had the door maintenance company's twenty-four-hour emergency number on a sticker right on the door. A hastily assembled wall of cardboard boxes, a cranked-up gas furnace, and the door maintenance person's prompt response saved the inventory from freezing.

The lesson: keep the emergency number of a reliable maintenance person for each operating asset handy where everyone can find it. Stocking certain critical parts or ensuring that the maintenance person in question can quickly access critical parts can also help to minimize the impact of an incident.

Cosmetic maintenance

While cosmetic maintenance is probably the least important of the maintenance types a small business needs, don't overlook it.

In the Janitor chapter, I discuss the importance of a clean and orderly business premises. In a similar vein, appearance affects how third parties perceive your business—third parties such as suppliers and customers upon whom the success of your business depends. For instance, cracked pathways, peeling paint (exterior and interior), broken windows, faded signs, and dented vehicles could present a bad impression and undermine your business.

However, by no means am I advocating carrying out cosmetic maintenance just for the sake of it, particularly if failing to do so won't adversely affect an asset's performance. I'm suggesting that you assess the impact of not doing cosmetic maintenance before spending money. A business associate taught me this lesson in New Orleans. I was attending a trade show and convention and, like everyone else who has ever attended a convention there, headed to Bourbon Street in the evenings to take in the bars, restaurants, and jazz clubs. One evening, a group of us wandered into one of the many dimly lit, packed jazz clubs.

On a small raised stage three or four musicians were belting out a tune while waiters manoeuvred crab-like between tables barely inches apart. As we stood pressed up against a wall waiting for a table to become available and clutching the plastic cups of weird and wonderful libations we'd acquired elsewhere on the street, I glanced up at the ceiling to find that there was no ceiling, at least not in the way that, say, an interior decorator would describe a ceiling. Instead, I saw what would normally be hidden from view by suspended ceiling tiles—several criss-crossing wooden beams and a mass of wires and cables, some probably decades old and no longer serving any purpose. The whole mess had been spray-painted black in a failed attempt to make it look less like a dog's breakfast.

When I noticed one of my companions also looking around taking in the scene, I pointed out the ceiling and suggested that if I owned the club, I'd do something about it. "Why?" asked Mike. "The place is packed in spite of that." He motioned at the capacity crowd with his head. "Think they care? It'd be a waste of money."

Mike was right of course. Anything spent on cosmetic maintenance for that ceiling wouldn't have garnered more business for the club—it was already enjoying capacity crowds. Obsessive compulsive cosmetic maintenance tendencies such as mine must be reined in; they must be passed through the business-sense filter.

Eyes and ears

Most small businesses are unlikely to have full-time maintenance people on staff. A more likely scenario is that they rely on a list of third-party maintenance people, each a specialist in a particular field. For instance, computer maintenance is quite different from furnace maintenance which is quite different from, say, widget machine maintenance—hence different maintenance people.

However, it doesn't follow that an absence of full-time maintenance people means an absence of maintenance awareness. Employees in all functions must be taught how to spot maintenance issues in the assets with which they perform their jobs. For example, a bookkeeper should know when his or her computer is making an unusual noise, behaving peculiarly, or in some other way indicating that it needs a maintenance specialist's attention. The same applies to factory workers, drivers, and all other employees using assets of any kind.

Be warned though that you can't assume employees will automatically pay attention to peculiar sounds that to you indicate a maintenance problem. People differ in their awareness of things mechanical—a lesson I learned the hard way. In one instance, one of my warehouse employees heard the faintest change in the noise emitted by a particular machine, found the failing part, and replaced it before the machine failed.

In another instance, an employee didn't react at all when a machine began making a noise of metal grinding on metal. By the time I heard it, a dislodged bolt was about to grind through another part and cause a costly failure. Take nothing for granted— teach all employees to understand that any unusual behaviour or noise is a maintenance red flag.

In small businesses, all employees must be the eyes and ears of the maintenance function.

Obligatory maintenance

Certain operating assets might require routine maintenance by law, lease, or warranty. These obligations are usually very specific.

You must schedule any obligatory maintenance and ensure that you comply fully. Noncompliance could mean serious legal, insurance, or warranty consequences in the event of an accident or a malfunction.

A record of the maintenance complete with supporting documents, such as correspondence and maintenance persons' reports, could be very useful and save a lot of time and angst in the event of an incident or dispute. An indexed three-ring binder stored safely off-site is a good way to keep this record.

Dangers

Maintenance projects can involve risks to life and limb and need to be assessed before the work commences. This might sound a bit alarmist, but even small maintenance tasks can cause serious accidents if the risks aren't considered. For instance, when preparing to dislodge a paper jam in a desktop printer (and this is directed to those people I've seen using pliers to dislodge bad jams), unplug the power cord.

Common sense and a few basic precautions when it comes to apparently simple tasks can prevent serious accidents. If you were a building maintenance person preparing to inspect a leaking pipe just below the twenty-foot ceiling of an industrial bay, would you ensure that the ladder was stable and properly secured? Would you ensure that a second person was present to hold the ladder and assist in case of a problem? After all, wrestling with a pipe while perched twenty feet up on a ladder isn't child's play. Of course you'd take these precautions, right? I know I would, assuming I could even be persuaded to climb twenty feet up a ladder. Well, Brian didn't.

Brian was the building maintenance person for the industrial park that housed our Calgary premises. He took none of the precautions that a quick risk assessment and common sense required. He was found unconscious on the concrete floor with, among other injuries, a cracked skull. What exactly happened nobody knows. To Brian it was all a blur and there were no other witnesses.

While quick risk assessments and common sense might be sufficient to prevent accidents during small maintenance tasks, larger maintenance projects involving complicated equipment will usually require a formal risk assessment before work commences. A comprehensive assessment will take into account heavy stuff, sharp stuff, moving parts, electricity, gas lines, and other dangers of which experts will be aware.

Working with competent maintenance people, particularly if you have large or complex equipment, will go a long way to ensuring that your small business avoids the dangers inherent in some maintenance tasks.

Managed maintenance

Maintenance will never be one of the more exciting aspects of small business management, but it will always be a vital one. Manage it properly and it will contribute to the making of your business; mismanage it and it could do the opposite.

Remember the ship and the ha'penny's worth of tar.

CHARACTER 23: SUPPLIER

A KEY CHARACTER

This character's influence will vary greatly but, in one way or another, every small business will encounter a supplier. Some may have just one while others will have multiple suppliers. Some may interact with suppliers only occasionally, others many times a day. Some may entirely rely upon individual suppliers while others may not rely on any at all. It all depends upon the nature of the small business.

The supplier is the source of finished goods to be resold, raw materials to be processed into finished goods, or equipment with which the small business carries out its work. For most small businesses this makes the supplier a key character who has considerable influence over its well-being and who can affect it for better or for worse.

STABILITY AND RELIABILITY

The daily challenges most small business-owners face are numerous and varied in a Jack-of-all-trades kind of way. One minute you're resolving an irate customer's problem and the next refereeing a difference of opinion between two employees. You're the owner. You're the go-to person when issues escalate and the last thing you need is for supply issues to escalate to where they need your attention—by that point, disruption of supply might be imminent. And what a small business needs from its suppliers is stability and reliability so that it may in turn offer stability and reliability to its customers.

But supply disruptions can happen for any number of reasons—manufacturing and delivery delays, inventory shortages, import paperwork errors, erroneous or incomplete deliveries, and defective products, to name just some of the common examples. Then there is the age-old overdue payment reason. Suppliers like to be paid on time and will readily withhold delivery to reinforce this point.

The degree to which supplier problems constitute a headache for you depends upon the degree to which your small business relies upon a particular supplier. This brings us to an important consideration: whenever possible, before choosing to do business with a supplier, weigh the make-or-break effect it can have on your small business. Select thoughtfully.

My small business was tied to just a single supplier for each of about a half-dozen product types. This was due partly to the nature of the textile screen printing industry, which has a limited number of competitive manufacturers, and partly to my belief that brand monogamy would foster a closer relationship with suppliers and lead to advantages not enjoyed by brand polygamists—in retrospect, a decision I now regret. The rewards for supplier monogamy did not materialize. Instead, my business relied heavily on those few suppliers when a broader range of alternatives would have given us a greater variety of prices and quality options and hence greater market-penetration potential.

If you're going to inextricably bind the future of your small business to the future of a single supplier and its brand, consider the pros and cons very carefully. It could be a double-edged sword.

Double-edged sword

While all is well with the sole supplier and its brand, you will likely enjoy a stable and reliable supply. Should the supplier's fortunes change for the worse though, stability may be threatened and alternatives may no longer be available. This could be seriously detrimental to your small business or, in a worst-case scenario, even break it.

At some point after I committed my business to the leading brand of textile screen printing ink, the competitive brands began to close the quality gap while maintaining much more favourable pricing. Our market share began to erode—but by then it was too late to acquire one of the major competitive brands.

I know the owner of a small ceramic business who also ran into the double-edged sword problem, albeit temporarily. It's worth noting her experience because in a different industry with a different product, it could break a small business.

Glazes are a critical part of ceramic production and the slightest change to a formula can cause a number of problems, from colour shifts to flaws. Over a period of years, Karen's small business became reliant on a single glaze manufacturer. As is the case for most ceramicists, her glaze formulas are a closely guarded secret. Her sole-source glaze supplier had worked with her years before to develop the glazes that impart the unique properties she requires of her finished products.

This supply stability continued until the supplier changed the glaze formulas. To Karen's dismay, the reformulated glazes no longer worked. She had no other source and her production ceased while the supplier worked on the problem. Eventually, after two agonizing months, she was able to call her staff back and resume production.

Karen's experience should be a warning for other small businesses with single-source suppliers of key materials. Circumstances change. It's a good idea to develop a plan B to ensure supply continuity.

Cultivating guardian angels

For convenience, I've been portraying suppliers as individuals. In the case of big companies, the individual with whom your small business deals will usually be a salesperson, a customer service representative or, in some cases, a technical expert.

Because these people have formal business relationships with your small business, they are likely to conduct themselves formally and with discretion. That's why it's useful to cultivate a friendly relationship with one or more of the supplier's employees other than your formal contacts. You might meet these people at trade shows, through mutual acquaintances, at company functions, or via social media. The friendship might have its roots in common interests, such as children, pets, or hobbies, and while conversations will revolve around these things, business will inevitably creep into conversations.

The business benefit of these guardian angels is that quite often you'll hear of impending developments such as staff and management changes, intended new products, and other information that might be useful to know but that's not yet intended for public consumption. It's surprising how indiscreet and loose-lipped some employees of big companies can be, particularly if they have reason to be disgruntled.

Disputes and disagreements

Disputes and disagreements between small businesses and their suppliers are bound to arise from time to time. Any of the circumstances I mentioned earlier—from non-delivery to late delivery and everything in between—can trigger a dispute or disagreement.

When blood pressures rise, the key to preserving an amicable supplier relationship lies in how the small business owner (or an employee) handles the dispute. If it escalates, you may need to consider who needs whom more. Quite often in a supplier and small business relationship, the small business is the junior partner and therefore the one with the most to gain by tempering its demeanour accordingly.

That doesn't mean you should allow your small business to be pushed around by bigger and stronger suppliers, but an abrasive or threatening stance will almost certainly be inappropriate, ineffective, and potentially destructive. Even in the most frustrating and trying of circumstances with a big-company supplier, there are alternatives. You can appeal to reason, cry for help, prod a conscience, or try humour.

Consider the story of one small business owner's response to a large supplier's indifference to his dilemma.

Shawn was very pleased with the latest equipment purchase for his textile screen printing business. Driven by a couple of good operators, the big blue computer-controlled circular T-shirt press could print a multi-coloured design on about six hundred T-shirts every hour. It cut an imposing figure on his factory floor—a giant blue octopus, twenty feet in diameter, with (in this case) sixteen tentacles evenly splayed about it. It was a T-shirt-spewing monster.

Shawn had a few other smaller presses bought over a period of years from the same supplier, a privately owned but big and successful equipment manufacturer in the US that we'll call P&T Equipment. All had been good investments and were still steadily printing T-shirts.

Sadly though, weeks after delivery, the monster had still not spewed a single printed T-shirt. It was sitting lifelessly on the factory floor—a comatose octopus—in need of certain vital parts that hadn't arrived with the main body of the press. And to add to Shawn's mounting frustration, even after the parts eventually arrived, two more weeks went by without any sign of the P&T technician who had to install them.

After many phone calls to various members of P&T's staff and management without result, Shawn's short fuse ran out. He fired off a fax to the owner of P&T (we'll call him Paul). They had shared a few dinners and glasses of wine at industry trade shows over the years and Shawn felt comfortable leading off with, "Dear Paul."

I saw a copy of the two-page "Dear Paul" fax, the like of which you'd be hard pressed to find in any business textbook, dispute-settlement manual, or business-school lecture. It began very politely on a positive note by tracing the history of Shawn's equipment purchases from P&T. It mentioned how well the previously acquired presses had performed and thereby allowed his small business to increase its production and grow. He then explained how, on the basis of his confidence in P&T's equipment, he took the calculated risk of investing in the recently acquired much bigger and more expensive press.

After the first page, the friendly tone of the missive began to slip as Shawn traced the process of the recent acquisition, from placing the order, to the incomplete delivery, delayed parts, and non-appearance of the technician. He mentioned how his initial excitement had turned to disappointment and, eventually, anger. And so it continued to deteriorate in tone until he ended the fax with the final blow in what had become a verbal beating: "I'm so annoyed that I will never, ever buy another piece of equipment from P&T. In fact, I wouldn't buy a fire extinguisher from you if my penis were in flames!"

The usually difficult-to-contact-and-slow-to-respond Paul called within minutes with an apology and a promise to personally intervene immediately.

So what should a small business owner conclude from that? Well, for one thing, sheer frustration expressed through humour got Shawn the result he was seeking. Would it have worked in a different situation with a different supplier? Perhaps not. This is why you'll want to consider the circumstances before deciding how to deal with the problem—you don't want to act hastily or thoughtlessly and potentially destroy a supplier relationship worth preserving.

The obdurate supplier

Unfortunately, there are no guarantees. Your thoughtful, diplomatic, and courteous approach to disputes and disagreements could all be wasted on an obdurate supplier.

If that happens, the see-you-in-court option might be all you have. At this stage the relationship is almost certainly over, at which point your lawyer comes into play. As I explained in the Lawyer chapter, I had to deal with just such a supplier and, refusing to be bullied, fought back. Justice prevailed and the supplier ended up paying for his obduracy.

You're not family

I have known small business owners, particularly new ones, to be quite naive in their dealings with large suppliers. You need to understand that it's all about the bottom line. Notwithstanding the best efforts of the public relations departments and advertising agencies, very little sentiment is involved in big business—it's ultimately about the dollar and the quarterly financial report.

Individual representatives of big companies assigned to your small business account will quite often be affable and even likeable, but they are the facade for something a lot less personable and potentially ruthless.

What I find particularly insidious is the supplier who portrays your business as a member of one big happy family. You might have already heard something like this from, say, the president of Friendly Company Supplies, "Don't worry. You're part of the Friendly family. We'll look after you!"

Baloney! It's a business relationship and nothing more. The supplier's priority is moving as much product out the door as possible at the best price possible. While you help further that end, you're "family." If your supplier is presented with a more attractive alternative that will move even more product out the door, or if you annoy the supplier in some way, your "family" status will be found wanting. To be lulled into believing the all-in-the-family deception is to set yourself up for disappointment.

It's best to make it a rule, for yourself as the owner and for employees, to treat every supplier cordially but on a businesslike basis. Because that's what it really is—just business. And you'll be better off not expecting anything more than that.

On rare occasions I've seen the rule violated without ill effect, but in those circumstances the supplier was usually a small business owner too. Among the suppliers my business dealt with over a twenty-year period, just one has shown an interest in maintaining contact as a friend—the owner of a small chemical factory in Santa Barbara.

Contact with the big suppliers ceased as soon as I no longer meant anything to their bottom line, and that includes the supplier who particularly promoted the "we're all family" myth.

David's defense against Goliath

When you're a small business David doing business with big-supplier Goliaths, you can't expect to meet force with force—you have to outwit them.

The rule in the business world is similar to that of the jungle: the strongest will prevail, unless the weaker are smarter. Large suppliers will use their superior size and strength to exercise influence and even intimidate small businesses when it suits them, much more so if the small businesses don't have alternative sources of supply.

My small business of eight employees couldn't have been more of a David in comparison with its main supplier, Goliath Ink (my pseudonym for them), a wholly owned subsidiary of a vertically integrated, publically traded, multinational conglomerate with over seven thousand employees.

Because of its dependence upon Goliath Ink, which would hear no criticism of its adverse pricing structure, my small business was at a disadvantage. Goliath Ink, through lack of Canadian market awareness and a lingering dose of arrogance born of being the industry leader for many years, dogmatically adhered to the belief that its product was vastly superior to all else in the market and therefore its significantly higher prices were justified. But market circumstances had changed.

Competitors closed the quality gap while maintaining lower prices. I was left no choice but to supplement our product range with a less expensive brand of textile screen printing ink to satisfy the demands of certain price-sensitive customers. However, I didn't want Goliath Ink to know this because I couldn't trust them to not turn nasty.

Soon after the first delivery of the new brand of ink to our warehouse,

Goliath's representative responsible for our account paid us a rare visit. So soon, in fact, that I wondered if he'd heard about the second brand of ink and was on a mission to investigate. It was, the representative said in the phone call from Los Angeles, to be just a quick, same day, in-and-out visit to review a few figures and compile projections for the coming year.

We extended the courtesy of a warehouse tour—a courtesy we extended to all our suppliers' representatives, even though we knew they were only interested in seeing if we were carrying competitors' products. To this day I don't know if he suspected anything, but the only ink the representative saw in our warehouse was Goliath's.

The day before he arrived I rented a one-ton cube van, into which our warehouse manager loaded the entire inventory of the new brand of ink. As she drove the van away from the warehouse's back door, I could hardly watch. It was so heavily laden with five-gallon ink buckets that the undercarriage was only inches from the road surface as it creaked and groaned its way to a parking spot just fifty feet away.

As soon as the representative was safely winging his way back to California, the truck was backed up to the warehouse. Unloading commenced and the suspension—creaking and groaning again—gradually resumed its normal posture.

A head-to-head confrontation that could have ended badly for my small business was avoided. When backed into a corner by a big supplier, a small business needs to be smart. Sometimes survival can depend upon creative solutions.

The cooperative supplier

Diplomacy when patience wears thin, courtesy when provoked, assertiveness without aggression, and a dash of humour when appropriate can go long way to maintaining cooperative supplier relationships. Though not guaranteed, stable and reliable sources of supply should be the reward.

Oh, and finally, don't forget that a cooperative supplier is a supplier paid on time.

CHARACTER 24: FRANCHISOR

Climbing Mount Start-Up

Small Business Owner Wannabe longs to dwell in the village of Business Bliss, where everyone makes handsome profits and lives happily ever after. But Mr. Wannabe knows from all he's read and heard that Business Bliss lies on the other side of Mount Start-Up, which looms large and menacingly in front of him. He also knows that vast numbers perish on the craggy slopes of Mount Start-Up long before even catching a glimpse of Business Bliss.

Just as he's pondering whether he has what it takes to conquer this mountain, an apparition—one that could easily have been created by J.K. Rowling—appears and makes Mr. Wannabe a very tempting offer. The apparition says that for a small fee (nothing is for nothing, even in fantasies), it can transport him over Mount Start-Up and deliver him straight to a business of his own in the village of Business Bliss. Mr. Wannabe is very tempted, but hesitates as he wonders: *Is this too good to be true? Could I be rushing in where angels fear to tread? And who is this apparition?*

Back in the real world, we know that Mr. Wannabe's apparition is a franchisor—a franchisor who, for a fee, promises avoidance of most of the blood, sweat, and tears associated with independent start-ups. And in the real world, seldom is anything in business as cut and dried as it may first appear. This is particularly true of franchising, which brings with it special elements that demand clarification and understanding. And the first thing to understand is that franchising is different from independent small business ownership in that the franchisor exercises influence through a franchise agreement.

So who is this franchisor?

A complex character

A franchisor is broadly defined as a company who allows another company or individual (the franchisee) to participate in its business. The franchisor retains ownership and control of the overarching business, the brand, trademarks, products, and—depending upon the circumstances—other assets such as buildings, but gives the franchisee the right to use these assets in return for fees (some up front and some ongoing). Therefore, while the franchisee may appear to be the owner of a business or brand, he or she is only operating it under an agreement with the behind-the-scenes owner.

Franchisors impose standards and rules by which franchisees must operate. Usually these are strictly enforced to ensure uniformity and consistency from one franchised location or service to another. Think about every McDonald's you've ever been to anywhere in the world. Was there a moment's doubt about where you were? The sign, architecture, furniture, décor, colours, and food: perhaps not the assurance of a gourmet experience but definitely the assurance of familiarity and consistency. This is a key advantage of franchise ownership—turnkey brand recognition not easily or quickly achieved by independent small businesses.

Franchising is simple enough in principle but often complex in implementation. So much so, many countries have deemed it necessary to regulate franchising. Other hints of potential complexity are found in words and phrases such as “franchise disclosure document”; “exclusive franchise”; “nonexclusive franchise”; “sole and exclusive franchise”; “master franchisors”; and “standards of performance.” There is much to understand before taking the franchising plunge. I wouldn’t recommend proceeding without first consulting two key professionals—a lawyer and an accountant.

Franchise lawyer

Franchise law is a specialized area of business best served by specialized knowledge and experience, hence franchise lawyers. As a prospective franchisee, you would be well advised to consult a good one. I assume of course that we’re talking about a small business person considering becoming a franchisee.

The franchisor will usually present a franchise agreement standardized to his, her, or its business. This agreement would typically leave little room, if any, for negotiation. While the franchise lawyer may not be able to influence the terms of the agreement, he or she will at least be able to provide the franchisee with a full and clear interpretation of the rules by which the franchisor will govern.

As I have noted throughout this book, forewarned is forearmed.

Accountant

Engage an accountant—and again, preferably one experienced in franchising—to review all the financial aspects of the proposed franchise. Even small variances in elements such as turnover, profit margins, royalty rates, and overhead expenses, for example, can significantly impact the bottom line. A good accountant will be able to provide insight into the credibility of all these numbers.

Undoubtedly, the franchisor will present income and expenditure projections as part of the sales pitch. But expect him or her to emphasize the upside—after all, this person is selling the franchise and therefore unlikely to dwell on the downside. That's the job of your accountant—to explore the full range of fiscal possibilities and consequences.

I once saw a John Louthan cartoon of two managers looking through an open door into a research and development department where people are excitedly high-fiving each other. One turns to the other and says: "Get someone from accounting to kill this damn excitement!" We make jokes about accountants' fiscally conservative orientation, but it could be incredibly useful to a prospective franchisee.

Research

In addition to consulting with experts, you must conduct your own research on the topic if you're considering the franchisee route to small business ownership.

There's no shortage of reading material (books, articles, blog posts, etc.), and you should access as much of it as possible. I only have space here to discuss two examples, and I recommend that you read them both. The first is a paper: *What the Hell Happened? When Franchisee Discontent Morphs Into Litigation*, published by Dickinson Wright LLP, a law firm specializing in, among other things, franchise law. The author, who presented the paper at the 2010 Canadian Franchise Association National Convention, Edward (Ned) Levitt, is a partner in Dickinson Wright's Toronto office. In addition to practicing franchise law, he served as general counsel to the Canadian Franchise Association and was a member of the Ontario Franchise Sector Working Team, which contributed to the creation of Ontario's franchise legislation. He is also the author of *Canadian Franchise Legislation*, published by Butterworths–LexisNexis. In other words, Ned Levitt knows franchising. And contrary to what you might fear, the sixteen-page paper is not written in legalese—it's particularly well written in layman-friendly English and is enormously informative. Available online, it's a must-read for small business franchisees and prospective franchisees.

My second recommendation is an article in the March–April 2014 issue of *Pacific Standard* magazine titled "Disenfranchised: Why are Americans still buying into the franchise dream?" Among a lot of other useful insight, it discusses how franchisor-imposed rules are becoming increasingly strict and how some franchisors are using minor rule violations to terminate contracts and seize the franchises without reimbursing the franchisees—a consideration not to be taken lightly.

Discussions with franchisees in businesses similar to the one you're contemplating running will almost certainly be worth the time and cost of a few dinners. What I'm encouraging here (not for the last time) is that you sign a franchise agreement under no illusions as to the risks and benefits.

The downside

You may be a little concerned about the cautionary tone of the preceding few pages. Your concern may grow if you explore Google and find, as I did, articles titled: "Discontent Simmers Among McDonald's Franchisees"; "Franchisee Discontent over Failure to Renew and Encroachment"; "Aaron's Runs Afoul of Its Franchisees"; "Subway Franchisees Unhappy in Germany"; and "Rumbles of Franchisee Discontent Growing in the Depths of Hell." I included the latter two to show that it's not just a North American issue—they're from Germany and New Zealand respectively.

Then there's that article I referenced earlier from *Pacific Standard*: "Disenfranchised: Why are Americans still buying into the franchise dream?" You'd expect the article to provide an answer to its own question, but it doesn't. It keeps us waiting for an answer right to the end and then disconcertingly concludes with the tale of a franchisee from Long Beach, California, who left suicide notes, one for his wife and one for the media. The article quotes from the note to the media: "In this franchise system the Franchisor has all the rights and no duties and obligations, whereas it is just the opposite for the Franchisee." Shortly after penning the note, he shot himself.

The downside can't go down much further than this. Fortunately though, as in most situations in life, for every downside there's an upside.

The upside

Franchising has a longer history than you might imagine—the concept was implemented as far back as the Middle Ages by the Catholic Church, which made franchise-like agreements with tax collectors, who retained a percentage of what they collected before turning over their proceeds. Modern-day franchising was first introduced in the United States by the Singer Sewing Machine Company in the mid-1800s, and it has expanded internationally and grown steadily since then. Today there are approximately 780,000 franchise establishments in the United States; 78,000 in Canada; 37,000 in the United Kingdom; 30,000 in South Africa; and 24,000 in New Zealand, to name a few countries for which the numbers are readily available.

Given these numbers, one can only assume that there is a considerable upside to franchising, but at this juncture it might seem to you that I've emphasised the downside. You'd have a point, but there's a reason for what might appear to be my excessive negativity.

You see, one can be blinded to the negatives when presented with the positives of franchising, especially with the high failure rate of independent start-ups at the back of one's mind. A turnkey operation with an established, tried-and-tested system and immediate brand recognition is an attractive proposition, particularly at the lower end of the franchising spectrum where the financial barrier to entry can be relatively low. According to the Canadian Franchise Association's website, you can invest in some opportunities for franchise fees as low as $5,000 and individual investments as low as $10,000. It's bound to be enticing to a would-be entrepreneur hoping for better odds than are generally associated with independent start-ups.

I just want to make sure you're aware that the shiny franchise coin has another side before you attend a franchisor's sales presentation. Don't expect him or her to focus on anything but the shiny side. This certainly doesn't mean to imply in any way that by attending a sales presentation you're in imminent danger of throwing your franchise fee and start-up investment down a dark hole. It merely implies the need for a careful look at both sides of the coin before reaching for your chequebook.

The delivery

So what should you expect the franchisor to deliver for your franchise fee and the ongoing payments? Well, first and foremost you should expect unfettered access to the brand, trademarks, products, and perhaps other assets, such as a building, as I mentioned earlier. But more than that, a good franchisor will provide the franchisee and his or her management with whatever training the nature of the franchise demands, and support such as consulting, marketing, an up-to-date library of operating manuals, and any other tools and materials needed to operate the franchise according to the franchisor's standards.

The appeal in all of this is the promise of a virtually trouble-free turnkey operation with systems, products, and brand recognition in place. Who wouldn't be tempted by the possibility of avoiding the craggy slopes of Mount Start-Up?

Where angels fear to tread

Just as it's certainly unfair to characterize small business ownership through franchising as a case of fools rushing in where angels fear to tread, it's also advisable to pause before allowing the apparition to whisk you away to Business Bliss.

Minimize your risk and maximize your peace of mind: do your research, ensure you're fully informed, and consult the right professional help.

CHARACTER 25: CUSTOMER

Inappropriate introduction

Universal Stores sold budget clothing in one of Cape Town's northern suburbs. It doesn't exist anymore but lives on in my memory as the place where I was introduced to the customer for the first time—during a Christmas vacation job in my last year of high school.

I'd had other vacation jobs, but you don't learn much about customers when you're stuck in a grocery store's stock room repackaging bulk dry goods. Nor do you meet customers while attending to animals in the back rooms of a veterinarian's practice, or in a stable hanging on to a twitch twisted around a horse's upper lip while a deworming tube is fed through a nostril into its stomach.

The customer care training on the first day at Universal was brief and to the point. I don't recall the training session having a title but it should have been: "Screw them before they screw you." And they meant it—I'd heard less aggressive pep talks in huddles before rugby matches!

So, under the watchful eye of the store manager, we were sent to do battle with the customers. I can still show you how to grasp the back of a too-large jacket to make it look and feel like a good fit. But by no means did we have it all our own way. We were up against a cunning adversary. In those days, South Africans did their weekend shopping on Saturday mornings because the stores closed at noon and didn't reopen until Monday. After the Saturday morning pandemonium, while tidying up and re-shelving inventory, we'd find stinking old shoes in some of the boxes—effectively a one-finger salute to our adversarial customer care policy.

Such was my introduction to the customer.

A warm body with a pulse

About twenty-four years later, when I opened my own business, my customer relations philosophy was a 180-degree departure from the Universal experience. The last thing I wanted was an adversarial relationship with my customers.

I didn't want my business to indulge in practices equivalent to taking up the slack in an oversized jacket. I also hoped that my customers would not indulge in the antics of the shoe bandits.

I visualized my typical customer as someone well-mannered, honest, patient, polite, and cooperative. Someone who'd come through the door smiling broadly and just itching to happily pay for my products and services. Like every new business owner, I needed customers—turning people away never crossed my mind.

Guided by that mindset, any warm body with a pulse qualified as a customer, no questions asked!

Reality dawns

With the passage of time comes awareness, and eventually I became aware that my customer base was not, and would never be, a legion of angels. It was instead a representative sample of the population at large, and we all know what a mixed bag that is!

Well-mannered, *honest*, *patient*, *polite*, and *cooperative* describe most customers but will never describe an entire customer base. (Rare exceptions may exist, but I'm not aware of any.)

And to make matters more challenging, small business owners' interactions with certain customers are tainted by a long-established myth-turned-mantra that serves to embolden the ill-mannered, impatient, impolite, uncooperative, and unreasonable in the belief that they are always right.

A MYTH DRESSED AS A MANTRA

It's one of the business world's most common mantras: "The customer is always right."

It's also nonsense.

The customer is not always right. Far from it. This slogan-turned-mantra was apparently popularized over one hundred years ago by renowned retailers such as Harry Gordon Selfridge, John Wanamaker, and Marshall Field. To be fair, these gentlemen couldn't have anticipated that their slogan—intended to positively influence the attitude of retail employees—would be interpreted by some customers as an endowment of infallibility.

This apparent infallibility and the often-repeated reminder that the customer pays the wages have subtly contributed to some customers presuming that they have the right to speak and behave as badly as they please.

I wonder how Messrs. Selfridge, Wanamaker, and Field would have reacted to the YouTube clip of the lady beating a takeout box on the counter of a restaurant to emphasize that she had been expecting red, not green, peppers on her kebab. The entire restaurant (and possibly people out in the parking lot) was treated to her berating the startled restaurant employees: "DON'T YOU KNOW THAT THE CUSTOMER IS ALWAYS RIGHT?"

Kebab Lady clearly believed that since the customer is always right, she was entitled to be as abusive as she chose, even if it was about something as inconsequential as the colour of a bell pepper. And she extracted every ounce of perceived entitlement out of the situation.

No business owner or employee should ever have to suffer such indignity at the hands of a customer. Never, ever!

Verbal abusers mostly get away with it, unfortunately. However, in Kebab Lady's case there was a deeply satisfying conclusion to the incident for all whose ears had been assaulted by the tirade. This always-right customer, unwilling to wait fifteen minutes for a replacement kebab, turned and stomped off still lecturing the restaurant employees at the top of her voice as she headed for the door. Perhaps distracted by her lecture, she forgot that the glass door was to be pulled, not pushed. *Thump!* She discovered her error at full throttle. Karma!

A similarly "entitled" customer phoned Simon Clifford, president of a chemical factory in Santa Barbara. The conversation was about an item of equipment the size of a domestic kettle, known as a spot gun, used to spray a chemical to remove unwanted ink spots from printed T-shirts.

The customer said that the trigger mechanism on his spot gun had failed and brusquely demanded to know what Simon was going to do for him. Simon suggested he send the gun back to be repaired. After the customer said he couldn't do that, further conversation revealed that he'd hurled it to the floor and then smashed it to pieces. In spite of this admission, the customer demanded a free replacement.

"I'm not going to do that," said Simon, "but what I will do is suggest anger management therapy."

Simon draws on more than twenty years of successful business ownership when he says: "The customer is always right, until I decide he's wrong."

I don't want to give the impression that people like the shoe bandits,

Kebab Lady, and the equipment abuser represent a broad swath of customers, but they and their ilk do surface often enough to warrant mention in any discussion about customers.

The lesson: unless you have a compelling reason to deal with bad customers, you're better off without them.

A bit later in this chapter I'll address weeding out the customers you'd rather not have. For now let's focus on the customers you would rather have—the great customers.

Great customers

Even though a slate of only great customers is unachievable for most small businesses, there's no harm in making it an objective to acquire as many great customers as possible—you'll be much better off economically and psychologically.

The definition of a great customer will vary from business to business. In my business it was a person of pleasant disposition who appreciated our commitment to quality at a fair price, who appreciated our reliable technical support, who was interested in a long-term relationship, and who paid his or her bills on time.

But of course this is not a one-way street. You have to encourage great customers. You have to make it worth their while to keep bringing you their business. How you do it depends upon the nature of your business, but for most it will involve high-quality products and services, a welcoming, helpful attitude, and a genuine interest in solving whatever need they've brought you.

Making your great customers feel that they're part of something special encourages loyalty. People like to belong. Involve them. Let them be the first to hear about your upcoming new products and services, and tell them about interesting and helpful developments in your industry. You're on the right track if you're regularly writing emails to your great customers that go something like this: "Hi, Marjorie. Attached is a (video/article/ TED Talk/link) I've just seen. I think you may find it (useful/helpful/informative)."

And remember that people prefer to do business with people they like. But there's a fine line between genuine likeability and faking it—customers can see through the latter and it turns them off.

Faking it—the big turnoff

How many times have you heard the mechanical "Have a nice day!" intoned by a customer-service person not even looking at you? Ten times? A hundred times? A thousand times?

Perhaps you're so accustomed to the mechanical intonation by now, you're no longer aware of it. Perhaps "Have a nice day!" passes for what it is—an insincere and meaningless formality. And perhaps you're not bothered by the insincerity. Well, *I* am. And unless I'm the only one, businesses should take note of my dog-biscuit experience.

At my business we kept a box of dog biscuits handy so visitors could treat the two company Jack Russells if they'd forgotten to bring their own. For instance, Darcy the FedEx driver, who had a biscuit-based bond with Cassie and Ryley, would occasionally forget. And the trouble is that Jack Russells don't understand forgetfulness. Keeping a stash of dog biscuits for forgetful visitors to use saved a lot of terrier angst.

When the stash ran out I would pop into the big-box pet store a few blocks away for replenishments. I'd observed over a number of visits that the staff on the cash registers engaged customers in conversation about their pets. If they noticed that you were buying dog food they would inquire about your dog's breed and its name. They all did it in exactly the same way, as if reciting a script. It was most likely a head office–devised idea for establishing a rapport with the customer.

Well, that type of scripted customer engagement doesn't work for me because it invariably becomes a meaningless, mechanical dialogue in which the customer is forced to participate for fear of appearing rude. I find this annoying, and I'll bet many other customers would agree.

Surely when this happens it's obvious to all but the most imperceptive customers that they're being subjected to a misguided management directive and that the employee so directed pays no attention to their answers at all?

I proved this one day while hurriedly dashing in for a box of dog biscuits in a distracted, irritable state of mind.

"Hi, what kind of dog do you have?" the employee asked as I placed my box of biscuits on the conveyor belt at her cash register.

"He's a cross between a Newfoundlander and a Chihuahua," I said, offering the first sarcastic answer to pop into my head. Such a cross is obviously as ridiculous as it is a physical improbability. A Newfoundlander weighs seventy kilograms and a Chihuahua three kilograms. I mean, come on, picture the honeymoon!

An appropriate response, if the associate had been paying attention, would have been "What!" or "You're kidding!" or "You got a picture?" But no, without hesitating for even a second, she said: "Oh, that's nice. What's his name?"

"Roger," I said, which is my middle name and all that came to mind in the moment.

She held out my cash register receipt and change saying "That's a nice name for a dog" as she turned to attend to the next person in line.

"Hello. How many hamsters do you have?"

Oh, please tell her five million and I'll bet she asks what their names are!

Isn't this a classic example of mechanical insincerity likely to result in exactly the opposite effect management would hope for? How can any business person think that a dose of insincerity will do anything but leave a bitter aftertaste? It's certainly not going to enhance the customer's shopping experience!

The customer is not the only victim of this kind of silliness—spare a thought for the employee. After all, the scripted questions were not her idea. And therein lies the lesson for small business owners: ensure that your business offers genuine, heartfelt customer care, and please, oh please, don't force your customers and employees into this pointless type of scripted dialogue—it's not going to do your business any good. Hiring front-line personalities naturally inclined to engage people in a sincere, intelligent way is a much smarter idea than issuing scripts.

If anyone in a small business—owner or employee—can't naturally take a genuine interest in the needs of his or her customers, bend over backwards to solve these needs, and delight in doing so in an attentive, spontaneous manner, a career change to something far removed from customers is probably overdue.

Bending over backwards

You will of course, like the rest of us, bend over backwards for great customers or even customers you think can become great customers. (At first we do this for all customers, but that's before we've learned to use the bending-over-backwards routine productively).

It's a necessary contortion we all undertake to acquire and retain desirable customers in a competitive market. Not only that, servicing customers well, experiencing their gratitude, knowing that you've made it easy for them to bring you return business, and turning them into word-of-mouth ambassadors is immensely satisfying to authentic customer-service providers. Anyone who doesn't derive satisfaction from bend-over-backwards service may be able to fake it for a while but in the longer term is not suited to serving customers—something to be kept in mind when hiring.

One Friday in the early days of my business, while still at the foot of the small business learning curve, I bent over backwards for a customer who could not get the in-time-for-the-weekend service he needed from his regular supplier. I expedited his order and then drove the five-gallon container of screen printing ink to the airport so that he could take delivery of it in Saskatoon, seven hundred kilometres east of my warehouse in Calgary.

Service doesn't get any better than that in the screen printing industry unless the vendor also picks up part of the extraordinarily high airfreight cost; I did that too. I believed that my business was making an investment in turning a hitherto minor customer into a major customer.

He didn't even thank us, took the extraordinary service for granted, and continued buying the bulk of his ink from the local supplier who had not bent over backwards in his hour of need. And then, to pile insult on injury, he had to be pursued for payment.

The hard lesson, later reinforced by similar experiences, was that appreciation and payoff for bending over backwards is not always guaranteed.

Experience teaches how to gauge the likelihood of payoff for bending over backwards. Over time, your intuition in determining how far to bend over backwards for customers and potential customers grows, as does your confidence in trusting it. Even then there will be disappointments from time to time. But don't let this get you down—occasional disappointments are part and parcel of dealing with customers.

Commercial or personal?

In the less-formal atmosphere of the world of small business, it's very easy to cross the fine line between customer and friend. It would be unusual to not encounter customers with whom you have enough in common to strike up a friendship. There are, however, pitfalls.

In a commercial relationship, issues such as pricing, delayed payments, discount expectations, defective products or services, and late deliveries can arise to test the relationship. In short, money can add volatility to a relationship, and a commercial relationship, by its very nature, is money based.

So, is it possible when a relationship crosses the fine line between customer and friend to leave the potentially volatile money element on the customer side of the line? Perhaps in some circumstances, but it's difficult.

Here are some of the thoughts that plagued me over the years in dealing with customer-friends:

- *She twice went on trips with my wife. She and her husband were guests at a family wedding. We've socialized together. We're supposed to be friends. So why would she only occasionally buy from us and instead buy the bulk of her supplies from our competitors? We've given her a special discount, as we do for friends. Does a slightly lower price for a lower-grade product from our competitor trump our friendship?*
- *We've had a customer-friend relationship for years. We've socialized and visited each other's homes. But through the process of selling his business he left us with an unpaid account. Why? Is it unreasonable of me to expect more of friends?*
- *Staying at his condo in Phoenix was great. I really enjoy his company. He's a good friend. But he's also a hard-nosed businessman, and when he keeps pressing for lower prices, I find it a bit awkward. I don't want to harm our friendship, but I also can't give away the product at the discount he expects. The customer-friend dividing line has become a bit blurred. Will one affect the other?*

There are other examples, but these three cover the most common types of situations I experienced. If there's a one-answer-fits-all solution to these dilemmas, I've certainly never found it. I wish I had a pat answer to the customer-friend dilemmas you may encounter. Unfortunately, I don't. But at least I've alerted you to a potential problem and, again, forewarned is forearmed.

Bad debts

If your business doesn't sell on credit, congratulations. I hope you appreciate how much of an advantage you have over those of us obliged to carry receivables. Here are the three significant disadvantages you're dodging: additional accounting and administration, additional working-capital requirements, and the risk of bad debts.

The worst aspect of selling on credit—the one small businesses tend not to plan for—is bad debt. It can catch you by surprise and is always infuriating, not to mention damaging. So damaging that, if big enough, it can break a small business.

Careful vetting of customers and tight credit management are absolute essentials if you sell on credit, but they're still not iron-clad guarantees against bad debts. If you're vigilant, you'll likely spot the red flags (slower payment patterns or rumours of problems, for example), and you can react to avoid, or at least minimize, a bad debt. But sometimes you can be caught unawares—even a historically stable customer might suddenly go off the rails.

My business's first significant bad-debt event cost seventeen thousand dollars; a long-time customer went bankrupt after losing his sole big account. We also lost seven thousand dollars when another hitherto good customer's Olympic program failed, and thirteen thousand dollars when a previously stable customer decided that partying with an expensive white powder was a lot more fun than running his company.

Some of your customers, even some of your favourites, are all but guaranteed to sooner or later cause you bad-debt losses if you sell on credit. The challenge is to keep these losses to a minimum.

Customers can be very persuasive, particularly when they're in financial trouble and you threaten to start tightening the credit screws. My best hard-earned advice is to follow your intuition. If that little voice is telling you to see the red flags and take action before you throw good money after bad, do it! If discussions with the customer don't calm your fears, cut off supply, take legal action or whatever other measures are appropriate, but don't delay.

Disengaging

Firing is a popular term used to describe the concept of disengaging from unwanted customers. I subscribe to the concept but prefer the term *disengage*.

Fire has a harsh, if not aggressive, connotation. If I had to depict it in a cartoon, I would draw someone with a face like thunder pointing to the door yelling, "Get out! JUST GET OUT!" and some pitiful soul submissively slinking towards the door. Now, while I'm sure that I'm not the only small business owner who has encountered a customer to whom he's wanted to show the door (Kebab Lady comes to mind), you must resist the urge to retaliate. I'm not discouraging you from disengaging (I've already said I'm an advocate), but I *am* discouraging you from upping the ante, no matter how aggrieved or indignant you may feel.

For one thing, it wouldn't be good PR to have your business associated with aggression, and you certainly wouldn't want to be seen frogmarching a customer to the door—aside from potential legal issues, word gets around. For instance, while Kebab Lady deserved to be confronted and told to leave, the other restaurant patrons would have felt very awkward, no matter how justified the restaurant owner was. Kebab Lady was handled calmly, with no retaliatory abuse or violence. She blew off steam, made a fool of herself, and then left. The situation didn't escalate.

Kebab Lady demonstrated what can happen in a retail environment, but what about situations where the customer isn't necessarily present in person and might even be on the other side of the continent? Shouting matches over the phone or rude email exchanges aren't helpful either. You don't want to commit defamation in writing or be recorded saying anything libellous. Remember that the purpose is to disengage, not to engage in the verbal equivalent of mixed martial arts.

So, what you do is stay out of the cage. Instead call, or perhaps email, and tell the combative customer in polite language that your business has tried but is apparently incapable of satisfying his or her needs and that you are therefore terminating the relationship to allow him or her to deal with one of your competitors. You may even offer names and contact information. And voila, you have one less headache and your competitor has one more—two birds with one stone!

Disengaging can also be appropriate in circumstances other than confrontation or dispute. You might apply the 80-20 rule to your customer list and discover that 20 percent of your customers provide 80 percent of your income. As other businesses have done, you may then choose to disengage from the less-productive 80 percent of your customers. An Edmonton decorative glassworks company made this decision and disengaged from the 80 percent of customers (mostly small gift stores) accounting for only 20 percent of its income and most of its shipping and breakage headaches. But it bears repeating that this must be done politely—it's good business manners, and also, burning bridges is not a smart business practice.

You may also have customers, even big customers, from whose business you cannot make a reasonable profit. If all other possibilities are exhausted, you may decide to disengage; again, politely.

Literature

The customer is a very popular topic in business literature. Read as much of it as you can. It's not all good and it won't all apply to your business's circumstances, but by discerningly picking and choosing, you can harvest useful advice and ideas.

You'll find though that business literature (very much like health and dieting literature) can be contradictory, particularly on some topics such as whether or not to keep certain customers. There are the advocates of firing customers and then there are the advocates of hanging on to customers, even those like Kebab Lady. The hang-on advocates quote statistics to support the keep-them-at-all-costs philosophy. They'll point out that the cost of replacement is up to 700 percent higher than the cost of hanging on to an unbearable customer.

Of course, the hang-on or let-go choice is not always just about economics. There's also the question of whether you want your business and working life spoiled by a few unbearable customers.

I was influenced by the business literature on customers. It's where I first heard about the concept of disengaging from certain undesirable customers, and I subsequently did so successfully. It's where I heard that customers who come only for a low price will leave for a lower price—something I found to be true. It's where I learned to never assume that I knew what my customers wanted and to instead ask them what they wanted. It's where I read how even small gestures of gratitude are appreciated by customers, and this inspired the candy-bars-with-every-delivery idea that brought us untold goodwill over a twenty-year span.

I recommend that all small business owners and intended owners develop the good habit of mining the business literature (books, articles, and blogs) for advice and ideas on customer management suited to their particular small business.

A MOST IMPORTANT INGREDIENT

Your type of business might make it unnecessary, even impossible, to be selective about your customers, but if you can do so without committing economic suicide, do it. A slate of great customers is a huge economic and psychological advantage—it's well worth making it a focus of your business.

Decide whom you want to do business with and do all that's necessary to help them feel that they want to do business with you. As for the troublesome minority, remember that while disengaging from customers may seem counterintuitive, it's a legitimate, albeit underutilized, business practice.

CHARACTER 26: TRUCKER

A COMPLEX BUSINESS

Picture our trucker as someone who typically drives a very large truck—a tractor and enclosed fifty-three-foot trailer. It's the eighteen-wheeler rig that causes your car to rock as it thunders by on the highway loaded to the gills with shrink-wrapped shipments on wooden pallets.

If the driver is a long-haul trucker, the tractor part of the rig will have a sleeper berth (living quarters) complete with bed, fridge, TV, air conditioner, microwave, and other home comforts. I once met a long-haul trucker whose sleeper berth included a bed for the Jack Russell terrier that accompanied him on all his trips. Truckers—men and women alike—tend to be tough, no-nonsense individuals; essential traits for coping with the demands of the job. But they are also highly skilled individuals, as you will know if you've ever seen a trucker handling a big rig in heavy traffic or backing up to a loading dock with the precision of a seamstress threading a needle.

My business dealt with truckers extensively for both incoming and outgoing shipments. If—as is often the case—their service is vital to your small business's operations, manage the relationship carefully. Trucking is a complex business prone to problems that can directly affect your business. When it all runs smoothly and shipments arrive on time and intact, it's a good day. When urgently required shipments are delayed, go astray, or are damaged, it's a bad one. Managing the relationship carefully helps to keep this kind of bad day to a minimum.

Work with a reputable trucking company

I found that working with an established, reputable trucking company was the best way to minimize the frustrations associated with this industry. Good trucking companies tend to attract good truckers, be they full-time employees on the payroll or owner–operators contracted to the trucking company.

The leading trucking companies maintain modern fleets in good working order, which is of course important to their customers, many of whom plan deliveries nowadays on a just-in-time basis. But stuff still happens. Extreme weather events, accidents, and breakdowns occur in spite of the best equipment, sophisticated scheduling systems, and excellent truckers.

And that's why you're better off working with a leading trucking company motivated to maintain a good reputation. A good company will dedicate the resources needed to quickly recover from problems. Nevertheless, I've known leading trucking companies to go through bad patches and have been forced to switch. However, finding an alternative is usually not difficult; it's a competitive business.

Treat the trucker well

Long-haul trucking is a tough job. In fact, it's been described as a lifestyle rather than a job. A long-haul trucker can be away from home for weeks at a stretch, dividing his or her time between the driver's seat and the sleeper berth. The only breaks in the monotony and loneliness are the occasional visits to truck stops or service plazas for showers, meals, and refuelling. A short break later, it's back on the road again dealing with inconsiderate, rude drivers until he or she arrives at a destination and something is found to be wrong with the shipment. Then they have an unhappy, rude customer to compound an already high level of stress.

I give you this insight into a long-haul trucker's life because it presents an opportunity for your business. Be the one customer who makes the trucker's day by being welcoming and polite. Offer him or her coffee and cookies in winter or bottles of cold water in summer. If the trucker arrives at lunchtime invite him or her in, particularly if it's pizza day at the office. Offer the use of your washroom for freshening up. Offer somewhere comfortable to relax and have a chat before he or she has to go back to the mayhem of the highway. In short, treat the trucker as you would appreciate being treated if you had a lonely, stressful job that most of the time involved dealing with bad drivers and irritable customers.

Do this even if you've just taken delivery of a damaged or partial shipment. Taking out your frustrations on the trucker is puerile. These things are hardly ever the fault of the trucker—he or she just happens to be the face of the trucking company at that moment.

You're going to do this because not only are you a generous, decent human being, but also because you know that generosity is met with generosity. And word gets around. My business benefitted in ways that reflected the amicable relationships we had with our truckers.

On many an occasion when we weren't ready for a pickup, rather than sit and wait in the cab, the truckers would help wrap and load pallets. They'd rearrange their schedules and go out of their way to make late pickups when we couldn't be ready on time. They'd also go out of their way to deliver to us first when they knew we were in urgent need of something on the truck, sometimes having to manoeuvre pallets around inside the truck to reach ours. When we moved our warehouse from one town to another about twenty kilometres away, our trucking company gave us the use of a fifty-three-foot trailer for a week and hauled it for us at no charge. These are the benefits of a great business relationship with your trucker—decency being met with decency, and generosity with generosity.

Inbound trucking

Even great trucking companies have mishaps. So inbound shipments must always be inspected for damage or partial delivery. Partial delivery is usually obvious, as is physical damage. But damage such as the freezing of non-freezable materials or the thawing of frozen ones, for example, is more difficult to detect. It's better to find out about hidden problems before the trucker leaves so that your company's representative and the trucker can agree and sign off on endorsements of the waybill.

It's important that damage endorsements and other comments be clearly noted on the shipping documents of both parties and signed off on. It's always a good idea for both parties to take digital images too. These are a great help later when the inevitable damage claim has to be filed.

Outbound trucking

The intent with every outbound shipment is that it arrives at the destination intact and on time. The incentive is customer retention—you want to retain your customer and the trucker wants to retain your business. You can help your cause by making the trucker's job easier, and he or she will respond by trying to please you.

The first important job is to prepare the waybill and other required shipping documents, such as dangerous goods declarations, completely and legibly. Truckers appreciate not having to spend time deciphering illegible handwriting or faint carbon copies.

Then pay a lot of attention to packing properly. When my business prepared a shipment on wooden pallets, the standard practice was to secure the goods to the pallet with strapping and then shrink-wrap it. As further assurance, we secured the loose ends of the shrink wrap with clear parcel tape to ensure that it didn't unravel.

In addition to the usual clear plastic shipping envelope that contained a packing slip addressed to the customer, we printed five sheets of letterhead-sized paper with the destination name and address—one for each side of the palletized shipment and one for the top.

I'd first decided to have my company label outgoing shipments this way when I saw a trucker crawling over the truck's contents looking for a particular pallet and being unable to find it because the destination labels on all the pallets were inconspicuous. It occurred to me that labelling conspicuously, and particularly on top of the pallet, would be a great help to a trucker.

In addition to all this, a great packing and labelling job will be noticed at the destination and can only enhance the customer's favourable impression of your small business.

Stuff happens

As I mentioned earlier, it's not a perfect world, and no matter how diligent your trucker might be, stuff will happen. And my business had its fair share of stuff.

Late December one year, just before we closed for the Christmas break, we received two fifty-five-gallon steel drums of freeze-sensitive, photo-sensitive emulsion. We'd paid extra for heated shipping—a necessity in Canada for about six months of the year—but something had gone awry with the truck's heating system en route from Texas. The contents of the two drums were frozen solid, like two big pink frozen lollies in their moulds. Once frozen, the emulsion could not be reconstituted—it was a total loss. Given that the drums cost over three thousand dollars each, the situation was serious enough, but worse than that, we needed the emulsion for when we reopened after the holidays.

The trucking company agreed to reimburse my business for the loss and made special arrangements to ship two replacement drums immediately. They arrived about a week later, but again, you guessed it, they were frozen solid. For the second time the trucking company reimbursed my business but apologetically declined to undertake a third shipment, admitting that they clearly weren't capable of properly handling a heated shipment on that route.

This wasn't the only temperature-related shipping problem we experienced. We'd made arrangements to ship a used textile screen printing press from Ontario to British Columbia in the middle of summer and had issued explicit packing and shipping instructions. We didn't, however, anticipate having to tell the trucking company (not one of our regulars) to not ship the press in a freezer truck with a load of vegetables. Why would we? Well, they did, and the seals in the press's hydraulic system froze solid and cracked.

While some items can incur damage during shipping, others can disappear entirely. And if and when they eventually turn up, it can be in the most unlikely places. Houdini Drum was such an item. We were expecting a delivery of four thirty-two-gallon fibre drums of emulsion on a single wooden pallet. When the pallet arrived, shrink-wrapped per the usual practice of the factory in Brooklyn, there were only three drums. Many phone calls later we discovered that the trucking company had dismantled the pallet at one of the hubs along the route in order to pack a new truck transporting our drums to the next hub. When they reassembled the pallet, the fourth drum was overlooked and then simply disappeared.

In a tongue-in-cheek email to the trucking company's management, I dubbed the missing drum Houdini Drum. What else could you call a drum capable of escaping from a shrink-wrapped and strapped pallet, hiding from trucking company staff, sneaking onto a different truck, and making it all the way across the continent before being run to ground in California? Houdini Drum eventually arrived at our warehouse a few weeks later, looking as though it had been mugged but with its contents unharmed. If drums could talk, Houdini would have had a tale to tell.

Less fortunate was a relative of Houdini's who made it all the way to the trucking company's depot within a stone's throw of our warehouse only to be impaled by a carelessly – driven forklift. Can you imagine cleaning up thirty-two gallons of emulsion with the consistency and stickiness of molasses?

If you do business with truckers, expect stuff to happen.

Claims

When stuff happens, another paper-pushing, time-consuming, administrative process is foisted upon the small business—filing a claim.

In our case it always involved completing a pack of documents known as the Claims Submission Form. Whatever the process might be in your particular jurisdiction, resign yourself to the fact that your small business will be spending otherwise productive time recovering money lost in an incident not of your making. To minimize the time spent on this process, make sure you complete it properly the first time. Don't neglect any part of the paperwork, attach supporting documents, and include digital images. Go for overkill; leave no wiggle room.

Before agreeing to a settlement, do something you should have done before shipping but, like many of us, probably didn't: check the standard coverage provisions (usually included in a terms of service agreement with the trucking company or sometimes printed on the back of the waybill) and make sure that the offered settlement complies with the coverage. Then make a point of keeping in mind the lessons learned from this claim process and apply them to the risk assessment of future shipments, before shipping.

Help the trucker help you

As a small business owner using a trucker's services, all you want is for your shipment to be delivered intact, on time, and at a reasonable price. The key to achieving this is to develop a good working relationship with a reputable trucking company and then work with the truckers to make their jobs as easy as possible for them. Oh, and have high, not unrealistic, expectations of your trucker.

CHARACTER 27: COURIER

Bike, vans, and planes

Unless your customers receive a service, take delivery online, consume your product on site, carry it away themselves, or have you deliver it with your own vehicle, you'll likely rely on a courier for your deliveries. And even small businesses that don't routinely use a courier are likely to need one from time to time for an important or urgent delivery.

Couriers, in which I include postal services, span a broad size-and-sophistication spectrum from small independent local operators on bicycles at the one end to huge international organizations with their own fleets of aircraft at the other. Your choice of courier will depend on the nature, distance, and urgency of your deliveries.

And here's something else to consider when choosing a courier. Picture yourself personally making a delivery to a customer you want to impress with your professionalism (which should be every customer). Notice your neat appearance? See how carefully you handle the parcel? Look how politely you greet the customer as you hand over the parcel and ask for a signature on the waybill copy or hand-held digital device.

Now, expect nothing less from your courier because if you're not personally making the delivery, the courier is the face of your business and can affect whether or not the customer does business with you again.

The courier and your business's image

I don't think most small business owners give much thought to how a courier can impact the impression customers have of their business. I didn't—until a customer made me.

In the early days we used a courier company for local deliveries within about a 150-kilometre radius of one of our warehouses. Each day they'd pick up our parcels in a van and take them back to their warehouse, where they'd be sorted by route and placed on the appropriate van and then delivered the next day. What more could you want from a courier service? Well, there was something that hadn't crossed my mind until I received a phone call from the owner of one of our bigger customers.

It started out well enough—with compliments about our sturdy corrugated cardboard boxes printed with our business name and logo and the neat and secure way we packed and labelled them. I was pleased to hear this because my intention was to indeed differentiate my business by demonstrating a degree of professionalism not evident in the way our competitors handled their deliveries.

Then he took me aback: "So why would you undermine all this by having your stuff delivered by a rude, don't-give-a-shit guy in a filthy T-shirt and jeans who hasn't showered for a week?"

I had no idea that my business was being represented by such a person. I also had no idea he didn't care about our parcels being soaked while he took his time stacking them onto a dolly next to his rusty, smoke-belching van in the pouring rain. And I could certainly sympathize with my customer's irritation at the courier's lack of effort to avoid walking mud into his reception area.

By the end of the call, I don't know if I was more embarrassed or furious. I thanked the customer for the feedback and assured him that, contrary to the impression he got from the courier, we really did "give a shit" and would be doing something about it.

We learned our lesson and, whenever possible after that, dealt with local courier companies that shared our standards. They dressed their employees in uniforms and drove vehicles that looked as though they'd recently come from dealerships, not demolition yards. Lower-than-appropriate standards is a situation usually confined to some local couriers. The large international courier companies pay a lot of attention to their public image with distinctive, neat uniforms and vehicles in corporate colours.

But this doesn't mean you'll never have issues with even the biggest and best of courier companies. YouTube can keep you entertained for hours with videos of outrageous mishandling of parcels by rogue—and hopefully shortly to be unemployed—employees of international courier companies. It explains what an ex-courier company employee meant when he told me that to a disgruntled courier, a "fragile" label reads "football."

Admittedly there's not much you can do about a courier somewhere along the line taking out his or her frustrations on your parcel, except to offset the possibility somewhat by selecting carefully and then hoping that respectful treatment of your courier will be reciprocated.

Treat the Courier Well

The points about treating truckers well, made in the previous chapter, hold good for couriers too.

It's no joke lugging a few hundred parcels each generally weighing anywhere between five and twenty-five kilograms in and out of a van, day in and day out, in all weather conditions. I knew a number of couriers who peppered their conversations with "my chiropractor" as easily as the rest of us refer to "my coffee shop" or "my supermarket." And when not carrying parcels, they're driving on congested roads keeping an eye on the surrounding traffic while simultaneously searching for parking spots into which to shoehorn the van.

All of this presents your small business with an opportunity to differentiate itself. In winter provide your couriers with, say, coffee and cookies and in summer with bottled ice water. We found that chocolate bars were particularly appreciated. Take a few minutes to chat about how their day is going, or about last night's game, or anything else of interest to them—you'll be amazed at what can you learn in these conversations about the courier industry and sometimes even about competitors on the same route. Help them load your parcels. Go out of your way to be considerate—be their welcoming isle of tranquility in a sea of sweat and stress. Become their favourite customer. It's not just common decency; it's also about knowing that building cordial business relationships makes good business sense.

Bolster your relationship further by properly preparing your courier packages. Strong boxes well packed and sealed and clearly labelled can make a courier's life a lot easier. I learned that lesson early in the life of my business after a package containing a poorly packed jar of sticky screen printing ink leaked in a courier's van making him as mad as a wet hen. I immediately established packing standards for the warehouse employees; these included sealing any liquid or paste products in heat-sealed, heavy-gauge plastic bags before packing them in sturdy corrugated cardboard boxes and then securely taping with water-activated reinforced parcel tape. I can't recall another parcel failure in the twenty-plus years that followed.

All of these simple measures will ensure that you become one of your couriers' favourite customers. Business is just more enjoyable when conducted in a cordial relationship, and you'll also find that people will reciprocate with favours and special consideration when you need it.

Problem resolution

In addition to a courier company's efficiency and attention to such things as representing their customers in a courteous, professional manner, another yardstick by which to measure them is problem resolution. All courier companies, no matter what size or how sophisticated they may be, rely extensively on human intervention—it's a very hands-on service. And humans, being humans, will make errors. Consequently, once in a while your parcels will be delayed, damaged, or even lost.

A good courier company will dedicate resources to dealing with these inevitable occurrences. And they will deal with them quickly, efficiently, and politely. If you incur a loss, they will reimburse you expeditiously. Anything less and they don't deserve to keep your business. And it doesn't matter who the courier is—the local inner-city courier on a bicycle or one of the giants flying your parcel to the other side of the world—they all have competitors more than willing to snap up your business.

Andy understood this. He owned a courier company that handled a lot of our daily local deliveries in Calgary. Andy was energetic, innovative, and Australian. Not just Australian but—and I write this with all due respect to Andy and my Australian friends—stereotypically Australian. That is to say, he pretty much told it the way it was and didn't display too much concern for the potential fallout. I had the impression that if fallout occurred he'd shrug his shoulders, open another beer, and forget about it, except when it came to his business—he took that very seriously.

In what was a rare occurrence, a parcel one of his couriers was supposed to deliver for us hadn't reached our customer by close of business on a Friday. I was still at the office after everyone else had gone home when our concerned customer called. He needed the delivery for an urgent job over the weekend.

I called Andy's cell phone. He answered immediately. I explained the problem. As I listened to his assurances that he would light a fire under someone, I wondered why there was an unusual echo on the phone. Then I heard what I thought was flushing. "Andy, tell me you're not on the toilet."

Unabashed and without a split-second's hesitation, he fired back: "Listen mate, I run a business. Ya gotta multitask!"

You have to love the no-nonsense, earthy way small business is conducted sometimes. Somehow I can't imagine a big international courier company CEO taking a business call on the john. Well, no-nonsense and earthy worked. Apparently a fire was lit under the right person because the parcel was located and delivered within an hour. Andy might not have cared about waiting to hang up before flushing, but he certainly cared about his business looking after its customers.

When a problem occurs with a local courier it's usually just one of two things: a late or a missing parcel. Problems with international couriers, however, can be more complex. You can easily run afoul of obscure rules and regulations so unexpected that it wouldn't cross your mind to even consider them before sending a parcel across international borders. Not only that, but the courier company's employees might not be aware of some of these rules either and so will fail to keep you from innocently stumbling into a frustrating, time-wasting, bureaucratic maze.

A syndicated cartoonist had sent me a copy of a business cartoon as a gift. To reciprocate I bought a very nice red wine and asked my warehouse manager to deliver it by overnight courier to the cartoonist in Kansas City.

The next day a representative of the courier company called from a depot in Kansas City to say that they were unable to deliver the parcel because it was illegal for a courier to transport wine across the Canada–United States border unless it was accompanied by the "proper paperwork" from a licensed wine merchant. The most annoying part of this was that the waybill, which identified the contents of the parcel as red wine, had passed through an untold number of hands who didn't care or didn't notice that it was wine or, worse still, didn't know that it mattered. At the last moment, just before it was to be put on the truck in Kansas City for delivery, it suddenly became an issue.

All reasoning with the polite but obstinate stickler for the rules went nowhere. While she agreed that it seemed silly to ship the parcel all the way back (and illegally) across the border, she stood firm. It seems that treating the matter as a bit of an "oops!" and just sending the wine a couple of miles down the road to its destination instead of back to Canada was unthinkable. Perhaps her job was at stake, who knows?

The wine duly returned to Calgary the next day, and then more of my time was wasted when I had to appear in person at the Canadian customs office at the airport to complete the appropriate paperwork authorizing the courier to release the parcel.

If your business is going to courier anything across international borders, know that rules, regulations, and restrictions are likely to apply and that it pays to make inquiries before shipping—it could save a lot of frustration, time, and expense.

Do what it takes

Always keep in mind what most small business owners don't even consider: the courier has a stressful, exhausting job. Do what it takes to lighten the burden a bit. Become his or her favourite customer and reap the benefits.

A good, reliable courier service doesn't only take another potential small business headache off the table—it can also help make your business.

CHARACTER 28: COMPETITOR

Broad brush

Pepsi has Coke, Apple has Microsoft, Ford has Chev, and the mom-and-pop corner store has another mom-and-pop corner store. Competition is as certain as death and taxes. I can't name a single small business without at least one competitor, so unless you own that elusive business (please let me know if you do), continue reading.

If you were asked to define "competitor" you'd probably suggest something similar to BusinessDictionary.com's definition: "Any person or entity which is a rival against another. In business, a company in the same industry or a similar industry which offers a similar product or service."

It's a bit of a broad-brush definition requiring closer examination. But right now, by way of setting the tone for this chapter, take special note of the word "rival" in this definition.

It's not a war

It's important not to misinterpret "rival." It doesn't mean mortal enemy. However, we can't ignore the fact that once in a blue moon you may encounter a competitor with an obnoxiously different perspective—a sort of North Korea of small business.

A malicious competitor intent on unfairly harming your business can be a serious and unsettling distraction. You have a couple of options. The first is a face-to-face conversation in which you politely appeal to reason. Often, and especially with bullies, a direct, polite confrontation will shoo off any bee in his bonnet. But if this doesn't work, rein in your justifiable anger. Don't be tempted to up the ante. Don't be drawn into a minefield of acrimony or a war of attrition. Instead, hand it off to your lawyer while you focus on advancing your business without the distraction. Your lawyer should be able to suggest suitable action depending on the nature and intensity of the competitor's bad behaviour. And it's amazing how effective an inexpensive cease and desist notice on a lawyer's letterhead can be in many circumstances. Suggesting this could keep a lid on legal fees. It could also further the cause of ethical competition.

The ethics of competition

Business should be conducted competitively but ethically. And while this chapter does discuss outwitting, outmanoeuvring, and outperforming competitors, it does so in the context of a competition, not a war. Think of small business as a game you plan to win. But even while basking in the glow of victory, be gracious enough to shake your competitor's hand and buy her a drink.

Underwriting this game is a set of ethics—a we're-here-for-fun-and-profit philosophy as opposed to a we're-here-to-kick-butt-and-take-names philosophy. The latter requires a commitment to aggression and acrimony. I would not advocate spending a small business life this way. Of course there's no official ethics manual for small business, but most of us intuitively know what lines not to cross in order to avoid unnecessary conflict with competitors.

Actual competition

Let's return to our broad-brush definition of "competitor" and focus on this part of it: "a company in the same industry who offers a similar product or service." Interpreted too broadly, this can be misleading. Much depends on what we assume "same industry" and "similar product or service" mean.

In the case of "same industry," you wouldn't normally think of, say, a coffee shop or café as being in competition with a supermarket. But on Fourth Street, Calgary, where I lived, five coffee shops and cafés in as many blocks sell pastries in competition with each other and the local supermarket's bakery. A literal interpretation of "same industry" doesn't necessarily suggest that a coffee shop and a supermarket are competitors, but clearly in this case they *are*, as portions of their otherwise disparate businesses overlap.

"Similar product or service" might make you think of competing clothing retailers. After all, they all sell clothes. But H&M isn't in competition with the Salvation Army Thrift Store. In this case, "similar product or service" doesn't place all retailers in the same marketplace.

It's necessary to identify your *actual* competitors. If you don't do this, you could end up like an errant Coonhound wasting your time barking up the wrong tree at the wrong quarry while the raccoon you should be watching sneaks up and bites your butt.

A coffee shop owner I met in Somerset West, South Africa, provides a good example of barking up the wrong tree. I'll call him Deon. He told me Starbucks was coming to South Africa and he was losing sleep over it. Deon had read *Onward: How Starbucks Fought for Its Life without Losing Its Soul* and *The Starbucks Experience: 5 Principles for Turning Ordinary Into Extraordinary*. Rather than enlightening him, these books made him feel great anxiety about the prospect of competing with a multinational giant. To hear Deon tell it, Starbucks was a vampire about to stroll into town and suck the lifeblood out of his small business.

I suggested that he think differently about potential competitors, particularly Starbucks, pointing out that the threat probably wasn't anything near what he was anticipating. His skepticism was still palpable even after I told him Starbucks was just one of the five coffee shops in as many blocks on Fourth Street, Calgary. And I'm not sure I dispelled any of his skepticism when I explained that the Purple Perk, a family-owned coffee shop on the opposite side of the street from Starbucks, is consistently busier than its famous neighbour. It seemed that Deon's biggest fear was the presumed aura of the multinational's iconic green mermaid logo and pretentious jargon.

The conversation with Deon reminded me of imagined competitor issues I'd dealt with while running my business, particularly in the naïve early years. It occurred to me there was a lesson about competitors for small businesses of all types in the Purple Perk and Starbucks rivalry. Back in Calgary, Paul Overholt, who co-owns the Purple Perk with his wife, Jane, agreed to talk about it.

Only minutes after I sat down with Paul in the Purple Perk, I noticed that his attitude to the multinational competitor across the street was diametrically different from Deon's. Far from being concerned about Starbucks, Paul saw advantages in having it close by. His well-reasoned strategy struck me as a classic example of how a small business can outmanoeuvre a large competitor—even a multinational corporation—by exploiting its weaknesses.

The surrounding neighbourhood, Mission, has been established for over 100 years. It's home to an eclectic population that Paul cleverly adjudged would favour a neighbourhood coffee shop reflective of the look and feel of Mission. One way he conveyed this was through incorporating ceramic tiles from buildings being renovated in the area into the floor of his coffee shop. His purpose was to subtly create a sense of familiarity for customers. By contrast, as Paul pointed out, the Starbucks across the street is cookie-cutter typical of the chain's standard architecture, standard interior, and standard corporate palette. I understand the cookie-cutter concept and the anywhere-in-the-world familiarity and confidence it purports to convey. But in *this* neighbourhood at least, the green mermaid seems to be thumbing her nose at the look and feel revered by the residents. As we were talking, I glanced around the Purple Perk—it was packed. Minutes earlier I had walked past Starbucks and noticed only a handful of customers. If this particular morning was anything to go by, Paul's fit-in-with-the-neighbourhood small business model was working.

I'm sure we all know at least one or two people who carry Starbucks cardboard cups with the green mermaid logo on display the way some people wear badges and ties to announce their membership in an exclusive club. Paul knows these are not his customers and that many of his patrons have an aversion to foreign-owned multinationals. This is what I mean by identifying your *actual* competition. There is bound to be some overlap of customers, but for the most part Starbucks is an *apparent* rather than an *actual* competitor. Paul's actual competitors are the other privately-owned coffee shops on the street. By not distinguishing between apparent and actual competitors, you waste time and energy barking up the wrong tree.

So rather than being concerned about the green mermaid across the street, Paul welcomes her presence, saying: "Her visibility raises the profile of coffee and the concept of coffee shops to the advantage of all five privately-owned coffee shops in the area."

Paul also quite correctly pointed out that in other industries, competing businesses are often located close to each other for the convenience of consumers and to focus attention on the product. "For instance," he suggested, "if you and I were to open a shoe store, where would we do it? Obviously at the local mall where all the other shoe stores are located. It's the same reason why most of the car dealerships are at Calgary Auto Mall." He was referring to an area with at least ten different car dealerships on a one-way circle.

The coffee shop lesson for all small businesses owners: identify your actual competitors, understand their strengths and weaknesses, and then adjust your business model to stay ahead. You should also know what your competition is up to at all times so you're not caught by surprise and end up with a sore butt, like an unobservant coonhound.

Binoculars

There are different ways of keeping an eye on your competitors. The specifics will differ depending on the nature of your business and industry, but we can address this in a general way.

I knew a service station owner in Calgary who kept a close eye on his competitors up and down the street. More specifically, he kept an eye on the per-litre gas prices they were displaying. This was what the binoculars under the counter were for. In the cut-throat gasoline business, prices can change daily (in volatile times, a few times a day). To remain competitive selling a common commodity in a price-conscious market, you have to know what the competition is charging. A few times a day he would reach for the binoculars and check the competitors' advertised prices.

While checking on competitors through binoculars might seem a bit James Bond-ish, I like it as a metaphor for the sound business practice of gathering intelligence on your competitors. I don't mean to suggest you should obsessively watch your competitors, but it should be part of your routine management activities—being oblivious could have consequences ranging from a slow deterioration in your competitiveness to a sudden, damaging, unpleasant surprise.

How you gather intelligence on your competitors is important. Keep good ethics in mind and definitely don't do anything illegal! All the intelligence you need can be gathered legally, inexpensively, and without having to invest in an Aston Martin. You can learn much about your competitors through trade shows, advertising material, websites, press reports, customer gossip, mutual suppliers, couriers, truckers, social media pages, and perhaps even surreptitious visits to their premises. Of those options, the surreptitious visit is potentially the most controversial. Be judicious. I've heard many surreptitious visit stories. Here's one my customer and friend Mac told me.

Mac built a successful transfer-printing business. Transfers consist of images screen printed onto paper for later application to garments (usually T-shirts) by a heat and pressure process. Transfer-printer businesses are very competitive and therefore usually guarded about their methods and materials. The biggest transfer printer in town was no exception. But when Mac was setting up his print shop, he needed information about materials and equipment.

So, one Saturday he went dumpster diving behind his competitor's factory while it was closed for the weekend and was astonished by how many discarded documents he found bearing useful information about customers and suppliers. But it wasn't all he needed. He wanted to know more about his competitor's equipment. This required a visit to the factory during business hours. Mac strode through the front door and past the receptionist with a cheery greeting. He headed straight into the factory. Nobody questioned his presence. He had a good look around before strolling out the back door—mission accomplished.

Some could argue that Mac's jaunts were skulduggery. Others might consider them merely creative, if not courageous. We could debate these points until the cows come home, but when I saw his cheeky grin and the glint in his eye, I knew Mac saw these escapades as akin to nothing more than schoolboy pranks.

Some competitors will test the ethical limits, but should *you*? And how do we judge the ethics of an incident—can it be merely intolerable or does it have to be illegal before the line is crossed? This is something for every small business owner to decide individually, but I favour competing fairly for no other reason than I want to see someone I can live with when I look in the mirror. By all means, find out all you can about your competitors, but do it ethically and avoid starting wars.

What and why

So what should you know about your competitors? The short answer is everything you possibly can to help you outwit, outmanoeuvre, and outperform them.

The first thing to understand is you're not going to outwit, outmanoeuvre, or outperform competitors by imitating them. You need to differentiate your small business from those of your competitors, and a "me-too" strategy is not the way to do it. If you haven't read Seth Godin's book *Purple Cow*, go do so (after you read this book, of course). *Purple Cow* is about standing out from the herd. It's a good philosophy, but it only works if you know what to stand out from. You must know who's in the herd and what they look like. You must know their strengths and weaknesses.

But let's not kid ourselves: this isn't a one-off exercise. In business, nothing is static. We have to be aware of changes as they occur. Among the boring brown cows in the herd are others aiming to stand out. Red, green, or orange cows are likely to pop up from time to time. When this happens, you need to know about it and reassess whether purple is still as noticeable as it once was. If it's not, make the necessary adjustments to once again stand out from the herd. So what do you need to know about your competitors?

A Google search will yield a treasure trove of good material on the topic. For example, a paper published by Leeds Beckett University provides a good summation. Here are some of the areas they list as important intelligence when gathering information about new and existing competitors:

- The products and services they provide
- How they market to customers
- The prices they charge
- How they distribute and deliver
- Their market share
- Their brand and design values
- Their staff numbers and the calibre of staff
- How they use IT

- Their management style
- Their media activities in local newspapers, radio, television, and any outdoor advertising

I would add "Business owner" to the list. You want to know about every key competitor's quirks, temper, personality, character, ethics, competitiveness, creativity, risk tolerance, and trustworthiness. These (and anything else you can think of that's worth knowing) are the pieces that create the full picture of your competitor. And you need the full picture for two main reasons. The first is that small businesses almost invariably reflect the personality of their owners. Therefore, if you know about the owner's personality, you'll have insight into the culture and personality of his or her business. The second, and probably more important, reason is that the day may come when you have an opportunity to negotiate with this person about collaborating, merging, buying, or selling. Negotiations are easier if you know as much as possible about the person on the other side of the table.

And competing is also easier when you know as much as possible about your competitors. Ultimately, competing is about customers. Competing is about winning in the marketplace, and winning in the marketplace is primarily about gaining and retaining more business, which usually means gaining and retaining more customers.

If you're fortunate enough to be in a new marketplace attracting new customers, then your task is to find as many of these new customers as you can before they find your competitors. But if you're in an established marketplace servicing an established population of customers—which is the case for most small businesses—your challenge is to woo customers away from your competitors. This is difficult to do if you don't know much about your competitors. We've been through a list of pieces needed to build a competitor's picture, but let's zoom in on something particularly important—indifferent or bad customer service (something often gifted to us by competitors).

Competing in customer service

The Leeds Beckett University list doesn't specifically mention "customer service," but a number of the items affect customer service—in other words, the customer's experience. Outstanding customer service is likely what many of your competitors think they provide. And it's likely that few actually do. If you're going to exploit a competitor's weaknesses, a good place to start is with the low-hanging fruit; customer service is usually low-hanging fruit.

Think of your experiences as a customer, of how you like to be treated when you're handing over your hard-earned cash. It sounds simple enough—treat customers the way you like to be treated—yet many business owners and their front-line staff still don't understand this. And I'm not talking about the superficial stuff like the smiley greeting as you come through the door, the cheery voice on the other end of the phone, or the thank-you email for the online order you placed. I'm talking about the whole customer experience, from the moment the slightest interest in doing business is shown to long after the purchase has been delivered. In short, great customer service means bending over backwards to meet the customer's needs while maintaining a helpful, friendly disposition throughout the transaction. If your small business does this better than the competition, it will stand out from the herd.

The price of war

So what's the takeaway? Compete hard but ethically and avoid warring with your competitors. In the short-term, there's no joy in conducting day-to-day warfare—it's debilitating, distracting, and counter-productive.

But there's also an important long-term reason to avoid warring with competitors. When the day comes that you need an exit strategy, you don't want to find that the obvious candidate to acquire your small business is the competitor with whom you waged bitter war. Now, instead of a potential acquirer, you have an enemy who'd rather gouge out your eyes than negotiate with you.

Intense but peaceful competition is a much better strategy.

CHARACTER 29: GOVERNMENT OFFICIAL

Compliance

We won't be spending much time on this character because there's not much to discuss. There are few options.

Wherever your small business is located between the two poles, from the moment you hang your shingle until the day you take it down, this omnipotent character, in all his or her incarnations, will never be far away. There's no place I know of where this is not the case.

That leaves your small business with two choices—comply with every level of government's dictates, on time and in full, or don't. But understand this about the choices: the former won't contribute to the making of your small business, but the latter can certainly contribute to the breaking of it.

Only exception

The only exception to total, unquestioning compliance is unfair, prejudicial, erroneous, or illegal treatment. In any of these situations, seek help from one or more professionals—accountants or lawyers for most cases. Depending upon their advice, the resources at your disposal, and the importance of the matter at stake, fight for what's right.

Critical message

To discuss this character any further would add nothing to the critical message—comply, comply, comply. And the brevity of this chapter is in no way a reflection of this character's importance to a small business. This is a very important character.

CHARACTER 30: GRAPHIC ARTIST

Communication

One of my favourite works of art hangs in the National Gallery, London. It's a painting of a horse named Whistlejacket. The horse's owner, the second Marquess of Rockingham, commissioned George Stubbs for the work in 1762.

I've had the privilege of spending time with Whistlejacket on a number of spellbinding occasions, and I'd like to describe him not only in the hope of encouraging you to visit him if you find yourself in London, but also because I want to make a point about the use of graphics in business.

The oil-on-canvas painting is 2.9 metres high by 2.5 metres wide, which pretty much makes it life-size. Whistlejacket was a thirteen-year-old chestnut Arabian thoroughbred with a long, flaxen-coloured tail. Stubbs painted him rising to a levade, which is to say that he's standing on his hind legs, with his forelegs raised and his body at about a thirty-five-degree angle. His head is turned towards the viewer. Stubbs's attention to detail is breathtaking. And the eyes … Oh, the life in the eyes …

I'll stop there because even if I carried on with this description for a thousand words—and assuming I didn't bore you into resorting to skimming—I'd still not be sure that your mental picture at the end of my description would be anywhere near a close resemblance of the painting.

In a moment I'm going to ask you to indulge me by putting the book down to Google *Whistlejacket*. I want you to understand my enthusiasm for the painting but, more than that, I want you to see how the actual image differs from the image I planted in your mind. And therein lies my point. No matter how many words are used or how skillfully they're crafted into a description, there is no way even a lengthy passage can accomplish what an image of the painting can in a fraction of the time.

Okay, you're ready to Google *Whistlejacket*.

Small businesses face this choice when trying to promote themselves and their services and products—words or images or both? I'm suggesting that in many circumstances, images (or perhaps images accompanied by some wording) will do a much better job. This shouldn't come as news to anyone; after all, how often have you heard the old expression "A picture is worth a thousand words"? And, by the way, wouldn't it make a great tag line for all graphic artists?

Clearly I'm of the opinion that a graphic artist is an indispensable resource for most small businesses (we'll discuss the few exceptions later). And it's not only because of the picture-and-thousand-words thing, but also because of another phenomenon in day-to-day business—avoidance of reading whenever possible.

Pictures in, paragraphs out

I experienced the people-will-avoid-reading-whenever-possible phenomenon over and over again after I first became aware of it while working for a major oil company, a number of years before becoming a small business owner.

I served on a project team whose mandate was to issue a report followed by a presentation to the management committee on the feasibility of overhauling a major accounting system.

The drafting of the report was shared by a number of us who were only too delighted to show off our business-writing skills. But one team member, Don, volunteered to assemble, print, bind, and distribute the report.

From the first meeting it was apparent that Don was less than thrilled to be on the project and didn't have much enthusiasm for anything but his upcoming retirement. And while we, the younger members of the project group, saw our participation as an opportunity to impress, Don saw it as another make-work exercise with the odds of implementation stacked against it. And who could blame him? After many years of trudging through the energy-sapping swamp of big-business bureaucracy, he'd come by his cynicism honestly.

After months of project work, we did our writing and Don did his assembling and distributing. A week or two later we presented our findings and recommendations complete with slides expertly prepared by the in-house graphics department. It soon became obvious from the nature of the questions that nobody on the management committee, from the president down, had read the report. Now, when you're a young professional with career ambitions, no matter how unpleasantly surprised you are, constraint is a good idea. Though sorely tempted, it would have been a bad idea, if not career suicide, to ask what the hell the point of a report was if it wasn't going to be read.

Don wasn't surprised though. He'd included a soup recipe in the management members' copies somewhere around page forty confident that nobody would notice. He was right. Nobody noticed.

Don's mischievousness showed that even in circumstances where you'd expect people to read, they don't. Business executives aren't going to read the report if they can wait for the slide presentation. People aren't going to read the book if they can wait for the movie. Prospective customers aren't going to absorb much information about you, your business, or your products and services if you present it in writing.

This is why advice abounds about keeping emails short, presenting information in bullet-point format rather than blocks of text, and illustrating blog posts with interesting images. In my own business I once solicited opinions from six different customers about four proposed container-label designs. All six chose the same label and offered the same reason—it had the fewest words.

In day-to-day business communication, pictures are in and paragraphs are out.

The fact that this is still surprising to some small business people is surprising to me. "A picture is worth a thousand words" has been around for about a hundred years. Nowadays it's only *more* relevant, as evidenced by the mind-blowing popularity of social media platforms such as Facebook and Instagram, where pictures are emphasized and writing is de-emphasized.

This avoidance-of-reading-in-our-day-to-day-lives phenomenon is intriguing, and you could be tempted to spend a lot of time trying to understand it. Is it our hurried lifestyles? Laziness? Information overload? But really, this isn't your mission, is it? Your mission is to promote your business. I think we should just concede that the phenomenon is what it is and go forth and find a good graphic artist. That is, unless you're a George.

Are you a George?

George's business was, in a promotional sense, an exception. Let me tell you why and you can decide if you too are a George. If you are, there'll be no need to stay with the rest of us in this discussion about graphic artists.

George had for many years been a chef at Cape Town's iconic five-star Mount Nelson Hotel before leaving to start a small business. He opened a Greek restaurant with just five four-person tables in a low-rent building in Mowbray, one of Cape Town's southern suburbs.

The decor and furnishings appeared to have been randomly acquired from flea markets and garage sales. The dim light fittings adorned with plastic ferns, the Formica tables with skinny chrome legs, the well-worn linoleum floor curling up in the corners, and the model Greek village with tiny twinkling lights and a slowly turning windmill were a far cry from the sumptuous furnishings of the Mount Nelson's restaurants. Yet, random, mismatched, and inexpensive as they were, the fixtures and fittings blended into an enchanting, remote-Greek-island shabby-chic restaurant atmosphere a few years before shabby chic was given a name and became a decorating option.

Dinner at George's was an all-evening event. Service was slow because he did everything himself. He presented the menu (a few traditional Greek dishes handwritten on a sheet of notepaper enclosed in a vinyl Pepsi folder), took the orders, served the wine (in mismatched glasses), cooked and served the food (on mismatched plates), and cleared the used dishes away. Later in the evening he turned up the music on the old Philips stereo set, smashed plates on the floor, and danced like Zorba.

If his quaint and unusual way of running a restaurant was the initial attraction ("You've just gotta see this place!"), it was the food that brought customers back regularly. George's cooking was, as they say, to die for. He was always booked well in advance. George didn't have to raise his business's profile, persuade anyone to visit, or impress customers with dazzling graphics. I'm not even sure he had a sign above the door, and I certainly didn't see evidence of any branding; this was not fertile ground for a graphic artist.

So, are you a George? Is your product or service so popular or unique that you don't have to compete for customers? If your business model is similar to George's, if your small business is in this contented place—full capacity, no growth intentions, and no need to brand or promote your business—you don't need graphic art. We're all a bit vain, so even if you are a George, seeing your business depicted in professionally-prepared graphics might make you glow with pride, but it would also be a waste of money. Don't spend money on graphic art if you don't have to.

If you're not a George and have to work hard at attracting attention and communicating with prospective customers, you're probably doing so in a competitive marketplace crowded not only with other small businesses but also with big businesses: big businesses gunning for attention with big advertising and PR budgets. And what's their main weapon? Eye-catching graphics. That's why eye-catching graphics—usually professionally-prepared graphics—are essential to competitive small businesses.

In addition to every other reason for using graphics in promoting our small businesses, we're forced to look the part we're seeking to play because the marketplace attaches a high value to appearance. And let's face it—we're conditioned to let appearance influence our assumptions about substance before we've even had a chance to consider it.

Looking the Part

Imagine yourself at a business networking event. You've mentioned that you're looking for a particular type of consultant—the type doesn't matter, it doesn't change the story—and in the course of the event, you meet two likely prospects.

The first prospect hands you a business card. You do what everyone does when handed a business card: you take it between your thumb and index finger, you feel it, and you glance at it. It's a graphically striking card with an embossed logo. You notice the high-quality stock as you feel it. Immediately you're on your way to forming a good impression. And as you know, first impressions are lasting impressions. You exchange a few pleasantries and agree to talk over the phone about your project the next day. Your first impression has you thinking, *Professional, capable, and successful.*

Later, the second prospect hands you a card. Same routine. You glance at it. You feel it. The stock feels thinner, the text is plain black, and there's no design element to the card. It looks and feels as though it was hastily prepared on a home inkjet printer.

I hardly have to speculate about what you'd be thinking or about who would have a head start before tomorrow's phone discussions. It's superficial and unfair but, I'm afraid, it's deeply entrenched conditioning.

A business card is just one example. The same concept applies to every other visual representation of your business: letterheads, envelopes, flyers, pamphlets, invoices, statements, postcards, product labels, shipping boxes, notices, menus, sandwich boards and other signs, websites, blogs, social media pages, television commercials, and a host more that could take us all day to list.

Whether your business gets a foot in the door depends on how well or badly you present yourself. Good visual presentation in all aspects of your businesses is important, and good visual presentation means professional-looking graphics by a good graphic artist.

A good graphic artist

It might be stating the obvious, but I feel compelled to point out that graphic artists differ greatly in ability, style, experience, cost, and value for money. The question is, what are the attributes of a good graphic artist? One might be inclined to associate *good* with awards and fame—with the type of graphic artist deep-pocketed big businesses seek out. But more realistically, from a small business perspective, a good graphic artist is one who can help you achieve an objective at a cost your budget can bear. It might sound like a tall order, but you can relax. Finding such a graphic artist isn't as challenging as you might assume.

Engaging big advertising firms or graphic houses is almost certainly out of the question for most small businesses which simply don't have the budget. However, creative and competent independent graphic artists are easily found by word of mouth or online searches. I've worked with a number of graphic artists but the most recent two are particularly competent independents; one was the son of a management consultant my wife met on a flight between Calgary and Toronto, and when he outgrew my small business (as I knew someone of his talent eventually would), I found another by a Google search.

Obviously you're not going to latch onto the first graphic artist you come across. You're going to do a little window shopping and snooping before meeting. I realize that nowadays it's easy to do business with independent contractors on the other side of the world particularly with Skype, FaceTime, and other similar technology. However, I like to deal with graphic artists face to face. I want to meet over coffee with a pad and pen. I want to get to know them. I want my graphic artist to get to know me and to get a feel for my business. I prefer the other side of a coffee table or office desk to the other side of the world.

I don't want to miss out on those sessions where a few swishes of a pen make what's in my mind appear on paper—as I watch with the amazement and delight of a child watching a few puffs and twists produce a balloon giraffe. It's magic!

But back to window shopping and snooping. A graphic artist's website is the obvious place to start. The portfolio page and perhaps the references page might be all you need before heading for the contact page. Check out a number of artists, narrow down the field to a promising few, and then set up meetings.

I've found that most graphic artists won't rely only on the impression you might have gleaned from their websites and will turn up at the initial meeting with a portfolio. This is a good sign. Take the time to examine it carefully; you're looking for a style to match your business's image and market. If your business is a hair salon with a focus on twenty-five to forty-five-year-old females not averse to funkier hairstyles, a graphic artist with a formal corporate-style body of work might not be an ideal match. Likewise, if your client base is primarily big corporations, your graphic artist probably shouldn't be one with a loose, folksy style.

Your graphic artist must also be somewhat thick-skinned; you don't want someone who is prissy about his or her work. He or she must be able to accept that you won't always like the first version of what you've asked for. But at the same time, you must be prepared to compromise between what you have in mind and what your artist produces, provided it's not outrageous or inappropriate, of course. Don't interfere with the creative process unless it goes right off the rails. You have to appreciate that you're entering a world of creativity where the graphic artist lives and works and where he or she must be allowed to exercise creative talent. After all, isn't that what you're paying for?

Mind the intoxication

Seeing your business's identity expressed in professionally prepared, eye-catching graphics is bound to evoke pride and excitement.

It confers an air of legitimacy, speaks to your professionalism, gives you the appearance of a serious contender, and perhaps even suggests a standing to belie your small size. All of this is good, but there's a potential problem—great graphics can become intoxicating, even addictive. As I mentioned earlier, we're all a bit vain. But vanity should not interfere with economic sense.

Paying a graphic artist to design must-have items such as business cards, letterheads, envelopes, product labels, and website banners shouldn't be difficult to justify. But what about promotional items such flyers, pamphlets, and postcards? It's not good enough that these items present an eye-catching impression of your business; they must justify their cost by producing income. They must come up favourably when put through a cost-benefit assessment. A cost-benefit assessment is easier said than done, however. Unless you're able to relate new business directly to a promotional effort, how do you know whether your snappy flyer is paying for itself? When it's not possible to measure cost-benefit directly, I think it's fine to rely on your entrepreneurial instinct—but be sure that graphics for graphics' sake, in other words, graphic intoxication, doesn't overrule gut instinct.

This is exactly what I allowed to happen on a few occasions. I used graphic artists very effectively for must-haves and some promotional items, but I also wasted money on other promotional items. And while I can say with confidence that the graphics associated with my business were always professionally designed and didn't do the business's image any harm, truth be told, many of them didn't contribute to the bottom line either.

A pink stress ball was my worst promotional misfire—it was a waste of graphics and environmentally inappropriate to boot. We were marketing a pink photo-sensitive emulsion when I got talked into the stress-ball promotion. I had appropriate graphics designed and printed on a large number of balls (I think it was somewhere around five hundred) and distributed them to screen printers far and wide. I eagerly awaited the curious inquiries. They never came. As time passed, it became apparent that the printers who'd bought the pink emulsion had bought it for technical reasons and that a pink stress ball was ineffective in raising awareness and irrelevant to the buying decision.

If I'd been more aware at the time, I would have asked myself the key questions I'm encouraging you to ask before undertaking a marketing project: Is there any reason at all to believe that this promotion will positively contribute to the bottom line after considering the effort and cost? Do my customers really need another trinket cluttering up their desks and drawers? Does the earth really need another indestructible rubber or plastic trinket that will end up in a landfill or, worse still, in waterways and the ocean? Can we find alternative promotions that are cost-effective and eco-friendly?

Effective portrayal

A graphic artist can be invaluable in helping to create the image you want your business to project and in helping to deliver your promotional message to your target audience. Just don't overlook the importance of a cost-benefit assessment in the excitement of seeing your business portrayed in professionally prepared graphics.

And, of course, success lies in those two words—professionally prepared. Poor or amateurish graphics can do your image more harm than no graphics at all.

CHARACTER 31: ONLINE MEDIA DEVELOPER

Not Uncle Fred

If your small business has an online presence, you're probably already familiar with this character. If not, allow me to introduce you to the online media developer.

Online media developers come in many guises including the neighbour's kid, your geeky niece, or retired Uncle Fred with too much time on his hands. These enthusiastic amateurs are not, however, the online media developers I have in mind for you. I'm talking about qualified, competent, professional social media developers who may work independently or be employed by a firm.

There are many areas in which thrifty, budget-conscious small business owners will try to get away with the cheapest option possible, but this must not be one of them. Cheap, particularly as in free from Uncle Fred, can turn out to be costly in terms of wasted time and business image damage.

The online media developer I'm introducing to you is knowledgeable about websites, blogs, and the many social media networks—LinkedIn, Facebook, Google+, Twitter, Instagram, YouTube, Pinterest, Vine, and Snapchat, to name just some of the better-known ones.

WHY ONLINE?

Invariably, discussions about whether or not a small business should consider an online presence focus on whether or not it will increase sales. While this might be the main consideration, it's not the only one.

Digital technology has become an integral part of how business is conducted, regardless of size. Increasingly nowadays, the first place people will go to find everyday information—address, phone number, email address, name of the owner, and even correct spelling of the business name—is a search engine (such as Google) or your website. It's become the convenient and quick way to find basic information about even the smallest of businesses. Without a website, this information isn't as readily available as the Internet has conditioned us to expect. So, being the Internet-centric people we've become, we equate the absence of an online presence (particularly a website) to an absence of serious business intent and will simply seek an alternative with an online presence, thank you very much.

In addition to convenience, an informative, well-presented website lends credibility to your small business. Potential suppliers, joint-venture partners, employees, and even potential buyers of your business are going to check out your website as a first step. What they find may determine whether they proceed with their inquiry. Without an online presence, significant opportunities could be lost.

I'll bet I'm not the only one who has declined to recommend a superb little business because it didn't have a website. The most convenient way to recommend a business to a friend or colleague is to drop him or her a quick email with a clickable direct link to the site.

Convenience—we're obsessed with it. The inconvenient absence of a website can frustrate us into buying or recommending something else.

Website

Your website must be graphically appealing, uncluttered, easy to navigate, and helpful.

Consider how you would feel if you needed a specific book and found the door to the recommended bookstore blocked by jugglers, clowns, and a mariachi band? Then once you battled your way past the noisy, animated entertainers and into the store, you found that the books weren't arranged by category, title, or author, or in any other organized way. Looking around, you couldn't see an assistant and realized you'd have to search without any help through thousands of books for the one you came for.

Would you stay? Or would you simply go to a store that didn't have annoying entertainers blocking the entrance and that had helpful assistants and inventory arranged in a way that enabled you to get in, find your item, pay, and get out in minutes? Exactly! You, me, and everyone else.

The same principle applies to websites, particularly e-commerce sites. Some online media developers are still dazzled by the clever animations and special effects modern digital technology allows them to create. Don't allow your developer to do this. Visitors want to get in, do business, and get out—as quickly as possible. They don't visit your site to be entertained, unless of course that's the sole purpose of the site.

Small business websites fall into two broad types. The first type is informational, and though designed to promote your business, it is not a vehicle for transacting business online. I refer to this type of site as an online pamphlet. The second type is specifically designed for transactions. This is commonly referred to as an e-commerce site.

Your choice of site will depend upon the nature of your small business. And your choice and the nature of your business will also determine the level of expertise you should look for in a developer. You might allow Uncle Fred to build a garden shack because he's handy with a saw and hammer (though I wouldn't recommend it), but you wouldn't think of letting him build your fancy new house. Yet, I've seen too many websites built by Uncle Freds, with predictably poor results. This aspect of your business is far too important for a cheap, slapdash approach.

It's true that you can set up a basic "pamphlet" website yourself with minimal expertise in under a half hour using various inexpensive templates, if this is all your business needs. Anything more than this though and you should be seeking the advice or assistance of a competent developer.

Blog

A business blog has a fourfold purpose: to position your business as an industry authority; to drive traffic to your website; to increase your SEO (search engine optimization); and to develop and maintain good customer relationships.

But in order to tailor a blog to its purpose, you need to keep in mind that a blog is not a book. People will settle down with a book and in one sitting read page after page, chapter after chapter. Not so with a blog.

A blog is more like a condensed glossy magazine—online. A good guideline for blog writing is to assume an audience of severely limited attention span. Blog readers prefer to receive information in short, sharp bites. They're turned off by anything more than this. This isn't difficult to understand if you've ever read the comments following an interesting or controversial online article. Don't you find that even when the topic is of particular interest to you and you're curious about other readers' comments, you find yourself reading the short ones and passing over the long ones?

I don't think many of us have much tolerance for windbags. From my perspective (and I don't believe I'm too different from most in this regard), more than a hundred words in a reader's comment on an article is flirting with windbag territory.

We, your potential blog readers, don't expect blog postings to be as short as readers' comments, but we are an impatient lot who believe we are very busy and don't have the time to read long blog posts, no matter how cleverly or entertainingly you might think you've crafted them.

So please keep them down to between two hundred and fifty and four hundred words to avoid testing the outer limits of our patience.

Something else you should know is that we'll be more inclined to read your blog posts if they aren't just a solid block of text but are broken up by one or more images (the more relevant and eye-catching, the better). Oh, and about your choice of words—please don't make us stop our reading and log on to our favourite online dictionary to figure out what you're talking about. We might just not bother to come back—we're very busy and terribly impatient, remember?

In addition to the key elements of brevity and eye-catching appearance, you must consider other elements if your blog is to fulfill its purpose. You'll find different opinions about these elements online if you Google "What constitutes a good blog?" Be selective about the tips and advice offered. Not all will apply to your particular readership, but you'll find a few common themes running through most of the literature on blogs. You should heed them.

Most advice discourages using a blog to sell products or services—it's widely believed that this turns readers off. On the other hand, helpful advice or useful and relevant information is appreciated. This is what promotes your business as an industry authority.

While a well-done blog makes good business sense for most small businesses, there is a caveat; it requires dedication, creativity, and writing skill. A blog must be kept current with regular posts—this requires dedication. It's necessary but difficult to keep finding fresh, relevant material—this requires creativity. Posts must be well written to draw in and hold a reader's attention—this requires writing skill. I say this with all confidence after blogging at least three times a week for ten years.

A lack of blog-writing talent or time is not an excuse for not having one. Blog-writing services, from independent writers to content development practices, are aplenty. As with all services though, do some research before selecting a suitable fit, both in price and competence.

Social media networks

In addition to websites and blogs, many small businesses promote themselves on one or more of the social media sites. I mentioned the better-known ones at the beginning of this chapter, but there are many others—by some assessments, hundreds.

An online search will disclose various periodic surveys that provide insight into the ever-changing state of the social media world. It's a good idea to keep current on which networks are best suited to your business's target demographic and which will give you the best return for your online marketing dollar.

Carsen Kendal, a social media marketing specialist with Vovia Online Marketing, an international online marketing consultancy firm headquartered in Calgary, says it's good practice to work with a limited number of well-chosen social media networks and manage them well rather than many and manage them poorly. This is particularly sage advice for small business owners with limited time and resources.

The expert

If you're one of the vast majority of small business owners who's not a trained website developer or social media expert—and unless you're in the enviable position of being able to take the time away from the day-to-day management of your small business to become one—you're going to need the help of a competent online media developer.

This may be an independent developer or an online marketing firm catering to small and medium businesses. It's here where the average small business is most likely to find an appropriate level of expertise at a manageable fee.

The process of finding candidates will usually include an online search, asking for referrals from colleagues and associates, website reviews, and meetings with prospective developers. I've found that the most productive way to conduct the initial meeting with a potential developer is to present a brief written outline of your business, your target market, and what you think you need for a website. If you can prepare an outline (with text and basic charts) of a full-blown online marketing strategy incorporating a number of social media networks, so much the better.

A neatly prepared document will not only facilitate communication but also signal clarity of thought and intent on your part. For website discussions, I found that clarifying my vision by drafting a rough page-by-page mock-up of the site I had in mind saved a lot of time when explaining it to the developer. I would also go armed with a list of sites with features I liked. All of this helps the developer understand your preferred direction and cuts down on the time wasted exploring blind alleys.

A developer should be prepared to spend up to an hour (a good developer won't need more) examining and discussing your concept. After that he or she should be able to indicate a ballpark cost. When it comes to cost, you shouldn't assume that the quoted price equates to quality. A few years ago I met with four website developers and gave them all exactly the same rough mock-up of a relatively comprehensive business consultancy site. The quotes ranged from five thousand dollars to twenty-five thousand dollars. I chose the developer who quoted six thousand dollars and was very happy with the result.

Always insist on a signed scope-and-cost-of-project agreement that provides remedies for noncompliance, particularly if post-launch maintenance of the site is included. Without it, your project can become a nightmare of unpleasant surprises and a bottomless money pit.

As I mentioned in the Burglar chapter, I once failed to insist on documentation regarding the various aspects of maintaining an e-commerce website—it cost my small business eight thousand dollars and two months of lost online business. My company's e-commerce site was hacked shortly after I shifted responsibility for maintenance from one developer to another. Each claimed it was the other's responsibility and I was left to carry the can.

Offline strategy to promote online presence

Your online media developer will have an array of digital tools for promoting your online presence, but there are additional things your business can do to direct traffic online.

Your company's website and blog addresses and references to any other online presence your business may have should be on everything a customer or potential customer is likely to receive in the normal course of doing business with you. This includes letterheads, envelopes, business cards, pamphlets, flyers, packages, product labels, waybills, packing slips, and any other documentation you distribute.

My business went a step further and had large numbers of eye-catching postcards—designed specifically for the purpose of encouraging visits to our website and blog—printed inexpensively by a gang-run printer. We included them with any mailed material as well as in every package we delivered.

The plan was to constantly remind our target market that we had an online presence in the hope that customers would pay us online visits. Marketers will tell you that the key to results with this sort of campaign is repetition, which is pretty much the same thing I first heard my father say when I was just a kid. I've never forgotten it: "If you throw dung at a wall long enough, eventually some of it will stick."

If you're going to consider the idea of including a token "thank you" of chocolate bars or cookies in every delivery, as my business did for over twenty years, promote your online presence the same way. Seal the chocolate bars or cookies in small plastic bags printed with a thank-you-for-your-business message and your various online addresses.

It's not difficult to find ways to promote your online presence and, in the process, differentiate your business from your unimaginative competition. All it takes is a little creativity.

There is of course the issue of ensuring that the benefit gained justifies the cost. All this creative stuff is fun—however, you're in business and the bottom line looms large. But weighing up the cost against the benefit in this area is a bit nebulous and not an easy task for a small business owner. How do you tell which promotional effort resulted in online traffic? It's one of those things that comes down to judgement by learned or innate entrepreneurial intelligence.

Email blasts

By monitoring blog visits (I use Google Analytics), I discovered that visits spike significantly immediately after I send out a personalized email blast framed as a monthly invitation to visit a particular blog. The spike then subsides over the next two days until visits resume their normal daily level.

What this means is that in spite of all ongoing digital and other efforts to direct traffic to your blog, some people will only visit if reminded. In addition to encouraging blog visits, a repetitive monthly email also keeps your business's name in front of the customer or potential customer (remember the dung and the wall principle?).

Before blasting out mass emails, you must familiarize yourself with any applicable anti-spam laws covering commercial electronic messages in your particular jurisdiction. Most jurisdictions, including all the G20 countries, have them. If you use a mass-mailing e-mail service such as say, Mail Chimp, they will usually have built-in safeguards to keep you on the right side of the law.

Of course, all of this assumes your blog is worth visiting. If you don't regularly (say, a few times a week) post interesting, helpful, and informative material, there's no point encouraging visits.

Keep it current or can it

Picture this. It's a magnificent midsummer's afternoon and you're strolling down Main Street with a new light cotton jacket on your mind. You stop outside a boutique. You pause to look at the store window before entering. You notice the mannequins. They're wearing last winter's insulated coats and knee-length boots. Taped to the inside of the window is a faded handwritten notice: "Christmas holiday hours." Then you see the potted palms on either side of the door—dead for lack of water.

The vibe isn't good. Even the expressions on the mannequins' faces aren't encouraging. "Listen to us. Don't even think of coming in here for a jacket. The owner doesn't care. She has so little enthusiasm for this business that we're still sweltering in last winter's down jackets. This attitude will be reflected in the poor service but, in any case, what are the chances of finding what you want in a neglected place like this?"

What do you do? What would anyone do? Yes, move on down the street to find another clothing store.

Expect a neglected online presence to have the same effect on potential customers as this neglected storefront on Main Street—be it a website, blog, or page on a social media site.

So here's the message: keep your online presence current with good material and fresh graphics to at least demonstrate that your business is dynamic. It's better to just have a single page with contact information that doesn't need regular updating or no online presence at all rather than a neglected presence. No vibe at all is better than a bad vibe.

Set it up properly

While you could probably quite comfortably set up social media profiles for your small business yourself—LinkedIn, Facebook, Twitter, and the rest—seriously consider hiring an online media developer to set up your business blog and website if it's to be anything more than a basic one-page information site.

No matter how modest your online media budget might be, there's a developer willing to tailor his or her services to accommodate you, without your having to resort to Uncle Fred. Advice on even just a few key elements could make your online presence a whole lot more effective.

On the other hand, if your business budget can accommodate it, hiring an online media developer to help you develop a comprehensive, coordinated online media strategy that incorporates a website, blog, and social networking sites could help make your small business.

CHARACTER 32: WEBSITE HOST

Choices

This character should be on every small business owner's contact list. Regrettably, this isn't the case. Nowadays, the cost of setting up a presentable website can start at under a hundred dollars. Reliable hosting can cost as little as twenty dollars a month. In spite of this, about 40 percent of small businesses still have no presence on the web. But enough tut-tutting about a discouraging statistic for now. We're here to discuss an important character—the website host. For the sake of convenience, let's think of this host as an individual, even if it's a big corporation.

Website hosts, just like any other service providers, aren't all cut from the same cloth. Selecting one isn't as simple as surfing the Internet and picking a name—the digital equivalent of throwing a dart at a list. Different options come with different offerings and vastly different price tags. It's therefore important to consider your web hosting options while keeping needs and costs in balance. You don't want to subscribe to an inadequate service, but you also don't want to pay for more than you need.

And in terms of accommodation for your website, unless the site is fairly basic (a digital flyer), consider getting qualified advice on suitable hosting. But more of that after we've discussed website accommodation options.

The options

Websites live on web servers, which can be configured in various ways to offer different types of accommodation. To make informed choices about website accommodation, we should have at least a basic understanding of what web servers are and what they do.

Let's start with a simple description. A web server is a computer or a device on a network that manages network resources. This may seem clear enough, but the digital world can be a mysterious parallel universe for many, and when we delve deeper into the different types of server accommodation for websites, we run into the dreaded technical terms and acronyms associated with all things digital. It can be hard for us non-techies to wrap our heads around what techies think are simple explanations of the digital wizardry of their world. But we shouldn't be discouraged from asking questions when our uncomprehending stares are met with smirks or, worse still, eye rolling. We shouldn't beat ourselves up over the implied lack of grey matter. Let me set your mind at rest—most often the problem is not our lack of grey matter. The problem is usually an inability on the techie's part to deliver an explanation in plain, layperson's language. Remember, these are the culprits who came up with bizarre terms like "cookie" for a piece of data stored on your computer by a website while you're browsing the Internet.

Be encouraged by the assurance that once in a while you'll find a gem among techies—one with a talent for translating tech-talk into plain language.

Some time ago I ran across a piece written by such a gem but unfortunately cannot remember the author's name nor where I read it. But I do remember the analogy well enough to have a basic understanding of server options available for housing websites.

You have a choice of three types of accommodation for your website: (1) a shared server; (2) a virtual private server (VPS); and (3) a dedicated server. Here's the clever analogy—think about the three server options as three different types of housing, each with a landlord (the website host).

In the server "housing" market, shared servers are the least expensive of the three options. They're akin to once stately, multi-roomed mansions turned into student accommodation, where utilities are shared. The landlord takes care of periodic maintenance chores such as lawn mowing, snow shovelling, and light bulb replacements. It's fine while there are only a manageable number of occupants, but as soon as additional roommates move in and everyone starts using the facilities, the water pressure drops and the Wi-Fi slows down. Shared servers are best for smaller websites, but a greedy landlord can turn a blind eye to intolerable overcrowding. If this happens where your website lives, you should find accommodation for it elsewhere.

The next step up from a shared server is a VPS. Think of it as a townhouse. You'll be sharing some resources with neighbours but less so than at the student accommodation. There will also be more room. And here too the landlord will take care of the periodic maintenance chores.

The third option, for those who want a lot more space, is dedicated servers. This is the equivalent of your own detached single-family dwelling. You will have all the space and independence you desire, but you could be mowing the lawn, shovelling snow, and replacing light bulbs.

Now what about the all-important budget implications of each accommodation option? I'm sure it will come as no surprise to you that, as with housing, the more space you enjoy, the more it costs. Shared hosting, like student accommodation, is the least expensive. Dedicated servers, like detached single-family dwellings, are the most expensive. For many small businesses with basic websites, shared hosting is adequate and easiest on the budget. Why pay for more than you need? However, nothing stays the same forever. Basic student accommodation may be adequate while you're a student, but when you graduate, circumstances will change and you may want to upgrade. Changing circumstances affect websites too, and may dictate that you need more space than your current host can offer. You may then have to consider relocating and even upgrading. But what might some of these changing circumstances be?

One reason to change servers is increased website size and activity. For instance, your e-commerce site may grow by the addition of a large number of products and by attracting many more visitors. It may outgrow its accommodation. Another possibility is that one or more of your neighbours may grow in size and activity. It would be the equivalent of a resident in the student housing acquiring more possessions and inviting more visitors than can be accommodated in his or her room. The only places for the extra possessions and people to go are the common areas. Soon the other residents and their visitors won't be able to move around the house easily. In web server terms this would be an overtaxing of central processing unit (CPU) capacity: i.e., slow service.

Sometimes you might not know why a website host's service deteriorates in vital aspects such as speed or uptime. The reasons don't really matter. What matters is that website visitors expect to find your site up and they expect it to respond with the speed of lightning. Otherwise, they'll move on to a competitor's site. I once had to relocate a website for speed and downtime reasons. A website developer had recommended a California-based website host after investigating a number of hosts for my business's new website. Speed, uptime, customer service, and, interestingly at the time, use of solar energy, were proffered as outstanding attributes. The hosting proceeded as advertised for a while, but then this privately-held hosting business was sold. Almost immediately, downtime increased dramatically. When the phones were no longer being answered and voicemail messages were ignored, it was time to relocate.

If any of these, or perhaps some other changes, affect your website's performance, it's time to find alternative accommodation. Technological advances and intense competition among website hosts have moved the service bar up high in recent years. You should expect superb service from your website host, but above everything else, you must have speed and almost 100 percent uptime because your website visitors are an impatient, fickle bunch.

That being said, this is a good time to recommend consulting with a web or IT expert.

Why enlist expert assistance?

Many small business owners have an I'll-do-it-myself mindset. It drives them to attempt unfamiliar and challenging tasks for which they may not be qualified, such as selecting a website host. It's probably the same mindset that drives many of us to only read the instructions of self-assembly items once we've failed miserably, yelled at the crying kids, chased the bewildered family dog out of the room, and reached for the Diazepam while calling Ikea names your family has never heard before.

As a neophyte embarking on an unassisted search for website accommodation, expect a similar degree of frustration. For a preview of the quagmire you're going to have to wade through, get your ankles wet right here on just a smattering of the terms and acronyms you'll encounter. I found these crammed into only two pages of a document by a website host explaining why you should choose them to accommodate your website: POPs; IXPs; bandwidth capacity; network redundancy; SSDs; 10 gigabit networking; time to first byte; HTTP; high cache hit ratio; application layers; HTTP–HTTPS load balancers; load balancing methods including round-robin, random, client, hash, and DNS; HTTP–2; CDN provider; A–B test; VCL; store raw customer files in S3; ELB; and HAProxy.

If this doesn't sound like Greek to you, you're probably equipped to go ahead with an investigation into the best host for your website on your own. However, if it does sound like Greek, engage an expert to assist in your search—it will be a lot more efficient and effective than attempting it on your own.

What will your website require of a host?

Whether you set out on your own or engage a specialist, the search has to start with a thorough understanding of your hosting needs, currently and down the road.

Early in the search is where the neophytes are separated from the specialists. The specialist will know where to search whereas a neophyte will likely stumble about in the dark and go down a few blind alleys before arriving at what might appear to be a good destination. And then, because of lack of experience, the neophyte might mistakenly think the place has all the required features: good response time; host reliability and uptime guarantees; upgrading options; add-on domain allowances; a user-friendly hosting control panel; technical support; terms of service; site backup; environmental friendliness; and reasonable sign-up and renewal costs. A website specialist will be aware of which hosts offer the features you require and will therefore be able to quickly locate a best-fit host for your site.

Engaging assistance doesn't have to be a major undertaking—even a half-hour consultation with someone knowledgeable could make the difference between a good and a bad choice. You shouldn't have to look beyond your web developer for host recommendations.

Moving day

The need to upgrade is usually indicated by something as obvious as poor response time caused by a significant increase in a website's size and activity. As we discussed, when this happens, it's time to find an alternative home with the help of a website specialist.

A less obvious indicator of the need for a moving day is the flip side of the growth reason—excess capacity. You might scale back the size of your site for any number of reasons. For example, you might sell part of your business, leading to a reduction in the complexity and activity of the site.

I had a multisite account with a large, reputable website host, Rackspace Inc. (www.rackspace.com). On the advice of an expert, I opened the account primarily to host my business's e-commerce site, but it also housed three of my other sites—an online art gallery and two blogs.

Six or seven years later, I disposed of the e-commerce site. Shortly afterwards I realized that the art gallery and blog sites were consuming less than 1 percent of the hosting capacity, for which I was paying about $2,400 CAD a year. However, this was the best deal Rackspace's business model could offer me. Obviously, but reluctantly, I had to part ways with Rackspace—they had been a faultless host, but their service became overkill for my diminished hosting needs. But, as Alexander Graham Bell said, "When one door closes another opens." And sure enough, an expert directed me to another door, behind which I found what's sometimes referred to as boutique website hosting.

Boutique website hosts

We're all familiar with the term "boutique" in conjunction with clothing stores, wine shops, and other retail outlets of a specialty nature, but lately it is also being used to describe niche web hosting services. Boutique website hosts usually offer hassle-free, turnkey service to owners of smaller sites. Some focus on particular types of businesses or communities. I'm going to tell you a story about one such host that piqued my interest—it's bound to do the same for you. It's Kim's story.

Kim Bruce is a designer, sculptor, and wizard in digital technologies. The short version of Kim's story is that after she sold her Calgary design business to concentrate on her art, she trained in web design and HTML code in order to build and maintain her own site. One thing led to another. Prompted by a demand from fellow artists looking for a website design and hosting solution that wouldn't cost an arm and a leg and could be self-maintained, Kim learned how to code WordPress themes. She then launched Artbiz.ca, her website design and hosting service primarily for artists. She'd found a niche.

In keeping with our housing analogy, Kim accommodates websites in a townhouse complex—in website terms, on a virtual private server. She serves as landlord, providing a bother-free existence after you select one of her clean, simple, and elegant WordPress themes. Here's what she does for her tenants: installs WordPress; sets up any plug-ins you need, such as SEO, sitemaps, or contact forms; keeps WordPress and the plug-ins up to date and secure; keeps the theme updated; and provides online instruction and support as part of the service. An additional benefit of this boutique type of hosting with pre-designed WordPress themes is that it's possible to have your website up and running within twenty-four hours.

I know all of this to be true because when I had to relocate my sites, I chose Artbiz.ca. The initial attraction was the $1,800 or so I was going to save on annual hosting fees, but the personalized service you'd associate with a boutique sealed the deal. As well, I found the WordPress and security updates part of the service particularly enticing.

A boutique website development and hosting service like Artbiz.ca is an attractive hosting option for small business websites. Cost, personalized service, and worry-free accommodation would be enough, but then there's the added bonus of participating in the noble cause of small businesses supporting each other.

Shopify

A small business web-hosting discussion wouldn't be complete without mentioning Shopify. Shopify was founded in 2004 to host e-commerce websites of all sizes and has since rocketed to success. In 2015 it went public and is now listed on the NYSE and the TSE.

At the time of writing, Shopify claims more than 377,500 online stores in 150 countries with a total gross annual volume exceeding $15 billion. Simple arithmetic suggests an average annual gross revenue of just under $40,000 per online store. As this falls well within any definition of small business, we can safely conclude that Shopify hosts a large number of small business's e-commerce websites. So now you're probably wondering what hosting with Shopify costs. The answer is that it depends on a number of variables, such as the plan selected and the volume of business conducted through the site. But by using some publicly available information we can arrive at a rough idea.

Shopify derives its income from a combination of monthly hosting plans (ranging from $29 to $299) and transaction fees (ranging from 2% to 5%). Shopify's revenue was $205.2 million in 2015, so a quick calculation suggests an average annual fee per customer of roughly $550. Admittedly, aside from the fact that it seems low, this number doesn't tell you much about what your particular e-commerce site would pay for hosting with Shopify. But given the membership numbers and the average gross revenue per online store, we can conclude that an awful lot of our fellow small business owners find it economically viable to have Shopify host their e-commerce sites.

An important character

Your website host is one of the characters you're unlikely to meet face to face, but this doesn't diminish his or her importance in the day-to-day making of your small business. Small businesses rely on their websites for business and credibility—a less-than-excellent website host can undermine both. Select a website host carefully and don't hesitate to seek specialist advice.

CHARACTER 33: TRADE SHOW MANAGER

Two purposes, one destination

It's been about a half hour since takeoff. Drinks have been served. The flimsy little fold-down tray can't accommodate both a plastic glass of chardonnay and a paperback, so she closes the book and puts it on the vacant seat between them. She stares out the window. There's nothing to see, but she's not looking, she's fretting. *God, I hope that missing crate turns up. If it's not one thing it's another. What's the point of sending two people ahead if they can't set up? Last year it was—*

"LA home for you?"

She turns to look at him. She's not surprised at the overture. He's been looking like he wanted to strike up a conversation ever since they boarded. *Why can't people on planes just mind their own damn business*?

"No," she says. "I'm actually going to Long Beach for a trade show."

"Really?" he says, his face lighting up. "Me too!"

"The screen printing show?" she asks, knowing Long Beach is the venue for all sorts of trade shows.

"Yes," he says. "I have to buy a new press and some other smaller stuff. I've never been before but I figured it would save me a lot of time and hassle if I could see and compare a few machines all in the same place at the same time. How about you? Also looking to buy something?"

"No, we're exhibiting. My company manufactures adhesives and cleaning chemicals. I've done the show for about six years now. Works out great for us."

"How so?"

"Well, every year we find new prospects and usually end up turning most of them into customers."

"You do any other marketing?" he asks, intrigued by her apparent enthusiasm for the show.

"Oh yes, we still do the usual stuff like flyers, email blasts, and phone calls. We've tried cold-calling prospects too, but we're a small company and that takes a lot of time and the returns aren't great. So shows make more sense for us."

"Maybe I should be thinking of exhibiting … is this is a good one?"

"Usually. And it should be another good one this year if the freakin' truck driver gets my crate there … But yes, it's really well managed."

Managed for success

The trade show manager is a catalyst. His or her job is to create an environment that facilitates interaction between exhibitors and attendees. Show organizers stage trade shows (local, national, and international), consumer shows, road shows, private shows, hospitality events, special events, product launches, seminars, and professional conferences. For simplicity's sake I'll refer to them collectively as trade shows—it won't change the essence of the discussion.

In spite of the sophisticated marketing and sales tools the digital age has given us, for most, face-to-face is ultimately still the most effective way of doing business. However, you simply can't do business with people who don't know you exist. While this may sound obvious, I know many small business owners who simply don't get it. Consequently, they don't do enough to expose their businesses to those people, particularly suppliers and customers, who influence their survival or failure. A well-chosen trade show is an effective way for both sellers and buyers—or, in trade show parlance, for both exhibitors and attendees—to address this.

Attending

You may have a specific reason for attending a trade show, such as to see an item, meet suppliers, or compare different brands of a commodity. Alternatively, your purpose may be more general; perhaps you want to be infused with new ideas, stimulated by interesting concepts, or apprised of your industry's state and trends.

Whatever your purpose, consider it carefully. For one thing, it wouldn't make any more business sense to spend time and money attending a show that isn't likely to benefit your business than it would to, say, buy an item of equipment you aren't likely to use. Both are a waste of money.

Before attending a trade show it pays to be prepared. A useful resource for just about everything you need to know about trade shows is Barry Siskind's *Powerful Exhibit Marketing*. This book is primarily for exhibitors but also includes a section on the personal benefits for exhibitors' employees. I find most of the items in this section to be equally applicable to small business owners, and I'd recommend they be included in any small business owner's checklist of reasons to attend a show:

- Learn new techniques
- Uncover industry trends

- Build a professional network
- Introduce yourself to industry leaders
- Attend industry events
- Meet competitors
- Develop new people skills
- Talk to industry media
- Talk to customers

The people who treat trade shows as entertainment and an excuse to take a trip or just get out of the office for a few days—and I've known many who do—have lost sight of the fact that a trade show is a business event: a serious, intense business event. How serious? Serious enough to convince large companies to spend millions of exhibiting dollars wooing small businesses, year after year.

There will of course be lighter moments. There will be jokes and funny stories, there will be belly laughs as you reminisce with old friends and associates, and there will be parties, dinners, and drinks (more on that later), but make no mistake, the underlying purpose is serious business.

Now, having preached about the importance of taking trade shows seriously, I'll confess there was a time when *I* didn't take shows seriously enough. For one thing, I made a common mistake—I rewarded a staff member who had been performing well with the opportunity to join me at a trade show in Atlanta. I saw it as a bonus trip and a chance for him to broaden his knowledge of the industry. However, I didn't spell out any objectives, make it clear I expected feedback, or in any way impress upon him it was first and foremost a business trip. I assumed this was understood. I was mistaken.

Well, as you might have guessed by now, he treated the event as more of a weekend away than a business trip. Rather than scouting the competition, new business ideas, and new textile printing techniques, his primary mission seemed to be scouting for hockey tickets. And it was mission accomplished when he saw the New Jersey Devils beat the Atlanta Thrashers 1–0. Admittedly it was in the company of an ex-customer (we'd had a payment dispute), but I'm not sure how much business was discussed or how much effort was made to mend fences because the ex-customer remained an ex-customer.

An executive with one of our major suppliers took note of Mr. Hockey's apparent priorities and later, much to my embarrassment, pointedly asked whether he'd come for the hockey or the trade show.

All of this speaks to the wisdom of careful planning and predetermined objectives to ensure maximum benefit is gained from a show—an exercise that should include everyone earmarked to attend. Document your objectives and prepare a list of assignments for each attendee. Following the show, review the results and prepare a schedule to implement any useful ideas and concepts. You may also consider regrouping during the show to gauge progress and perhaps adjust the assignment lists.

Small businesses can greatly benefit from attending shows, but, like anything else you undertake in your business, do so thoughtfully and with an eye on the bottom line.

Exhibiting

Exhibiting at a show is quite different from attending one. For one thing, your primary purpose is to show rather than see. But since you're already there, you should do some seeing too (more about this later).

The time and money can be significant, but so can the returns. Any opportunity to show your company and its products or services to a large audience gathered for a few intense days for the express purpose of seeing what's on offer, should be an attractive proposition. It's certainly a lot more attractive than cold-calling. However, don't jump boots and all into the first show that comes along. A careful review and selection process will help ensure the best bang for your exhibition buck.

Don't lose sight of the fact that show organizers are in the business of making profits and will therefore promote their shows in the most enticing ways they can dream up. This means you have to cut through the hype and get to the nub of the matter—what's being offered, is it what you need, and what's it going to cost you?

Barry Siskind recommends asking yourself some key questions before attending any trade show as an exhibitor:

- Why am I considering doing this show? The show should complement your overall marketing plan, including your marketing strategies (e.g., advertising, direct sales, direct mail, telemarketing, and social media).
- What do I want from this show? With each show you may have a different business objective, such as to gather leads, create an image, meet the media, introduce new products or services, find dealers and representatives, or conduct market research. The trick is to pick one objective and focus all your efforts on achieving it.
- Is this the best show for my market? Have you checked out alternative shows in this market? The biggest shows aren't always the best. Don't limit your exhibiting opportunities by jumping at the first show that comes along.
- Who are the other exhibitors? Who is exhibiting at this year's show and who has exhibited in the past? The answers not only let you plan your exhibit properly but are also a good indicator of what the visitors expect.
- What do I know about the show manager? A lot depends on the show manager's expertise. Check his or her experience carefully. Does this person have the credibility to deliver what's promised?
- Are my products and services ready for this market? Have you done your homework? This is particularly important when you're new in a market. For foreign markets, price should include freight, insurance, duty, and brokerage. You should understand terms of credit, packaging, and labelling requirements. You will have to understand how business is conducted in the market, all the local customs, and the environmental considerations.

- Do I have resources to do the show properly? Unless you're prepared, don't waste your time. The proper "resources check" includes such things as money, time, personnel, and product readiness.

- Do I have a follow-up plan? Before you exhibit you'll need a follow-up plan in place. In addition to personal visits, you should consider follow-up through direct mail, telemarketing, and other sources. Your first contact should be two to thirty days after the show.

- Are you show-ready? All too often exhibitors work a show with the same skills they use in other areas of marketing. Shows are different, requiring a unique set of skills. Honing your sales expertise for a situation where time is an obstacle is the real challenge, and unless exhibitors understand this, trade shows won't work. Shows have reached a level of sophistication that has left inexperienced exhibitors in a quandary. Some are disillusioned and others limp through the exercise and never realize their potential. But if you're prepared, a well-planned show can put the world at your doorstep.

Not much needs to be added to Siskind's list other than the fact that for many companies, a significant aspect of exhibiting is capturing leads. Lead capture efficiency has come a long way since technology first replaced the clipboard and handwritten list. The key to efficient lead capture is a badge issued by the show manager. This badge records all an attendee's contact information in a microchip, barcode, or some other similar technology. Exhibitors can then access this information instantly via any number of scanning devices—in some cases, even through smart phones.

Explore lead capture technology fully before you exhibit. First, call the show organizer to ask if lead capture technology is provided or whether you should provide your own. And, as Siskind recommends, follow up with the captured leads two to thirty days after the show.

Siskind's book should be compulsory reading for any small business owner preparing to exhibit. Much of the book is aimed at large exhibitors, and while I don't think this should deter you from reading it from cover to cover, you would still benefit greatly if you skimmed over the parts you feel are not directly applicable to your particular small business and studied those that are.

EXHIBITING *AND* ATTENDING

A large manufacturer with which my business was associated exhibited at a number of trade shows each year. The management required the employees to take breaks from their booth duties and walk the show for the particular purpose of snooping on the competition.

To ensure this requirement was taken seriously, the managers would debrief the employees back at the office after the show. It's an excellent idea for small business exhibitors to emulate these managers. It just makes sense to take advantage of being at the show as an exhibitor and an attendee.

Here's a warning though: a show booth can keep you very busy, and before you know it, the day will have flown by with your only absences from the booth being trips to the toilet and the fast-food concession. If you don't specifically schedule times to walk the show, it won't happen and you'll lose an opportunity.

PERIPHERAL ACTIVITIES TO BE SOUGHT OUT

Most trade shows, particularly the bigger ones, spawn numerous peripheral activities. There may be dinners, drinks, meetings, lectures, presentations, seminars, factory tours, parties, and entertainment and sporting events—each one will afford learning or networking opportunities.

You and your employees should seek out and attend the events most likely to benefit your business. Admittedly, networking (as in actively approaching strangers and striking up conversations with the intent of making a contact or extracting information that could be benefit your business) isn't everybody's cup of tea. It's not mine. I hate it. But even those of us reluctant to force our way into conversations will find it's still worthwhile attending these kinds of events. You don't have to be a pushy extrovert to benefit from a networking event.

I've long suspected all mothers of reading the same what-to-tell-your-kids book, so I'll bet your mother also told you eavesdropping is bad manners. But my second bet is that, like my mother, yours forgot to add, "Except at trade show networking events."

If you haven't discovered this already, you'll find you can learn a lot by keeping your ears open, particularly if drinks are being served. Early in my career I realized the more people drink, the less they care about confidentiality and the more invisible bystanders become. Impending product releases, research and development in progress, key appointments, key firings, and gossip about competitors are some among many topics you might pick up on at peripheral events. It never fails to astound me how indiscreet some people can be with what should be confidential information—indiscretion for which you should be grateful, particularly if it can benefit your small business.

The point here is if you don't seek out and attend peripheral events, you could be missing out on opportunities, information, and contacts to advance the cause of your small business. The only proviso is you have to be selective about which events to attend and which to avoid.

Peripheral activities to be avoided

"What Happens Here, Stays Here" is the famous slogan used to promote Las Vegas tourism. It was the product of a brainstorming session in 2003 by advertising agency R&R Partners and has since given rise to the popular expression "What happens in Vegas, stays in Vegas."

The message is clear—feel free to indulge in activities that may be frowned upon back home because nobody back home will hear about it. Well, it's utter BS of course because among humanity's flaws is an inability to keep secrets or suppress bragging. How many times have you heard this whispered: "Don't repeat this because nobody's supposed to know, but …"? And think of all the times you've heard of criminals being caught because they just couldn't shut up about their "accomplishments."

Well, the same flaw was evident at trade shows long before Sin City began assuring its visitors that what happened there stayed there. Over a span of twenty years attending big trade shows, I've seen people tarnish their reputations and those of their businesses because they foolishly hoped that what happened at trade shows stayed at trade shows.

Call me a prude if you must, but do you really want to attend a serious business event and have suppliers, competitors, and customers remember your small business for your or your employees' sexual exploits, heavy drinking, or drug use? Worse still, while it might be all tee-hee, ha-ha at the time, once those labels are hung on individuals or businesses, they're not easily shed; I know of incidents almost two decades old that are still mentioned in conversations as if they happened just the day before.

It's best to avoid those peripheral events and activities where you might end up under the wrong spotlight. There are usually plenty of events where you can have a lot of fun and party your face off without crossing the line.

Back to the Office

A busy airport isn't the best place for a hungover trade show attendee. He's just endured a long lineup at check-in and now, boarding pass in hand, he joins the back of another long line slowly and hesitantly snaking its way towards LAX passenger screening.

Oh, man! How long's this gonna take?

"Hi there!"

He turns slowly. "Oh, hi!"

"So, you buy your press?"

"Yes. Well … I know which one I want, just have to see the bank manager now. How 'bout you? Have a good show?"

"Actually, yes," she says with a big smile. "Sold all the inventory we had in the booth, which is nice because it covered most of the show expenses and, better still, we don't have to ship it back. We were really, really busy!"

"I know," he says, "I went by your booth a few times and it was always packed. Get any good leads?"

"Tons!"

"You know what I picked up?"

"What?"

"An exhibitor's package for next year."

"Good for you!"

"Yep. Met the show manager. What a guy!"

"Sure is! Like I told you, he's most of the reason this show runs so well."

They've reached the entrance to the security area, where a bossy woman in a white and black uniform tells him to take line two and sends the businesswoman to line five. "Tell you what," she says as they part, "meet me over there at duty-free. We'll find a bar and do a bit of celebrating. And maybe I can talk you into automating your adhesive application."

"Okay, sure!"

He turns in the direction of line two but, in his fragile condition, far too quickly. *Oh shit, my head!*

CHARACTER 34: FISHING FRIEND

Why a fishing friend?

Harbouring regrets is unhealthy—I get that. But if I were allowed to harbour one regret, it would be that I didn't routinely schedule whole days off from my business for recreation.

That's where the fishing friend comes in: a character who embodies a commitment to time off from your small business. I now know that one day a week away from my business would have alleviated a lot of accumulated stress.

Working excessively can become a bad habit, even to the degree that you feel guilty if you're not at the office or staring at a spreadsheet on your computer. And I can't claim that those days when I worked when I should have been spending time with my fishing friend (or family and Jack Russell terriers) were productive. In fact, my presence on those days didn't do me or my business any good.

You may have no interest in fishing at all, but that's not the point. You can have a cycling friend, hiking friend, skiing friend, running friend, swimming friend, sailing friend, boating friend, mountain-climbing friend, dog-enthusiast friend, and so on and so on. If the activity involves the outdoors, so much the better. But you have to commit to a designated day—no excuses.

My lack of regular fishing friend activity can't be blamed on lack of opportunity. The area around Calgary, where I lived, couldn't be better suited to outdoor recreation if it had been designed that way. Mountains, foothills, lakes, rivers forests, and prairie all within easy day-trip distance of the city provide endless recreational opportunities. Yet even with all this available I found myself messing about at the office—unproductive messing about is really all it was—on days when I should've been outdoors forgetting about the office.

It's not that I never took a day off with my fishing friend; it's just that I wasn't committed to the day, and consequently it happened far too infrequently.

Wading in crisp mountain streams with fly rod in hand, lying on riverbanks watching beavers swim back and forth with branches in tow, crouching in forests with binoculars trying to spot the woodpecker drumming away somewhere in the distance, or sprinting after my Jack Russells at a field trial—these activities would've done more good than habitual, unproductive overtime at the office.

Anne needs a fishing friend

While writing this chapter I had a conversation with Anne, the owner and manager of the coffee shop where I did some of my work when I needed a change of environment. I was curious to know how she coped with illness and stress seeing that she works eleven hours a day, six days a week, assisted at any one time by only one of a roster of part-time employees.

Her story is worth telling for two reasons. The first is to illustrate how a facade of happiness and prosperity can conceal the challenges in the backrooms of a small business. The second is to give aspiring small business owners pause for thought, not to discourage business ownership but to encourage putting aside the rose-coloured glasses and entering business ownership cautiously and in possession of as much knowledge as possible. It can be dangerous to disregard the potential for stress when running a business—excessive, unanticipated stress can undermine good mental health. With some idea of how much stress is likely to come with the business, you can take preventative measures such as, among other things, committing to a fishing friend.

Anne's coffee shop is inviting. The furniture and fittings are tasteful. The decor is attractive. It's cozy but not so cramped that you feel you're sharing your conversation with the next table. The atmosphere is warm and comfortable. Background music, clinking china, droning voices, and bursts of laughter waft through the shop as the charming host and efficient and friendly baristas attend to customers' beverage requests. Some patrons are there to chat, some to read, some to tap away at laptops, and some to pore over folders of business documents. As some pack up, button up their coats, don their scarves, and head out into the cold, crisp Calgary air, others arrive anticipating their favourite mug of warmth and comfort.

It's no wonder people think of Anne's coffee shop as a fun business to run, and say so. But in our conversation, Anne rolls her eyes in an if-only-they-knew kind of way. I suspect she's referring to the long hours. We laugh knowingly when I tell her about how a business owner I know responds to nine-to-fivers who envy him for being able to pick and choose his own work hours. "You're right," he says. "I get to choose whichever sixteen out of twenty-four hours I prefer to work!"

Then Anne tells me about the reality that the facade of smiling baristas and comfortable, relaxed customers conceal from view. Some people might know that she opens the coffee shop at seven o'clock every morning and works until she closes at seven o'clock in the evening, six days a week. What very few know is that she sleeps with her cell phone under her pillow—she says she can't afford to miss those occasional late-night or early-morning calls from employees to say that they can't work as scheduled. She must always be ready to scramble to rearrange the schedule after calling around for a replacement. Anne sees her cell phone as a necessary constant companion, not just to ensure that she's on top of her employee roster, but also in case of possible after-hours emergencies at the shop. She notices my wry smile and says, partly indignantly and partly defensively, "I run a business!"

The other bit of information that the having-your-own-coffee-shop-must-be-such-fun crowd doesn't know is that Anne considers the demands of her business to have been a major contributor to the failure of her ten-year marriage.

It's been four years since she opened the doors, and while it seems to me that the coffee shop is quite well patronized—though she would like it to be busier—she says that the first two years were much tougher than she'd anticipated. But, she says, with four years of an eight-year lease still to go, she's resigned to keep working at it.

When I mention that since the coffee shop is closed on Sundays she at least has one day off to relax and recover, she tells me that she works in her parents' restaurant that day. She says that she doesn't take time off because she wouldn't know what to do with it, and besides, she makes more money working in the restaurant than she would if she kept the coffee shop open on a Sunday. Furthermore, she adds, she can't sit still and read because her mind keeps going over business issues.

Unfortunately I've met many small business owners in similar circumstances—burnouts or worse waiting to happen. If only I could convince Anne and the others of that. If only it were as easy as saying, "Here, log on to this site, fishingfriend.club, and find a fishing friend: a business owner just like yourself who also needs a rejuvenating day a week away from the business." Who knows, maybe one day there will be such a site for small business owners.

YOU NEED A FISHING FRIEND TOO

You might not think that you need a fishing friend or equivalent as desperately as I think Anne does, but think again.

Couldn't you benefit from more time away from your business? Wouldn't a fixed date with a fishing friend be relief to look forward to, especially on those days when you wonder what on earth made you think that running a small business would be fun? And even if you're fortunate enough to run a business that's more fun than one person can handle, don't you think that a break now and then to do something completely different would be rejuvenating and lead to a more balanced life?

Take some time to think about it if you must, but then do it.

Just do it

Find that fishing friend or preferred equivalent and spend a day a week (or at least a day every couple of weeks) with them as far away from your small business as possible. For that day, occupy your mind with something recreational, anything recreational—anything other than business.

Do it for yourself, do it for your employees, do it for your family. Do it for everyone who will benefit from being around a less-stressed, less-uptight you.

CHARACTER 35: HEALTHCARE PROFESSIONAL

Not only a Wall Street issue

Thomas was twenty-nine years old. On the morning of May 28, 2015, this Wall Street investment banker stepped onto the windowsill of his twenty-fourth-floor Manhattan apartment and jumped.

Thomas's death and the deaths of a twenty-two-year-old banking analyst and a twenty-one-year-old investment banker were the subjects of an October 2015 article in the *New York Times.* The article focussed on the potentially dire consequences of long hours spent in a grueling workplace: "Thomas died at a time when sensitivities about the pressures of Wall Street on young professionals are acute."

Career-induced suicide is both unspeakably tragic and paradoxical—a career chosen from among many alternatives for prosperity and happiness should not instead hasten death. Because of the mainstream media's focus on big business, it might be assumed that these sad stress-related incidents don't happen in the small business community. Well, they do. It's just that they don't usually make it onto the six o'clock news.

Many people view small business ownership as a stress-free, fun existence based on encounters with smiling receptionists, cheerful customer service representatives, or chatty technicians. Who can blame these people for not realizing that the facade of smiling faces can conceal financial worries, long hours, illness, and a fistful of other stress-inducing circumstances?

These situations in small businesses can be more dangerous to an owner's health than similar situations in big businesses. Big businesses offer paid-for employee assistance programs and other resources that a small business owner might not have access to. Small business owners are very much on their own in times of crisis, and that's when a healthcare professional becomes an important resource.

My own experience with business-related stress, the suicide deaths of three small business associates, and the near suicide death of another all underscored the necessity to include a healthcare professional as a character in this book. In the context of this chapter, "healthcare professional" includes any healthcare professional appropriate to the malady—general practitioners, specialists, psychiatrists, chiropractors, ophthalmologists, and so forth.

When business is going swimmingly

When business is going swimmingly and you're in good physical condition and a great frame of mind, the last character you're likely to give thought to is the healthcare professional. That's a mistake.

Just as a small yacht is dependent on a sailor with a firm hand on the tiller, most small businesses are dependent on a mentally and physically healthy owner. Usually, the smaller the business, the more critical the owner's health is in regards to keeping it on course. But even in a small business with good support staff, prolonged absence of the owner's guiding hand can be detrimental. Preventative maintenance is key. It's not just machinery that breaks down if poorly maintained.

Regular routine checkups and visits to the dentist at the first sign of common ailments are easily overlooked in the hurly-burly of day-to-day business. Murphy's Law has a way of ensuring that preventable health issues such as the flu or an abscessed tooth will throw you out of commission for a few days just when you're about to close that big order, when you're short staffed, or when something else critical requires your presence.

When business is not going swimmingly

Unless you are exceedingly fortunate, there will be times in the life of your small business when things will not go swimmingly. Problems can range from temporary issues such as periodic cash-flow shortages and inexplicable sales slumps to persistent longer-term concerns such as steadily declining market share.

Any number of sudden isolated setbacks such as a large bad debt, a key employee's resignation, critical equipment failure, loss of an important customer or client, fire, flood, theft or fraud may cause an owner's stress level to rise. Some stress is to be expected, but when it's prolonged or reaches a level at which the capacity to cope becomes questionable, red flags should be raised.

At this point you're probably wondering why someone whose stress is driven to dangerous levels by the normal trials and tribulations of small business ownership would own a business. And while this is a fair question, it's not the important question. The fact is that the small business community includes a lot of people not suited to business ownership, but for one reason or another, they're in it. Therefore, the important question is, "What can be done about business-related stress before it leads to a tragedy?"

Even among small business owners who handle stress quite well, there are those—particularly men—who are foolishly macho about their health and seek help from a healthcare professional long after they should have, if they seek it at all. Don't be one of those people.

Timely consultation and intervention

It would be naive to assume that consulting a healthcare professional when ill, physically or mentally, guarantees a return to good health and normal business activity in all circumstances. But it certainly improves the chances.

In the case of relatively minor physical illness, healthcare professionals can help minimize the effects, discomfort, and duration. Although mental illness such as depression obviously presents a more complex situation than, say, the common cold, the principle remains the same; the chances of managing the illness or recovering from it are improved by timely consultation and intervention.

While my focus in this book is small business ownership, preservation of life is a priority above everything else—business concerns pale into insignificance by comparison.

It shouldn't come to this

If you've ever been to a memorial service for someone who committed suicide, you'll know that it's different from other services. There's the grief of course, but there are also the questions.

At one memorial service for a customer who took his own life, I glanced around at the assembled family, friends, and business associates—a silent, sombre, and uncomprehending sea of faces—each person probably struggling with the same tormenting questions that were running through my mind. *How did it come to this? Could I have done something to help prevent it? Did I miss any signals or perhaps even cries for help?*

I can't claim that this customer's suicide and those of certain other associates were entirely business related, but I know that business-related stress and depression were contributing factors in every instance. In one case the suicide note referenced a key person insurance policy; it was offered as a gift to his two partners to help them save their faltering business.

In another instance, a customer who'd been receiving treatment for depression related to a business failure parked his vehicle in his warehouse one night and gassed himself. A day or two later I saw a card he'd mailed to someone with whom he'd been having acrimonious business dealings to assure him that he harboured no ill feelings and that this person should not assume that their conflict had anything to do with his suicide. Others received similar cards. I don't know how to adequately describe the emotions of the moment while holding that card other than to say shivers ran down my spine. And again, there was the recurring thought: *What could have been done to prevent this?* Maybe nothing, but maybe, just maybe, self-diagnosis could have detected the early onset of symptoms and immediate treatment could have prevented an escalation that ended in a memorial service.

Self-diagnosis

Without access to formal programs normally available to big companies' employees, small business owners must recognize the symptoms of extreme stress and even mental illness in themselves.

Most of us have no trouble recognizing when we are physically ill, but how are we to recognize the symptoms of much more nebulous issues such as excessive stress or mental illness? I was told by Dr. Lowinger, a Melbourne-based MD, coach, and writer with a particular interest in the mental health of small business owners, a number of symptoms are recognizable. Emotional numbness, conflict with family and colleagues, and loss of motivation at work can all indicate stress and burnout and should serve as a cue to find help before the symptoms worsen.

Dr. Lowinger suggests that feelings of worthlessness, difficulty sleeping, appetite changes, and suicidal thoughts can be symptoms of depression. She says that if any of these types of symptoms interfere with your life, your work, or your relationships, and especially if you experience thoughts of suicide or harming yourself, then it's time to seek professional help. Your family doctor, a walk-in clinic, or even the emergency department of a local hospital are good places to initially find help.

The cause of small business owner stress

Angela Martin, an associate professor for the Tasmanian School of Business and Economics at the University of Tasmania, has conducted research on the topic of stress in the small business community. She told me that small business owners face a number of unique risk factors for mental illness. These risk factors, which apply equally to the single-person, home-based small business owner and the small business owner with large premises and multiple employees, include:

- financial stress due to unpredictable income;
- high levels of uncertainty due to not knowing where the next job is coming from;
- heavy job demands and multiple responsibilities in the workplace;
- isolation and lack of social support;
- high-level responsibility to others, including employees and family;
- "presenteeism," which involves working even if you aren't well because if you're absent the business doesn't run;
- long hours, which may be even a bigger problem in small business than in the corporate world;
- blurring of boundaries between home and work: finding it difficult to separate yourself from your work and not taking time out for yourself; and
- business failure, which also carries a suicide risk.

Martin adds that depression in small business owners can be particularly dangerous if they're unable to work and lose their source of income.

Managing day-to-day stress

In addition to sudden significant events, there are the day-to-day sources of stress. On their own they may hardly be noticeable, but compounded, small doses of stress may reach significant and potentially harmful levels.

The day-to-day stresses that owners endure differ from business to business, as does each owner's capacity to deal with stress. This makes it impossible to devise a blanket stress-management solution to suit all small business owners. The fact that the resources at the small business owner's disposal differ greatly further complicates the matter. For instance, there's no value in recommending a vacation to a small business owner if he or she can't afford it, or in suggesting that more tasks be delegated if there is no one to whom to delegate. However, in these cases, the stress-relieving suggestion may still have merit if it can be adapted to one's particular circumstances.

Dr. Lowinger offers a number of tips for managing day-to-day stress as a small business owner. Some may not apply to your particular circumstances, others may have to be adapted, but all these tips are worth considering if they can help keep your stress at a manageable level:

- take regular breaks—set an alarm to remind yourself;
- take a lunch break—don't keep working while eating;
- schedule holiday breaks throughout the year;
- learn how to say no and outsource tasks whenever possible;
- set times to have your phone and email turned off;
- make time for enjoyable activities;
- look after yourself by getting enough physical activity and sleep and eating healthful food;
- learn some relaxation techniques, such as simple breathing exercises;
- build friendships and work relationships;
- look for creative or practical solutions to problems; and

- try to accept the things you can't change or control, so you can focus on changing the things you can control.

If, in spite of following all or some of these tips, you sense that you're not managing your day-to-day stress levels well, consult a healthcare professional before the cumulative effect of daily stress leads to serious symptoms.

It's your responsibility

As the owner, your health and that of your business are inextricably entwined. That makes this an important topic. Sadly, it's also a neglected topic. Don't add to the problem by being a stranger to your healthcare professional. Not just for your own sake but also for the sake of your loved ones and your small business, you must keep an eye on the state of your health. You must talk to your healthcare professional as soon as you have reason to suspect that you may need help.

Small business ownership can be a lonely existence. There are some things for which only you can take responsibility. Your health is one of those things.

CHARACTER 36: TRAVEL AGENT

IT'S ABOUT MENTAL HEALTH MAINTENANCE

If I asked you what words came to mind when I said "travel agent," I bet your response would include *fun*, *cruise*, *relax*, and *travel*. These would all be valid, but in a small business context, aggregated they'd indicate the real role of this character: to provide stress relief, which, less euphemistically, is mental health maintenance.

In the Healthcare Professional and Fishing Friend chapters, I addressed how important it is for small business owners to take care of their mental health. The Travel Agent completes the trinity of characters who help maintain a small business owner's mental health. Short breaks and longer vacations are a vital part of a good mental health regime. A vacation's purpose is to give you an extended break from the stress of the business ownership routine. It must be extended though—a weekend on the slopes or beach is not a vacation.

Extended break

Even as I write this I can hear a chorus of resistance. And if I listen carefully, I can hear that this resistance to an extended break, even one that's just a couple of weeks, is almost exclusively due to two items—time and money. But sorry, neither are valid excuses. I know this because I was once a member of that choir. Actually, I could have been the choir master.

The time excuse

I can't explain why I believed I had no time for an annual vacation, particularly in the earlier years, which are often the toughest in the life of a business. Ironically, it's during this time that you most need the vacation you believe you can't take.

My problem might have been the affliction from which many small business owners suffer—the belief that my business wouldn't operate without my presence and would simply unravel if I weren't there to hold it together. It's utter nonsense of course. It might be valid to believe that your employees can't run the business as well as you can, but believing that they can't do it well enough to avoid disaster for, say, two weeks is ridiculous (in most circumstances).

If you can't take two weeks off because you and only you can run the day-to-day activities of the business, and you also can't close the business for two weeks, you're in the wrong business. You should get out. You can't live a healthy life this way—it will eventually break you and your business.

You may want to take a cue from Karen, who needed a break badly while running her retail ceramics gift store in Calgary. She was in a predicament. She was determined to take a rejuvenating trip to Canada's east coast but had no one to run the store for her. And so, she decided to close the store for three weeks. Closing a small business for a few weeks to take a vacation may not be unusual—but *how* she did it certainly was.

Driven by a concern that customers would be angry and perhaps wonder if she'd gone out of business, she hired a graffiti artist to paint a cartoon mural in her store window: a graphic depiction of her doing vacation things (sitting on the beach, eating lobster, etc.), along with the dates she planned on doing them. It worked as intended. Far from being angry or concerned, customers were amused and told a rejuvenated Karen so after she returned.

You too may have to conjure up a little creativity to make it work, but you absolutely must take the time for at least a two-week vacation at least once a year. And when you do, never, ever do what I did on my first family vacation as a business owner and call in a couple of times a day—paranoia does little more than annoy everyone around you.

The money excuse

The "I have no money" excuse isn't valid either. I think it's a common misconception that vacations have to be expensive. Remember that the primary purpose of a vacation is not to spend money but to remove yourself from your small business and into a totally different environment where you can forget about work for a while.

Money for vacations is way down on the priority list at budget time for many small business owners, particularly in the early days. That's understandable, but it doesn't follow that a vacation can't be near the top of the must-do list. Many low-cost vacation options exist. If money is your concern, save the bespoke bike tour of Provence for when your business is thriving—for now, settle for a borrowed cabin in the woods, a hut at the beach, a friend's houseboat, or a camping trip, to name just a few options. But whatever you choose to do, do it far enough away from home to overcome temptation to pop into the office for something.

Manage your brain on vacation

In reality, despite our need to forget about business when on vacation, most small business owners cannot fully accomplish this. It's impossible. We're business owners; we can't turn off the part of our brain labeled "Open for Business 24–7." We're creative and entrepreneurial. Ideas find us at the most unlikely times. However, we need to manage what we can't turn off or we'll undermine the purpose of taking a vacation in the first place.

Managing your brain on vacation means managing a paradox. We take vacations to relax and put business out of our minds, but when we're in a relaxed state, business ideas find us more easily. The way to manage this paradox is to establish a to-be-dealt-with-later depository. You need some place other than your brain to lodge the inescapable ideas that come looking for you. The best tool for this purpose is a notebook. No, not the kind of notebook with a monitor and keyboard—in fact, you shouldn't pull out anything with a monitor and keyboard on vacation. I mean the familiar, inexpensive notebook with ruled pages between two covers and bound down the left side.

When an idea strikes, instead of annoying your family and other vacationing companions by allowing it to distract you, scribble it down in the notebook. This isn't a new concept but it's a good one. It's founded on the same principle as the old idea of taking a board and wax crayon into that other generator of creativity—the shower.

Once the idea is captured and securely incarcerated in your notebook, you can confidently forget about it and return to whatever relaxing distraction your vacation has to offer. After your vacation, back at the office, release the ideas from your notebook and work on them.

Resolution

Nowhere is it stipulated that resolutions are reserved for January 1. So seize the moment and resolve right now that an annual recuperative vacation will be in your business plans. In fact, go ahead, pour a glass or cup of something and plan a vacation. Make it work time-wise and money-wise. It can be done and must be done.

Not only will you benefit from your resolution to get lost for at least two weeks, but your employees, family, and everyone else around you will also benefit from a more balanced, less uptight you.

CHARACTER 37: GRAFFITI ARTIST

THE WRITING ON THE WALL

You may be wondering about the relevance of a graffiti artist in a book about business characters (unless of course your business is graffiti removal), but bear with me. I'm going to use the "writing on the wall" as a metaphor for everything from a gut feeling or sixth sense to input—observed, written, or spoken—that sets off an alarm or raises a red flag. And who better to represent writing on the wall than a graffiti artist?

FROM MINOR TO PROFOUND

A real-life graffiti artist's writing on the wall is quite often profane and unworthy of attention. By contrast, our metaphorical graffiti artist's writing on the wall is always worthy of your small business's attention. Some messages warn of impending doom while others point to profitable opportunities. They also range in significance from minor to profound, and ignoring any of these messages could have consequences. However, I'm going to discuss the effects of ignoring the profound ones here.

By profound, I mean serious enough to make or break a small business—the type of writing on the wall you can't afford to ignore. In some cases where businesses collapsed, the writing on the wall would have been visible to even the most willingly blind. On the other hand, we'll never know how some small businesses might have blossomed had they seized the opportunities mentioned in the messages. It has always been this way—some consider the writing and react while others suffer the consequences of embodying the old proverb: "None so blind as those who will not see."

Reading but not Reacting

Typically, over the life of a business, the writing on the wall will appear regularly; it was no different in the case of my business. I considered most messages, reacted to some, and failed to react to others. Unfortunately, a few to which I failed to react were profound, such as one particularly important message in 2004.

In 1994, the World Trade Organization members agreed to eliminate the use of quotas in all textile trade between them within a decade. One day in early 2004, the writing on the wall appeared in the form of a lengthy article in a local newspaper; it spelled out in great detail the implications and consequences of implementing the WTO agreement.

The article's overall message was as unmissable as the boldest graffiti you've ever seen: "Your business supplies Canadian textile screen printers, who will be affected when textile trade quotas expire on December 31 this year. From January 1, 2005, clothing will increasingly be imported without restriction from low-wage jurisdictions such as China, Bangladesh, Honduras, El Salvador, and Vietnam at a fraction of the cost for which it can be manufactured in Canada. This will include screen-printed garments currently printed in Canada. The larger-volume orders are likely to quickly be lost to low-wage regimes. This will decimate the Canadian textile screen printing industry by leaving it with only smaller local print jobs. Larger printers will be forced to close or relocate offshore, and you will therefore be left with only smaller customers in a downsized market. You can't follow the work offshore because you're confined to Canada by distributorship agreements."

By the time the predictions started coming true, the time to react to the writing on the wall, i.e., sell the business, had passed. My folly is just one example; the landfill of small – business failures is full of examples of the folly of ignoring the writing on the wall.

In the bag?

The vast majority of small businesses don't enjoy coverage in the business press. When one does, it's usually because of significant success. Tamrac earned this kind of coverage.

The Tamrac story is about a small family business that started manufacturing backpacks and camera bags on a kitchen table in California about thirty years ago. The creatively-designed and well-made products quickly caught the market's eye.

Camera bags in sizes and configurations catering to all photographers' needs became the range's mainstay. The business grew steadily. Eventually there was a factory in California, followed by one in China from where orders were shipped to retailers in Europe, Japan, and North America. This was a business enjoying the type of success small business owners dream of.

The writing on the wall began appearing around early 2004: "Last year 80 million cell phones with built-in cameras were sold worldwide. The quality of these phones and their cameras is rising and the price is dropping. People may discover that they don't need all the bells and whistles on large SLR cameras, and that their cell phones will do an adequate job for the type of snaps they take of their kids, dogs, and relatives. The day they won't need big, expensive camera bags anymore might be just around the corner."

There was more writing on the wall in 2009 to suggest that the photography industry as we had known it to date was in trouble: "Ritz Camera and Image, which just last year claimed to have 1,200 stores, filed for chapter 11 bankruptcy. Think about whether there's a message in this for all camera and allied businesses." The company later emerged from bankruptcy, but then there was more writing on the wall in 2012: "Ritz Camera and Image has filed for chapter 11 bankruptcy for the second time in three years. Shouldn't you now be thinking about what this says about the prospects for consumer cameras?"

Prior to the Ritz failure, dire warnings about the traditional consumer photography industry had appeared on the wall—that is to say, that part of it not incorporated in smart phones and other multipurpose digital devices, such as iPads. Digital technology was shaking up the photography industry in all aspects (not just in regards to SLR cameras), and giants such as Kodak and Agfa-Gavaert were faltering and scrambling to adjust. It's hard to imagine how the writing on the wall for the smaller allied businesses like camera bag manufacturers could have been any clearer.

In June 2014, citing weakened demand for point-and-shoot cameras, economic recession, and a shrinking number of specialized retail outlets, Tamrac declared chapter 11 bankruptcy. Perhaps the announcement should have included: "The writing on the wall warned that a market switching from bulky cameras to pocket-sized devices requires fewer camera bags. Our reaction could have been more timely."

Not always crystal clear

I don't mean to imply that all writing on the wall is crystal clear and you just need to read it and react. While quite often time is of the essence, a knee-jerk reaction can be as damaging as no reaction at all. Investigation, consultation, and consideration should precede reaction because the writing on the wall is frequently subject to interpretation.

At the time of writing, the watch industry provides a good example of how the writing on the wall can be interpreted in different ways and thereby elicit different reactions.

In his TED talk of February 2010, educator Ken Robinson points out that watches (single-purpose devices) are losing their popular appeal, particularly in the younger generation, due to the capability of digital alternatives (multipurpose devices) to perform a long list of handy tasks. But not everyone agrees. Some argue for an enduring and strong demand for wristwatches.

Regardless of differing opinions about the industry's future, even casual observers will be able to see a shift in watch-marketing strategies. Nowadays the advertising focus is on higher-priced watches, which are typically promoted in glossy magazines. Is this a normal adaptation to a slight market shift or a last-ditch effort to save an industry? Is the writing on the wall urging a strategic shift or warning of impending doom?

Time will tell whose interpretation is more accurate. There will be winners and there will be losers, but that's part of the challenge all small business owners face—we must interpret the writing on the wall.

Tsunami!

Picture a small business owner sitting in his or her office; writing suddenly appears on the wall: "There has been a market development of seismic proportions. It could trigger a reaction which could, like a tsunami washing ashore, swamp your small business."

If history is anything to go by, many a small business owner will be alarmed, but not alarmed enough to immediately spring into action. After all, scooping up valuables and heading for higher ground is a drastic step and a huge inconvenience. Sure it *could* trigger a "tsunami", but then again it might not, as previous false alarms would suggest. The small business owner, fuelled by a large dose of skepticism and reluctance to be inconvenienced unnecessarily, decides that *could* isn't definite enough and, without further investigation, hopes for a follow-up and perhaps more definite message.

But then, in due course and without further warning, the metaphorical "tsunami" arrives and swamps everything. If, instead of just hoping for the best, the small business owner had investigated the message on the wall and tried to verify it, he or she might have been able to save most of the business instead of losing most of it.

The lesson of course is to investigate rather than ignore the writing on the wall, particularly if it hints at something we'd rather not face, and then take appropriate action. But the question is, why do many of us have a tendency to not investigate in a timely manner, if at all?

Human nature

A precise, scientifically-established answer to the question of why we tend to fail to believe the writing on the wall is beyond the scope of this book and probably best explored by someone with a specialist knowledge of human nature, such as a sociologist or psychologist. However, as a small business owner who experienced the phenomenon and repeatedly saw it affect others, I'd suggest that it boils down to an inherent reluctance to first, believe, and second, react to, warnings of impending disaster. Perhaps it's an inbuilt mechanism that drives us to hope for the best because we'd rather not contemplate the disastrous alternative, albeit the more likely outcome.

On the flip side, the writing on the wall may spell out an economic opportunity with the potential to propel our small business to new heights and be ignored because it requires action that may take us out of our comfort zone. It may be that we are reluctant to take risks even though the spoils are promising or, in some cases, it may even be something as simple as laziness or procrastination.

As a small business owner I don't think it's as important for you to understand why you might suffer from this phenomenon as it is to know that you do. Knowing is the first step to corrective measures.

Status quo should never appear in a lexicon of business terms. Business is dynamic. Change challenges us and survival requires response and adaptation. The writing on the wall is the notice of impending change and a call to action.

Heed, investigate, and react

In my experience, spotting the writing on the wall is not the challenge—small business owners are easily able to see, read, and understand it. The challenge lies in granting the metaphorical graffiti artist credibility and taking the writing on the wall seriously enough to heed it, investigate it, and react appropriately.

The graffiti artist's lesson: pay attention to the writing on the wall. Don't ignore your gut feeling, your sixth sense, or whatever you choose to call the intuitive awareness we all possess but tend to ignore or overrule, particularly when it's sending messages we don't want to hear.

The last word

The second-last word goes to Ivern Ball, the mysterious poet to whom many quotations are ascribed but about whom very little information is available: "Most of us can read the writing on the wall; we just assume it's addressed to someone else."

The last word goes to me—don't assume the writing on the wall is addressed to someone else. The making or breaking of your small business could be at stake.

CHARACTER 38: ACQUIRER

A BAG OF MONEY

Meet the character many small business owners have in mind from the day their business opens—the person who's one day going to take it over and send them on their way with a bag of money.

This is the acquirer.

The only reason for shunning the acquirer would be an exit strategy of bolting the doors and walking away—no muss, no fuss, no bag. If that's your plan, it doesn't necessarily follow that you should skip the rest of this chapter. Stay with me for a while yet and perhaps you'll be persuaded to consider a more rewarding alternative: building your business with an eventual sale in mind.

So, that settled, we'll assume that your exit strategy is to one day dispose of your small business to an acquirer. We'll also assume that you're not going to be one of the few lucky owners to be approached by a potential acquirer and that you'll have to initiate the sale of your business by finding one.

However, before we go any further, there's an important topic we have to address. Discretion.

The importance of discretion

Even the slightest hint that you're considering selling your business will almost certainly be unsettling for your employees, customers, and suppliers. Obviously at some point these three parties will need to be told and possibly involved in the process, but until the time is right, it would be better for the selling process if you were discreet.

The time for telling each will likely differ, depending upon the circumstances and nature of your business. The employees are likely to be the most perturbed by the news and, to put it bluntly, you risk a potential acquirer's enthusiasm for the deal waning rapidly if he or she has any indication that key employees are likely to quit. Acquirers worry about smooth ownership transitions—key employee departures can mean a rocky start for a new owner.

Employees value security and are wary of change, and change of ownership is big change. They must therefore be handled with sensitivity and discretion. When the time arrives to take the employees into your confidence (usually some time before announcements to anyone else), break the news thoughtfully, keeping in mind the concerns and insecurities that have to be allayed. If you and the acquirer are able to jointly provide assurances, so much the better.

One technique for retaining key employees through a transition is for both you and the acquirer to demonstrate that you value their ongoing participation in the business. A good way to do this is to jointly offer a generous cash bonus. You could pay half at the time of the sale and the acquirer could pay the remaining half after, say, a year if the employee is still there. I found that this worked very well.

Now, primed to proceed with discretion, you're ready to consider the all-important question of value.

The question of value

You must have a reasonable idea of your business's value before entertaining any serious thoughts of selling it. This might sound obvious, but during the business and share valuation part of my career, I discovered that small business owners have little idea what their businesses might be worth. For instance, do you know the value of yours?

Furthermore, I also found that when pushed during a pre-valuation meeting, owners invariably estimated a number much higher than that of the subsequent, professionally-conducted valuation.

This all makes the argument for establishing an objective, well-reasoned, theoretically sound business value before planning the sale of your small business. Now, please understand that I do not include in "objective, well-reasoned, and theoretically sound" some of the glib, off-the-cuff, "instant" formulas you hear about from time to time from self-styled "experts." My favourite cringe-worthy "instant" formula is the multiple-of-sales one: the annual sales figure is multiplied by a factor (insert any number) to give a value. Profitability be damned! On the brink of bankruptcy be damned! Just pick a multiple, do the multiplication, and there you go, *voila*, your business's value. You might as well read the leaves at the bottom of your next cup of tea—it would be just as reliable.

There are tried and tested methods for valuing businesses, but placing these methods in the hands of anyone but skilled professionals is like placing a scalpel in the hands of anyone but a skilled surgeon. This is why I favour a fair market value prepared by an experienced expert as the first step on the road to disposing of your business. I cannot overstate the benefit of a fair market value as a starting point for a buy-sell negotiation.

Fair market value

The following well-considered, sound definition of fair market value has been in use in Canada since at least the mid-1970s and is endorsed by the Canadian Institute of Chartered Business Valuators. It holds that fair market value is "the highest price available in an open and unrestricted market between informed and prudent parties, under no compulsion to act and acting at arm's length, expressed in terms of money or money's worth."

In other words, fair market value is a theoretical value determined in ideal conditions with no extraneous influences. The actual price determined later by negotiation will invariably differ from fair market value because of the extraneous influences that are all but guaranteed to arise in the actual market place. Nevertheless, fair market value is a good place from which to launch a buy-sell negotiation.

Fair market value and your small business

A skilled valuator can quickly and quite accurately estimate a small business's value using a few key pieces of information. On a number of occasions I saw one of the senior partners of our valuation group calculate the value of a small business on the back of his cigarette box immediately after our first meeting with the client. A month or six weeks later, when we'd finished the formal valuation and presented our findings, he'd point out how his cigarette box calculation fell in the range of values the formal valuation had determined.

This doesn't mean that all small business valuations can be calculated on the back of a cigarette box. In fact, when a business valuation is the subject of contentious circumstances such as divorce, expropriation, succession, and probate, authorities typically require a detailed examination followed by a lengthy valuation report supporting the valuator's determination of fair market value. This is understandable. But I'm not convinced that determining a fair market value for the purpose of negotiating a small business sale requires a full-blown valuation project and detailed report.

It didn't escape my notice at the time—and you're probably thinking the same thing now—that informal consulting and guidance from an expert should be sufficient to establish a fair market value as a buy-sell negotiation launcher. I suggest you find a valuator willing to work with you in this way.

The Valuation Process

At the risk of being annoyingly repetitive, I'm going to remind you throughout this chapter that the information I'm discussing here is only intended to promote a basic understanding of business valuations and is not a substitute for the input of the experts you must engage from the moment you decide to sell your business.

Your valuator will tell you that most small businesses fall into one of three categories for the purposes of valuation: going-concern value, asset value, or liquidation value. But for our purposes, we're going to assume that the acquirer you're seeking will only be interested in your business as a profitable going concern.

A going concern is most commonly assumed to be an enterprise cruising along routinely doing business and, ideally, turning a profit. One could easily become mired in a discussion about the definition of *profit*, but let's say that it's the net income (gross income less expenses) adjusted to normalize expenses to market value levels—for instance, the owner's salary would be adjusted to a market value wage for the work performed in the day-to-day running of the business. The same applies to other expense items that may not reflect market values for any number of reasons—small business owners have considerable latitude in the charging of expenses.

Going-Concern Valuation

Let's say you're in conversation with a potential acquirer who tells you that he or she has two options for the money it would take to buy your business: buy your business or park it in a bank or some other blue chip investment.

What this person is essentially saying is that two key elements are weighing on his or her mind—risk and the rate of return on the investment. And, as we all know, the riskier an investment, the higher the expected rate of return.

So, for instance, if the money were invested in a low-risk blue chip investment, in today's market it would likely earn a relatively low return of, say, about 2 or 3 percent per annum. However, if it were invested in your small business, the acquirer would require a higher return because, almost without exception, a small business is a higher risk than a blue chip investment—often much higher.

Another way to illustrate this is by a question: If a sum of money invested in a high-risk small business paid the same return as a low-risk blue chip investment, why would you risk your money on the small business?

The sensible answer of course is that you wouldn't. But you might invest the sum in a small business if it paid a return higher than the blue chip investment to reflect appropriate compensation for the additional risk and stress. The question then becomes, how much higher?

This is where we need help from an expert, who would consider such elements as the current and expected future circumstances of the business and the industry, and who might conclude that, given the risks, 20 percent per annum is an appropriate return. Now we'd have one of the two key elements required to calculate a fair market value for the business.

The second element in the calculation is the expected return in dollars on the investment—in other words, the expected future pre-tax profit of the business. This is referred to as demonstrated sustainable earnings and is calculated using the net earnings for perhaps the past five years (or some other credible method) as an indicator of future sustainable earnings.

Let's assume that the sustainable earnings number is $60,000 (i.e., the expected annual pre-tax profit). So now that we know what we are going to receive as a return on our investment, we can calculate what that investment should be if the $60,000 is to equate to a 20 percent annual return. Do the math and you'll find that the investment should be $300,000. This is the fair market value of the business.

In other words, the investment of $300,000 will return $60,000 per annum, and this equates to our 20 percent per annum return requirement.

You can see why a fair market valuation is very much more an art than a science. Selecting the rate of return and the sustainable earnings demands skill and experience, which is why the result will invariably differ from valuator to valuator. However, whichever route they take, experienced valuators should arrive in the same ballpark.

Goodwill—the Intangible Asset

The term *goodwill*, in a business sense, refers to that invisible ("intangible") element of value ("asset"). Goodwill and net tangible assets together constitute the business's total value.

The value of the goodwill in our example is the amount by which the value of the business as a going concern ($300,000) exceeds the value of the net tangible assets. This would be the value of the tangible assets such as equipment, inventory, cash, vehicles, and furniture less the aggregate value of the liabilities. If we assume the net tangible assets in our example to be worth $100,000, then the value of the intangible assets, or goodwill, is the remaining $200,000.

Same thing from a different viewpoint: we've determined that the business has a going-concern fair market value of $300,000, which consists of $100,000 in tangible assets and $200,000 in intangible assets (all goodwill).

Nature of Goodwill

Think about goodwill as the aggregate of intangibles such as reputation, established customer relationships, convenience of location, special expertise, and brand familiarity—all these things contribute to the success of a business.

But knowing that goodwill is indicated won't be enough for an astute or well-advised acquirer. He or she is going to want to know what constitutes the goodwill value. It's legitimate to pay for goodwill if it's expected to continue to exist after the business has changed ownership. However, if any elements that contribute to the value of the goodwill before the business changes hands disappear after the business changes hands, that's a different matter. An acquirer won't want to pay for something he or she won't have after the takeover.

A common problem with small businesses is that some goodwill can be what's known as personal goodwill—sometimes as much as all of it. Personal goodwill describes the portion of goodwill attached to the presence of a particular individual or individuals, usually the owner. That is to say that the success of the business directly depends on the owner's presence. This might be because of a particular skill set, personality, or some other unique factor that attracts customers. When the owner leaves, the source of the goodwill leaves. In this case, the buyer would obviously be foolish to pay for the portion of the goodwill deemed to be personal.

By now it should be clear that if you plan to sell your business as a going concern at a value that includes goodwill, you must avoid confusing your identity with that of your business. You don't want the success of the business to be associated with your persona—that's creating personal goodwill for which a buyer should not be willing to pay.

The "potential" argument

Many an owner has told me that his or her small business should attract a good price because it has amazing potential. It's often true that a business has good potential—we've all visited a business and speculated on how we'd realize its full potential, as we see it. But why would a buyer pay for the potential?

If the potential hasn't been realized and the acquirer will have to do the work to realize it, why would he or she pay *you* for it? It's a bit like a house seller expecting the buyer to pay a premium for the house because it has the potential to look fabulous with new windows and a coat of exterior paint. Why would the buyer pay a premium for potential if he or she has to spend time, effort, and money realizing it? That's not to say that you won't be lucky enough to persuade a buyer to pay for potential but, barring extraordinary circumstances, I just can't see why anyone would.

FAIR MARKET VALUE VERSUS ACTUAL VALUE

As I mentioned earlier, a fair market value is only the starting point. Price negotiations can begin with the fair market value if it has been properly prepared using a fair set of assumptions.

However, those assumptions about (1) the highest price available, (2) an open and unrestricted market, (3) informed and prudent parties, (4) no compulsion to act, and (5) dealing at arm's length, don't necessarily apply when it comes to arriving at an actual price. The ideal conditions envisaged by a fair market value are unlikely to exist in reality. Then there can also be the impulsive and unpredictable elephant in the room affecting the eventual negotiated price—individual priorities.

You may be keen to sell for any number of compelling reasons. You may be tired of the business and the industry and impatient to undertake something completely different, or you may have health or family reasons, to name just a few. In such cases you would likely be prepared to settle for an amount less than the fair market value, just to conclude a deal.

The acquirer may be determined to buy the business for as many reasons as you want to sell. He or she may have an opportunity to integrate your business with an existing business to realize economies of scale, or may have always harboured romantic notions about owning a business like yours. There could be any number of circumstances motivating the buyer, so he or she may be prepared to pay a premium over the fair market value, just to conclude a deal.

These and other influences, when introduced into the negotiating process, inevitably result in a final settlement different from the fair market value. This is normal.

Now you're ready for the acquirer.

FINDING THE ACQUIRER

Unless you're one of the lucky few to be approached by a qualified acquirer, you're going to have to find one when you decide that the time to sell your small business has arrived. You will have to be proactive. Sitting waiting for an approach might mean a very long wait.

A good place to start your search is within your own industry. Sometimes you need look no further than a competitor or even employees. A business broker is another option. But *please*, regardless of the route you choose, ensure that absolutely everything is documented, and have a trusted lawyer review it all—*your* lawyer, not the broker's and not the acquirer's.

Your professional business valuation advisor may be your accountant, but if he or she isn't specifically familiar with business valuations, ask for a referral to a business valuation specialist. As I mentioned earlier, various "experts" use various methods to value businesses, and I'd much rather you benefitted from the opinion of a properly qualified and experienced business valuation professional. But again, *your* advisor, not the broker's and not the acquirer's.

Between your lawyer and accountant you should expect to be covered in such critical areas as confidentiality agreements, determination of value, and sale agreements. *Remember, don't do this on your own without proper professional assistance.*

A good way to initiate a discussion with a potential acquirer is to prepare a package (customize it to suit the particular potential acquirer) that makes the case for why acquiring your business is a good idea. This initial package doesn't need to be very specific as to numbers, but a well-worded document with well-chosen images and persuasive arguments can help smooth the passage to the next stage of the discussion. Don't underestimate the good impression a document of this nature can convey.

A word of warning on the topic of potential acquirers—qualify the inquiry before giving access to proprietary information. Be careful of fishing expeditions, particularly by competitors. Some expressions of interest may be more about interest in your proprietary information than interest in acquiring your business. In these cases a confidentiality agreement is of little protection. It can't stop them from stealing ideas and information for their own use.

Exceptions

You may be wondering how all I've discussed here squares with the multimillion-dollar acquisitions of small businesses by big businesses we hear about from time to time.

It doesn't.

Those are exceptions. They are few and far between and usually involve a small tech company with a specific invention that a large player wants to incorporate into its own business before one of its competitors does. If your small business is fortunate enough to find itself being pursued by an acquirer with deep pockets and an eye on your great invention, you can quite comfortably ignore this chapter, except the part about expert help. Yep, always the expert help!

This chapter is for the rest of us, who constitute more than 90 percent of all small businesses. We're the norm. We're the boutiques, coffee shops, machine shops, retailers, wholesalers, restaurants, paint stores, interior decorators, painters, florists, corner grocery stores, printers, renovators, couriers, delicatessens, cake shops, butchers, fish mongers, IT service providers, dry cleaners, screen printers, pet stores, funeral homes, car repair shops, garden service providers, and so on, and so on, and so on. We're unlikely to ever open the door to a Google or Apple representative with chequebook in hand. We have to build profitable businesses with the intention of one day making them attractive to acquirers.

The devil's in the details

When an opportunity to sell your business presents itself, by all means grab it with both hands. You built it, you rode the roller coaster of small business elation and anxiety, and you catered endlessly to the whims of a cast of characters. You've earned the right to that bag of money.

CHARACTER 39: YOU

Finally we come to the last character in this book. The character with the ultimate ability to make or break your small business—you!

It rests on your shoulders how your small business interacts with the other thirty-eight characters in this book who can individually or collectively make or break it. Interact wisely and they can make your small business. Interact foolishly and they can break it.

It's all up to you.

CONCLUSION

Small business ownership can be fulfilling, rewarding, and fun. It can also be the exact opposite. There may be times when you're too excited to sleep, and others when you're too anxious to sleep. Some days you might hop out of bed hardly able to contain your excitement at the prospect of another day at work. Some days you might not want to get of bed at all.

The truth is, small business ownership is not all fun and games. Your local bookstore will be well stocked with books of the "start your own business and get rich" variety which can cause people, prospective owners in particular, to view business ownership through rose-coloured glasses. This is dangerous. You need to be cautious. However, I don't want you to interpret caution as discouragement.

Follow your dream. Start a small business. But do so with your eyes wide open. Give yourself the best chance at building a successful business—one that fulfills you, rewards you amply, and is fun to own. First, choose your industry and business carefully. And then? Well, by now you know what comes next: identify those characters who can make or break your business and how they might do it. With this understood, interact with them accordingly.

Some small businesses become extraordinary—yours could be one of them. And if yours doesn't turn you into a billionaire but puts food on the table, clothes and educates your kids, and provides for your retirement, all while giving you the occasional laugh, that's extraordinary too! You can still consider yourself a successful small business owner.

And if this book has helped lower the incline of your learning curve, my mission will have been accomplished.

WHAT NOW?

Let's keep the conversation going. Learning is an ongoing process, and I'd be delighted to entertain your questions, comments, and feedback.

I also welcome opportunities to talk about the book's contents, as well as small business in general, at conferences and everywhere else small business owners gather to share knowledge and experience.

Drop in for a visit anytime at www.smallbusinesscharacters.com, or write me at michael.best@michaelbest.ca.

www.ingramcontent.com/pod-product-compliance
Lightning Source LLC
Chambersburg PA
CBHW021029210326
41598CB00016B/956
* 9 7 8 1 7 7 5 3 0 7 7 0 9 *